D1058959

*f*P

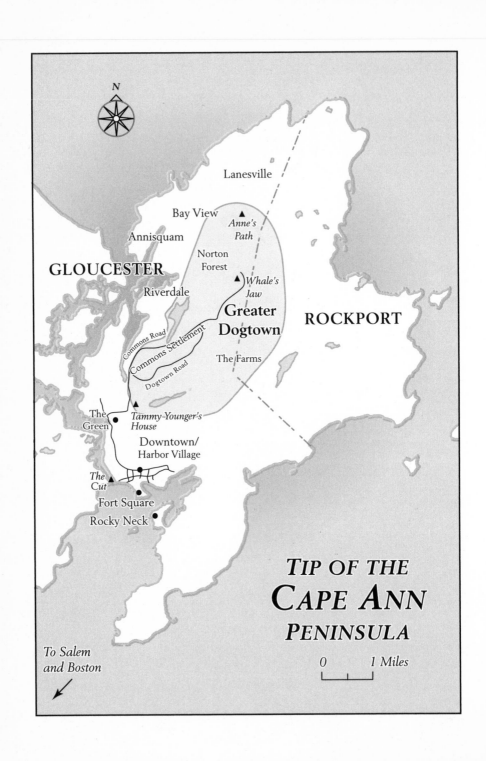

N

Lanesville

Bay View ▲ *Anne's Path*

Annisquam

GLOUCESTER

Norton Forest

Riverdale

▲ *Whale's Jaw*

Greater Dogtown

Commons Road

Commons Settlement

Dogtown Road

ROCKPORT

The Farms

The Green

▲ *Tammy Younger's House*

Downtown/ Harbor Village

The Cut ▲

Fort Square

Rocky Neck

TIP OF THE
CAPE ANN
PENINSULA

To Salem and Boston

0   1 Miles

DOGTOWN

Death and Enchantment in a
New England Ghost Town

Elyssa East

Free Press

New York London Toronto Sydney

FREE PRESS
A Division of Simon & Schuster, Inc.
1230 Avenue of the Americas
New York, NY 10020

First Free Press hardcover edition December 2009

FREE PRESS and colophon are trademarks of Simon & Schuster, Inc.

For information about special discounts for bulk purchases, please contact Simon & Schuster Special Sales at 1-866-506-1949 or business@simonandschuster.com.

The Simon & Schuster Speakers Bureau can bring authors to your live event. For more information or to book an event contact the Simon & Schuster Speakers Bureau at 1-866-248-3049 or visit our website at www.simonspeakers.com.

Manufactured in the United States of America

3   5   7   9   10   8   6   4   2

Library of Congress Cataloging-in-Publication Data

East, Elyssa.
Dogtown: death and enchantment in a New England ghost town / Elyssa East.
        p.   cm.
    1. Dogtown Commons (Gloucester, Mass.)—Description and travel.
    2. East, Elyssa—Homes and haunts.   3. Gloucester (Mass.)—History.
        4. Ann, Cape, Region (Mass.)—History.   I. Title.
                    F74G5E27   2009
        917.44'5—dc22   2009017197
                ISBN 978-1-4165-8704-0
                ISBN 978-1-4165-8718-7 (ebook)

To my teachers,
and my parents,
Nancy McKinley East
and
Sanders Roland East

Contents

PART TWO

. . . as with sacred places, so with the murderous spots. The record of events is written into the earth.

—HENRY MILLER,
The Colossus of Maroussi

Prologue

The Prophetic Pictures

A FTER CROSSING THE Merrimack River, I turned onto Route 1A, continuing south through the picturesque towns of Massachusetts' North Shore. I was traveling on a hunch in search of an abandoned colonial settlement called Dogtown Common, or simply Dogtown, though it was not identified on any map I could find at the time. It was one of those October days that inspire thoughts of harvest, not a battening down for winter. Traffic slowed through Newburyport, an archetypal New England town that keeps its collar buttoned. Kids sporting shiny jerseys in bright colors spilled out of cars parked roadside at a soccer tournament. Beyond the playing field and farm stands with pumpkins piled high, the landscape opened to tidal estuaries where gulls were lighting over mudflats and marsh grass in shades of golden taupe. The amber light warmed my skin, bringing a flush to my cheeks. I was feeling rapturous and inspired, dreaming of paintings coming to life.

I was on my way from Portland, Maine, where I lived during this 1999 autumn, to Gloucester, hoping to find the site that had inspired a series of paintings by Marsden Hartley. The *New York Times* has called Hartley "the most gifted of the early American Modernists," while *New Yorker* critic Peter Schjeldahl has written, "Hartley's best art looms so far above the works of such celebrated contemporaries as Georgia O'Keeffe, Charles Demuth, Arthur Dove, and John Marin that it poses the question of how his achievement was even possible." The answer, I had learned, was to be found in Dogtown.

1

Hartley, a peripatetic, lonesome soul, had been obsessed with Dog-town's primordial, highland expanse, which he painted on three separate occasions in the 1930s. And while his Dogtown paintings helped lay the foundation for some of his later, greatest work, Hartley also claimed to have been forever. changed—and possibly healed—by his time there. As for me, I was obsessed with Hartley, these paintings, and the 1931 summer he spent in this forgotten corner of America.

By official estimation, Dogtown is an unpopulated, roughly three-thousand-acre expanse—some say more—that fills most of the geographic center of the island tip of Cape Ann, a crooked peninsula extending ten miles seaward from Massachusetts' North Shore, twenty-five miles northeast of Boston. The end of this peninsula, where the city of Gloucester (population thirty-one thousand) and town of Rockport (population eight thousand) are located, is an island settlers created in 1643 by cutting through fifty yards of marsh in the Annisquam (or "Squam") River. For most of American history, this island, which is nearly the same size as Manhattan, was accessible only by boat or a short drawbridge that crosses the colonial canal known as the "Cut." Though the nearby towns of Essex and Manchester-by-the-Sea and parts of Gloucester are also situated on the peninsula, when people say "Cape Ann," oftentimes they are referring to the island alone. For added emphasis, people on the island may say "this side of the Cut." No matter where Cape Ann officially begins or ends, most everyone feels that the air is different after the Cut is crossed. Perhaps because Gloucester and Rockport extend so far into the Atlantic Ocean, something does change. It is the end of the line. Beyond the roads and the railway there is nothing but the sea.

The main roads around Cape Ann crest and fall over steep hills and tack hard on sharp corners as they follow the island's fifty miles of shoreline. Along them, smaller roads leading into the inland heart of this place climb steeply, if not suddenly, before narrowing, turning to dirt, and disappearing behind locked gates into the wilds of Dogtown.

Dogtown's terrain varies from forest to field where one can stumble upon stone remnants of colonial homes, to swamp and bog and hill and dale. Much of this highland area, the former pinnacle of an ancient pre-Cambrian mountain, is strewn with giant boulders. These boulders, some of which measure more than twenty feet in height, are glacial erratics from the Laurentide ice sheet, the continent-size Pleistocene-era glacier that once covered half of North America. Abandoned granite quarries pockmark the area's northern end. A commuter rail track that runs between Rockport and Gloucester before continuing south to Boston cuts through its eastern edge. The Babson and Goose Cove Reservoirs demarcate Dogtown's border to the southeast and west, respectively. These features define an area that's roughly three and a half times the size of Central Park.

Today Dogtown is heavily forested—much like it was before settlers cleared the forest primeval in the 1600s—which lends it a wilderness-like feel. But the area remained treeless for nearly three hundred years. This sere, barren wasteland was the "most peculiar scenery of the Cape," as Henry David Thoreau put it, noting its "hills strewn with boulders, as if they had rained down, on every side" in his *Journal* on September 23, 1858. These same rocks captured Marsden Hartley's attention seventy-three years later.

There is nothing majestic or idyllic in Hartley's gloomy paintings of Dogtown's large boulders. In his images, these rocks look like colossal macaroons, bones bleached from sunlight, gargantuan cheese cubes, smoked marshmallows, or giant chewed fingernails; one resembles a whale rising from the earth. A work called *Flaming Pool—Dogtown* stands apart from Hartley's other images of the area. *Flaming Pool* shows a small, gently hued body of water surrounded by brilliant red and orange flora and a pink and green sky. The place appears otherworldly, inspired, as if it could spontaneously catch on fire the moment a viewer walked away. Hartley's Dogtown paintings are altogether unusual, a little clunky—even as early modernist paintings of a primitivist style go—hauntingly lonesome, and entirely unpicturesque. But these images of rocks and earth thrive with profoundly felt distillations of energy. Though they evince a spiritual intensity that comes from Hartley's deep meditation on form, shape, texture, color, and place, they are so strange as to seem almost unreal, as if they could be found only in ultima Thule, the far-flung, ancient mythical land believed to exist beyond the "borders of the known world."

If Dogtown were indeed a life-altering place "so original in its appearance as not to be duplicated either in New England or anywhere else," as Hartley claimed and his paintings suggested, I wanted to see it. When I told friends about these paintings, their responses reminded me of a question posed by Elinor Ludlow in Nathaniel Hawthorne's "The

Prophetic Pictures." Before she sits for a celebrated portraitist (a fiction-
alized version of painter Gilbert Stuart), Elinor asks her fiancé, "Are you
telling me of a painter, or a wizard?" "In truth," he answers, "that question might be asked much more seriously than you suppose. They say
that he paints not merely a man's features, but his mind and heart. He
catches the secret sentiments and passions, and throws them upon the
canvass, like sunshine—or perhaps, in the portraits of dark-souled men,
like a gleam of infernal fire." Hartley's Dogtown pictures had their own
strange, brooding gleam, that flaming pool, those talismanic rocks.
Hawthorne's magic painter has the ability to "raise phantoms at will,
and keep the form of the dead among the living," whereas Hartley's
paintings seemed to have raised the unseen spirit of an ancient place
and made it visible. Under Hartley's brush Dogtown was shadowy, nu-
minous, transformative. This was the Dogtown I wanted to find. Like a
doubting Thomas, I hoped to finger its wounds.

I made for Gloucester's downtown with its wide harbor, close-set
brick storefronts, mix of Georgian, Federalist, and Victorian architec-
tural styles, fishing boats at their moorings and waterfront warehouses.
There were signs offering deep-sea fishing trips, whale watches, and
schooner rides, but no roadside markers leading visitors to Dogtown.
The lack of Dogtown signage had much to do with the fact that
Gloucester, which was initially settled in 1623 and incorporated in
1642, is America's oldest seaport. For over three hundred seventy-five
years, this small city's livelihood and identity have come from the
ocean, not its hardscrabble interior. But there was more to the story.
Many considered the place I sought to be dangerous. But I carried on,
wandering into and out of shops on Main Street. No shopkeepers
seemed to be paying their rent selling reproductions of Hartley's Dogtown paintings or Dogtown-themed postcards or pet rocks. The free
tourist maps did not list Dogtown in the area attractions. I approached
a middle-age man heading toward a Sicilian café to ask him about the
region. He waved his hand at me as though shooing off a fly, muttered
something indecipherable, opened the café door, and yelled "*Buon
giorno!*" with gusto.

I walked the full length of Main Street and had nearly given up on
my search when, out of the corner of my eye, I noticed a wooden sign
down a little side street. An image of one of Dogtown's most famous
boulders—the Whale's Jaw, a rock cleft like a whale breaching twenty

feet up from sea—advertised the Dogtown Bookstore. Hartley had made multiple drawings and paintings of this monolith. I ran down the street and found a set of stairs leading to a low-ceilinged, seemingly endless cavern filled with used books. Floorboards creaked and shelves sagged underneath the weight of titles about fishing knots and barn-raising guides, Harlequin romances, and old, leatherbound copies of Cotton Mather's treatises. An Arctic Studies section filled a high shelf over the entry into a second, smaller, more densely packed room, but I could not find any books about Hartley or Dogtown.

Behind a glass case filled with scrimshaw, intricate knots, and old brooches, the proprietor, a man named Bob with a salt-and-pepper beard and a wooden pipe, sat reading the newspaper. I asked Bob about Dogtown. He kindly told me a less detailed version of what I had read in Hartley's writings and a Massachusetts guidebook: in the 1600s, an estimated forty to sixty families fled pirate and Indian attacks and created the highland Commons Settlement. After the Revolutionary War, this village was deserted but for some destitute war widows, witches, former slaves, and the dogs they kept for protection; the area became known as Dogtown at this time. By the late 1830s, it was abandoned. Dogtown has remained unpopulated and relatively unchanged ever since.

I continued flipping through a box of handpainted postcards of Gloucester Harbor and asked Bob if he went to Dogtown much. He replied with a flat "Nope." When I asked Bob why he chose the name Dogtown for his shop, he simply stated, " 'Cause I liked it." Then my fingers landed on just what I had been hoping for: *The Dogtown Common Trail Map*. I bit my lower lip in an effort to suppress my excitement. Bob slid the map into a thin paper bag and handed me my change.

Today I find it ironic that I located a detailed map of this obscure setting in a bookshop. Dogtown is as much a labyrinth of stories as it is a jumble of alternating topography; I was about to discover that it is easy to get lost in both.

As soon as settlers cleared the land, stories—mostly tragedies and mysteries—took to seed and started to propagate. People would eventually tell me about a horrific event that took place in Dogtown on a rainy summer morning in 1984. When tragedy heaved its way into action there that year, the setting imposed an unofficial narrative on this event that would reach back through the centuries and forward into the future, which is where I stood, merrily counting my change and itching to explore the place Hartley had compared to Easter Island and Stonehenge.

I bounded out of the bookstore and crossed the street for the Sunny Day Café, spread the map across a small corner table, and ordered some coffee. Knobby, twisting, green contour lines wrapped around abundant little hills and depressions. Trails drawn in black wound in myriad directions. Dogtown existed on a more modest scale than the wilderness areas I had hiked in Maine, but the map was mesmerizing; I wanted nothing more than to lose myself in this place.

The map gave driving directions to an entrance and parking area along with some trail descriptions. It also listed a series of elementary precautions: carry a map and compass, wear bright colors and a "blaze orange hat" during hunting season, use insect and tick repellent. Two of the warnings struck me as odd, unless they had been intended for children, which seemed unlikely: "Don't go out alone" and "If you must explore by yourself, leave a note with location and estimated time of your return." I had hiked and backpacked alone in remote wilderness areas and had never seen such warnings printed on a map before. What could there be to worry about on an apparently densely populated island? There was no reason for alarm unless people were the cause for concern, but this possibility did not occur to me with any seriousness at the time.

I asked the waitress, a woman with short, spiky blond hair, if she ever went to Dogtown. "We used to go up in high school to party," she replied while refilling my coffee, "but not anymore." She turned to fill another customer's cup, then looked over her shoulder at me and said, "No one does."

That was just what I wanted to hear. Solitude would increase my chances for meeting Hartley's ghost, or so I hoped. I tried to picture Hartley, with his piercing blue eyes, aquiline nose, and the hangdog expression for which he was known, studying this place. He would be in Dogtown. At the very least his paintings and the traces of his brush would be recognizable there.

As I exited the café, I noticed a lady with gold-spun hair sitting near the door. Her face was buried in a book titled *Simplified Magic*.

I got in my truck and threaded my way through the city streets, passing a sign saying, "Have a Whale of a Time!"

If I had known then what I do now, I might not have been in such a rush. There is something different about Dogtown. It is not simple and it is not magic in the strict or literal sense of the word. The place transcended the events of that rainy 1984 Monday when a single human agent changed this place. This particular individual is now long removed from the setting, but this tragedy tapped Dogtown's centuries-old legacy of peculiar, melancholic tales, as if an aquifer had been filling up with such stories through the centuries, just waiting to be divined.

Years after this initial trip to Dogtown, I pieced together what transpired that 1984 day and the reasons why this rare colonial ruin had become neglected like a secret meant to be kept and hopefully forgotten.

The story goes like this.

PART ONE

Chapter One

The Birth of Tragedy

DURING THE EARLY MORNING hours of Monday, June 25, 1984, a chorus of howls rippled across island Cape Ann. After the first alarm rang at three-fifty in the morning, sirens wailed and flashed into the rain-drenched night as fire trucks raced up Massachusetts's North Shore to put out the largest blaze in recent Gloucester memory: a six-alarm fire on Main and Porter Streets in the heart of downtown. Tenants in apartments over the Mark Adrian Shoe Store rushed to safety just seconds before an explosion blocked the exit. The fire burned through the dawn as smoke mixed with fog and heavy rain brought visibility to a minimum across much of Cape Ann. But the winds were blowing to the southeast and, five miles away, on the northwestern side of the island, just beyond the ancient woodlots of the abandoned colonial settlement known as Dogtown, there was no sign or smell of fire, just the lingering echo of sirens and howling dogs in the gray light of dawn.

Rainy summer mornings on Cape Ann inspire sleeping late and staying indoors, but Erik Natti got up early, met his carpool, and traveled twenty miles for an end-of-the-year teachers' meeting at Marblehead High School. Matthew and Diana, Erik's two children from his first marriage, were at their mother's house in Salem. Erik would later recall driving away that morning and hoping that his second wife, Anne, "would enjoy a good day of being by herself" at their summer camp, an Airstream trailer at the northern edge of Dogtown.

The bulk of Cape Ann's population and development are clustered along the shoreline, but the Nattis had recently settled into these high-land woods at the end of Quarry Street to be as far away from civilization as possible and still remain on the island. They preferred the relative isolation of Dogtown's quiet expanse to inconveniences such as being awakened by sirens in the middle of the night.

The Nattis, who had a house in the village of Annisquam where they lived during the school year, may have told you that their summer camp, which filled a woodland meadow on land where Erik grew up, was in a part of Gloucester known as Bay View. This would not be untrue, but the top of Quarry Street, where houses disappear behind denser and denser woods the higher one climbs, also marks an unofficial entry into Dogtown—an invisible threshold to the island's wilderness interior.

Dogtown's colonial ruins, which cover half of the region's official three thousand acres, lie south of the Nattis' summer place, but people generally use the name Dogtown when referring to the entirety of the island's unpopulated center, a region that covers approximately five thousand acres. These malleable boundaries suggest that Dogtown is larger than any strict interpretation of history or land survey that tries to pin it down. It also implies that the name "Dogtown" stands for something too complex and elusive to be contained by the four roads around which the colonial village was created.

In Friedrich Nietzsche's *The Birth of Tragedy*, tragedy stems from the conflict between mankind's civilizing, Apollonian desire for order and our yearning for wild, Dionysian abandon. At the time of its inception, this colonial village represented an Apollonian ideal, but by the turn of the nineteenth century, when the Commons Settlement became known as Dogtown, the Dionysian impulse had overtaken the place. The region may indeed have been overrun with dogs back then, but it also began to inspire a certain type of human wildlife. Many of Dogtown's "witches" made fiery home brews, told fortunes, hosted buccaneers and gambling parties, and profited from prostitution. The folkloric record maintains that a couple of these women cursed anyone who attempted to enter their desolate village. Even in 1984, Dogtown remained a place where people escaped civilization either by going there to party with abandon or to lose themselves peaceably in nature.

By the twentieth century, Dogtown had become a unique land-scape, an isolated, municipally bound wilderness—not a manicured park—and a ruin-filled ghost town where the Dionysian principle with its knife's-edge balance between creative inspiration and destructive madness seemed to prevail. Dogtown enabled both Marsden Hartley and the influential postmodernist poet Charles Olson to cross the internal wilderness of their respective creative crises. Others, less fortunate, did not safely traverse either the actual, physical wilderness of Dogtown or the mental one it could impose. This wayward quality may have been the reason why a Bible-thumping millionaire named Roger W. Babson decided to have twenty-four large boulders hand-carved with Protestant prescriptives during the Great Depression. The lessons imparted by Babson's boulders—"USE YOUR HEAD," "TRUTH," "BE ON TIME"—stand out boldly against this confusing landscape as patent guideposts for those who may wander too far astray.

Over the years, most Cape Anners, being oceangoing people, ignored Dogtown. Of those who actually paid attention, some looked at the ruined settlement and saw a wasteland where civilization had died; others saw a life-affirming place where nature triumphantly resurged from the dead; many saw both things at once, as though the area represented all parts of the cycle of life.

The Nattis subscribed to the "cycle of life" point of view. Rumors and folktales about witches had long been the stuff of legend and did not bother them in the least—in fact, one could almost say such stories conveniently helped keep outsiders away. Not that the Nattis were misanthropes; though Erik was an especially private individual, both he and Anne were well-liked teachers. Anne taught in nearby Prides Crossing at the Landmark School, which specialized in instructing students with dyslexia, and took her own private tutoring pupils as well. One of these pupils, a challenging little boy named Daniel Bulba, wanted nothing more for his tenth birthday than to have Anne attend his party. Anne was just the sort of person to honor such an invitation, her deep brown eyes lighting up with pleasure. Erik was equally devoted to teaching biology and chemistry at Marblehead High School.

At about the time of her engagement, Anne, who was in her late thirties and had never been married, wrote to a friend and confided, "Everything I've been running away from for the last many years I now find I'm running after." In a subsequent letter she stated, "I feel kin to a whole history of waiters on the eve of The Day—a bridegroom on his last fling, a graduate carousing, a king before coronation, a soldier before battle, expectant father, sacrificed virgin, all of them attending their souls to time, while time moves deliberately on to meet one marked spot where the world will suddenly change."

Time moved ahead to Anne Phinney and Erik Natti's wedding on Saturday, August 20, 1983, a memorable event for all who attended. The couple hired a band that transported a thousand-pound piano up Quarry Street, a particularly steep and treacherous dirt road, to their ceremony and party at a clearing in the woods. At their reception, Anne and Erik, who is of Finnish descent, marked their commitment with a group sauna, a Finnish ritual observed on occasions both venerable and mundane, which meant before long, Anne, Erik, and their guests were "taking the heat," cleansing and purifying themselves in this time-honored way, and following it with a cooling swim in Blood Ledge Quarry, one of the many abandoned granite quarries that dot the Cape Ann highland.

Life had finally, pleasantly caught up to Anne Theresa Phinney, now Natti, as she walked through these ancient woods with her husband at her side, like Adam and Eve, neither unwise nor wholly innocent.

It was a fitting image: if anyone belonged in these woods, people believed, it was Erik, who had grown up in them, and Anne, who had grown up in a family of outdoorsy, educator parents in western Massachusetts. Then there was Erik's mother, who liked to tell people that she was a witch.

Once, when Erik was a little boy and had been the object of wrongdoing by another kid, his mother marched over to the offending boy's house, pounded on the door, and cursed the child's mother in Finnish. She didn't just swear, either. She moved her hands to conjure a whole variety of spirits, and from what young Erik could make out, she threatened to turn the woman's ovaries into walnuts. Mrs. Natti raised even more eyebrows when she took Erik and his sister Isabel out of Sunday school because she did not want them to be corrupted by the Bible. The Natti family's holy book was the *Kalevala*, a Finnish creation epic full of nature, magic, and shamanism. The *Kalevala*, like the Natti paterfamilias, originally came from Karelia, a heavily forested region divided between eastern Finland and Russia that is culturally distinct from western Finland. The Natti family tradition holds that Erik's paternal great-grandfather was sold into slavery in St. Petersburg, but managed to escape and eventually found his way to Cape Ann in the late 1800s to work in the granite quarries. If there was anything from the Old

World this Natti forebear was going to pass along to his descendants, it was a love for the *Kalevala*, and the shared Finnish and Karelian belief that the forest is enchanted and sacred, especially the birch and the blueberry that thrive in northern Dogtown. While there were other Finns on Cape Ann, most hailed from the western part of the country and considered Karelians to be unsophisticated backwoods people. One Cape Anner of Finnish descent says that his mother used to refer to the Nattis by a Finnish word that translates loosely as "forest people" or "leprechauns" and sounds like "met-tah buuloo," from the Finnish word for forest, *metsä*.

Although Erik's family wore their eastern Finnish culture proudly, they were no hicks. Erik's maternal grandfather was the sculptor Paul Manship, whose most famous work is the bronze Prometheus carrying fire in hand as he soars above the ice-skating rink in New York City's Rockefeller Center. Manship and the extended Natti family were central figures in a vibrant community of artists, writers, and designers on Cape Ann.

The Nattis had another claim on this forgotten corner of the world. After the quarrying industry went bust during the Great Depression, Erik's father, Ilmari "Jimo" Natti, and uncle Robert "Bob" Natti had bought some acres on the cheap and transformed this decimated land into a forest. Jimo could have charted his son's growth next to the white pines he planted four years before Erik was born. Though a day came when the forest outgrew the boy, the man never outgrew the forest. It was Erik's and, by extension, his wife's.

ON THE OTHER SIDE of the island, the Main Street fire continued to gorge itself on wind, metal, plastic, and wood. Eighty-four firemen, including additional crews from six surrounding towns, attacked the blaze. The sounds of shattering windows and splintering doors punctuated the fire's roar. News crews arrived, trailed by insurance adjusters who worked the crowd of spectators that was pinned behind police barricades, searching for business owners such as shoe-store owner Mark Adrian Farber, who watched as the apartments above his store disintegrated before his eyes.

Later that week, Gloucester would celebrate its annual St. Peter's Fiesta, a traditional Sicilian festival honoring the patron saint of fishermen and keeper of keys to the heavenly kingdom. The novena, a time-worn Sicilian ritual in which fishermen's wives and mothers pray to the saint for nine days, was already under way. In two days the novena would end and Gloucester's summer tourist season—so vital to the town's economy—would begin. But for now, downtown was burning in the rain, and all people could do was watch and worry.

On this day, more so than on any other, Dogtown could not have been more remote.

WHEN ANNE AWOKE she called her friend Linda Ryan, who worked as a flight attendant and had the day off. Anne and Linda, former room-mates, were as close as sisters. Cross-Dogtown walks were part of their bond, as was their unique communication system. If either Anne or Linda were passing near the other's home, she would leave a woodland calling card such as some pinecones or flowers to say hello. On Sunday Linda had ridden by the Natti camp on horseback and left a branch for Anne, who placed a bough and a small present on the porch of Linda's Rockport home later that evening.

That Monday Anne planned to walk through the woods to Linda's house—the same house they had shared for three and a half years be-fore Anne moved in with Erik. Anne's normal route usually took just over an hour, but right before hanging up the phone, Anne said she might try an alternate way, potentially delaying her arrival. It was the start of her summer vacation. She had time to wander.

Anne Natti was not the sort of woman to forgo a walk in the woods, even on this dreary Monday morning: it would make for an especially solitary, peaceful experience of the kind that only Dogtown could pro-vide.

Anne dressed in multiple layers to protect herself from the ele-ments, which bore down heavily. She sealed her slender, petite frame inside a pair of yellow rain pants and matching hooded slicker, snaked her feet into a pair of rag wool socks, and stuffed them into tall rubber boots. She placed her and Erik's puppy's red leash for use in Rockport inside a Ziploc plastic bag, stepped outside, and closed the door behind her. The puppy, a German shepherd mix named Woofer, bounded into the fog. It was between 9:15 and 9:30 A.M.

Though parts of Dogtown lie just beyond backyard swing sets and raised garden beds where bees cling to bright flowers, the rest of Cape Ann seems far away. The region may fill the geographical center of the island, but it is cut off from Gloucester and Rockport. Its elevation (between 150 and 180 feet above sea level) and awkward and sometimes impassable terrain add to its aura of remove, but the region's colonial ruins easily give one the impression that Dogtown is separated from society by time as well as geography. The area is an island within an island, riddled with a labyrinth of sixty miles of trails that appear and disappear, depending on the season, and that seem to multiply into endless wilderness. It is easy to get lost in Dogtown for extended periods—when one woman went missing there in 1951, the police had to borrow a map so they could find their way around. But Anne Natti regularly walked these myriad paths; she was an unlikely candidate for going astray.

This morning she chose a route that wound through what she and Erik called the "deep woods," a copse of hemlock, white pine, and cedar that a retired NASA physicist and MIT professor named Frederick Norton had started planting in the 1930s. This 121-acre stretch of Dogtown woods feels prelapsarian, though every bit of it was designed, sprouted, and planted by "the professor," as he was called. Such is the illusion of an expertly engineered and carefully managed woodland; though it is one of the most cared for parts of Dogtown, the Norton Forest looks like primeval wilderness.

Like a latter-day Johnny Appleseed, the professor, who was eighty-eight years of age in 1984, nearly always went barefoot, and shod his feet only when they hit the pavement. He did not even put on his L.L.Bean mukluks the previous September when he walked through the forest to Anne and Erik's wedding. Erik was like a son to the professor. They shared an intense love for the land; to them, it was sacred.

As Anne walked through the Norton Forest this blustery Monday, the wind gusted heavily, as it is prone to do on this exposed promontory during a storm. It howled and rattled through the trees, shaking their branches to create a sudden deluge. The hood of Anne's yellow rain slicker muffled her hearing and cut off her peripheral vision. The steady patter of rainfall intensified, drowning out the distant rumble and whine of a dirt bike.

The dirt bike rider had altered his course after seeing a home-made sawhorse made out of birch logs blocking a trail and marked with a sign saying NO BIKES. Making his way down a path that had turned slippery with mud, he stopped under a tree to wait out the pelting rain.

Woofer appeared through the trees, pranced up to the man's bike, sniffed the front tire, and darted away. The man watched the dog sally to a bush, a tree, a rock, and trot back to its master, a small figure dressed in yellow walking a nearby path. Moments passed. A tiny fragment of a single day gave life to an idea that would change two lives and a place forever.

Anne had no idea what was behind her. The man was careful not to make a lot of noise as he crept in close and planted his large palms against her back, shoving her forward. Trees whirred by. The ground came up to meet her.

Anne struggled to get up. The man grabbed a rock sitting alongside the trail. The rock was large enough to make a cornerstone, broad and heavy enough for crushing things. He heaved it with all of his might onto the back of Anne Natti's head.

The human skull, designed to cradle and protect the brain, is durable and difficult to break, but Anne Natti's skull immediately fractured upon impact.

This blow was survivable in and of itself, but no trauma of such magnitude exists in isolation. A shuddering, domino-like effect traveled down Anne Natti's spine. The degree of force her brain experienced would have immediately sent a cascade of opiates through her nervous system. Her brain most likely shut down in a self-protective mode, making her lose consciousness almost immediately. Pressure and fluid would have begun to build inside her cranium, causing her to moan and writhe involuntarily. She began to hemorrhage.

The man wrapped his long arms around her and dragged her to her feet and off the trail. She continued to moan and writhe. He dropped her among the trees just beyond the edge of the path and swung at her face with another rock. The blow broke her jaw and her nose. It pushed her left eye deep into its socket. Her movements slowed.

The man checked her pockets for money. Peeled the rain slicker off without unzipping it. Stripped away her vest. A sweater. He lifted an-other sweater, chamois shirt, and turtleneck off her body in one efficient stroke, pulled off her boots, and rolled down her socks, one by one. Then came her yellow rain pants, belt, and dungarees. He stripped off her tights. Unhooked her bra. Slid off her underwear and placed it in the Ziploc with Woofer's red leash. It would stay dry and relatively clean, though her exposed body was now wet, dirty, bloody, and going cold.

He had been thinking about raping her. Rain continued to fall heavily. Blood seeped into the earth. The rainwater diluted it until there was no longer a trace.

Suddenly, something snapped inside him. All of a sudden he came to and realized what he had just done.

He moved quickly. He tied the yellow rain pants around her neck and used them to drag her naked body deeper into the woods. Her breasts scraped up and over rocks and twigs. Briars and thorns scratched the skin around her ribs, back, and buttocks.

He pulled her into some dwarf pines growing on the edge of Professor Norton's land. Working her body underneath some thick growth, well out of sight, he laid his large hand at the base of her skull and shoved her face deep into the soft, damp earth until the mud reached her ears. If the pants around her neck had not cut off any remaining supply of oxygen to Anne Natti's brain, the mud would soon do the job. He gathered handfuls of leaves and scattered them over her body.

Anne Natti lay prostrate and moaning in a comatose state at least a mile and a half from the nearest house. She was bleeding to death, but still alive.

ANXIOUS AND TERRIFIED, the man ran from the scene. He knew these woods better than most, but nothing looked familiar in the downpour. Perhaps he thought the woods were playing tricks on him. He would not have been the first person to think that about this place, nor the last.

Eventually he came to some blue trail blazes, which he followed to the dirt bike. He traveled the many trails that criss-cross Dogtown until one of them deposited him onto a downtown street where he disappeared into the smoke-filled air without a trace.

———

THE MAIN STREET FIRE was still smoldering but finally under control. Policemen blew whistles and diverted traffic as people continued to arrive and stare.

Mark Adrian Farber, the shoe-store owner, now soaked to the skin with rain and spray from the fire hoses, watched a crane clear charred siding, a broken door frame, fried electrical wires, and shards of glass from the road. He buried his face in his hands and wept.

Chapter Two

Follow the Brush

T HE SMELL of fried fish and salt air dissipated as I drove inland. Traffic stopped in front of a restaurant called Scroo Cooking— an image of a screw adorned its sign—to allow a seagull carrying a chicken bone in its beak to cross the road.

I made my way to the corner antique store marking my turn. Driving slowly up a steep hill with ranch-style homes, I saw nothing that anticipated Dogtown except for a house that was decorated for Halloween. Three jack-o'-lanterns sat on the front steps, a ghost made from a white bedsheet hung next to the door, a scarecrow stood on the front lawn. A stuffed witch in a black cape and pointy hat had flown her broomstick into a tree. Her face was flattened against the tree trunk. The handle of her broom extended out from the tree's other side, as though it had impaled the trunk. A few moments later, a brown sign with yellow lettering appeared: DOGTOWN CONSERVATION AREA/ESSEX NATIONAL HISTORIC SITE. I turned on my blinker. My heart flashed with anticipation.

A large boulder sat near the entrance like a good host, poised to welcome visitors. In the woods along the narrow, potholed road, two tall rocks angled toward each other as though in close conversation. Fewer than a hundred yards from the turnoff two modern houses seemed out of place from the undeveloped, ancient landscape I had expected, however unrealistically, from Hartley's paintings and writings about Dogtown. I pulled into a small empty parking lot next to a derelict sign box. An overstuffed garbage bag sat nearby. Bits of old, unidentifiable trash were scattered around. It looked as though few people ever came this way.

I got out of my truck, opened the tailgate, and sat down to study the map, skipping over sentences such as, "In the early 1980s Dogtown Common was under attack on several fronts. . . . Walking Dogtown trails was dangerous." I missed the reference to Anne Natti, about whom I knew nothing at that time. Eventually, I came to understand what these lines really meant: Dogtown was more than the setting of a horrific crime; this transgression had seemingly become one of the region's defining narratives. But for now, I blithely plotted my route through Dogtown. I had made this journey for two reasons: Dogtown had changed Marsden Hartley, and his Dogtown paintings had changed me.

WHEN I FIRST saw pictures of Hartley's work in a book five years earlier, I was enrolled in a college painting class that was required for my degree in art history. I had always wanted to paint, but all of my prior attempts at making anything that advanced beyond a doodle merely confirmed my belief that artistic skill was something you were either born with or not. Thus far, the class had reinforced this belief. I could not draw anything resembling a straight line or a perfect circle. I was not merely a novice, I was absolutely terrible. It was hopeless.

When an instructor gave us an assignment to re-create a painting by a known artist as a still life, I knew I was doomed. How we might interpret these compositions was open-ended: Picasso's *Les Demoiselles d'Avignon* could be arranged with torn baguettes, toothpaste, buttons, and hair combs as one student had done. I could have chosen any image, but knew that it would be hard enough to make my effort look like an actual *painting*, let alone something recognizable. I needed to find something obscure that I could get away with botching entirely.

The night before we were expected to assemble our still lifes, I pulled dozens of monographs off the library shelves until I came across books about Marsden Hartley. I had never heard of Hartley, but his paintings captivated me immediately. His Dogtown landscapes were unlike anything I had ever seen. I was immediately taken by a picture titled *Mountains in Stone, Dogtown.*

In *Mountains*, a large boulder writhes up from a horizontal jumble of dark rocks. Autumnal red and orange plants sprout upward between the rocks, pointing in different directions, as if resisting their own weight. It appears that if one rock moved, the others would tumble out of the picture. Another row of rocks (or perhaps mountains) lines a distant horizon. A slender, stylized tree resembling a cross fills the left side of the image. A long, white cloud stretches across a turquoise sky. Another cloud hovers above it expectantly.

The painting is full of contradictions. It is an empty, lonely setting crowded with rocks and plants. The sun's amber glow illuminates autumn's brittleness but also suggests warmth and abundance. The clouds appear as lightweight but solid forms, while the rocks look to be liquid, as though recently poured from the earth's cauldron. The rocks are monumental, like mountains rather than stones, dense sculptural volumes that evoke Cézanne yet surge upward energetically. With such vigor bound up in these rocks, it was not hard to sense some desperation behind the painting's creation. I felt as though I could never tire of looking at this picture. I knew right away that this was an image I had to learn how to paint.

The next day I arranged a group of root vegetables to create my still life in imitation of Hartley's composition. Every so often, my painting instructor lingered by my easel, stared as though deeply absorbed, and said "strange" or "peculiar," then walked away. I took this to mean I was on to something.

There is a style of Japanese calligraphy called *zuihitsu*, which translates literally as "follow the brush." In zuihitsu the calligrapher surrenders to the brush rather than consciously trying to control it, allowing the brush to tell its own story. Inevitably, the brushwork becomes both the journey and the destination. The more I allowed Hartley's original to guide me in this spirit of zuihitsu, the more painting began to feel natural to me, as if the gestures Hartley had used to create his image were embedded in some latent part of my muscle memory. Soon I was painting every day. Slowly the rutabagas, turnips, and potatoes I selected for my still life had turned to stone. A head of garlic rose into a mountain. Peeled onionskin morphed into papery, brittle shrubs.

Two weeks later—and much to my amazement—I had successfully reproduced the original. I had finally made a painting, something I had always wanted to do but never believed was possible.

Suddenly I was willing to follow Hartley anywhere. And in the spirit of zuihitsu, I began to wonder what kind of story a place named

Dogtown would tell. I imagined that one day I would find this unusual landscape and the source of Hartley's inspiration as if doing so would complete some undone part of me.

After I graduated, Hartley and Dogtown simmered in the back of my mind until I moved to Maine, Hartley's birth state, two years later. When friends asked me to join them for the opening of a Hartley retrospective at the Portland Museum of Art, I put them off; I wanted to go alone. I fantasized about Hartley, my imaginary friend and mentor, dressed in a white suit, cravat, and spats and meeting me at the door. Together we would saunter through the galleries, arm in arm.

One winter night when the air smelled of snow that had not yet begun to fall, I entered the museum hoping to watch his life unfold through a series of images that would build to the climax of his 1931 summer in Dogtown, which had been pivotal for him personally and artistically. I had faith in the alchemy of stories, and Hartley's, in particular, which included his struggles with identity, depression, and creativity.

MARSDEN, NÉ EDMUND, HARTLEY was born in 1877 in the mill town of Lewiston, Maine. His mother died when he was eight, and soon thereafter Hartley's father moved to Ohio with a new wife and his daughters, leaving his only son behind and in the care of an older sister. Young Hartley was forced to leave school at age fifteen to work in a shoe mill to help support his family.

When he was sixteen, Hartley's father summoned him to Ohio, where Hartley worked in a quarry office and began to paint. In time, he managed to save enough money for formal painting lessons, and before long his teacher arranged a scholarship for him to attend the Cleveland School of Art. After one semester, Hartley received a scholarship to study at William Merritt Chase's prestigious art academy, the New York School of Art.

After he finished art school, Hartley began to use his stepmother's maiden name, Marsden, which his friends convinced him had a more glamorous ring than his given one. Hartley moved back to Maine, explored one alternative spiritual community, then another, and wrestled with his sexual identity. Hartley's homosexuality most likely contributed to the loneliness and alienation he experienced in early-twentieth-century New England and throughout his life, but he also sought out desolate, remote settings for the sake of his art. In 1908 he moved to Maine's White Mountains, where he lived in isolation in order to paint.

Hartley entered these mountain paintings into a show at Boston's Metaphysical Club, where critic Philip Hale praised their "fine insanity." At about the same time he met Charles and Maurice Prendergast, who encouraged him to return to New York for the sake of his career and furnished him with letters of introduction to the painters William Glackens and Robert Henri. Not long after Hartley moved to New York, he was introduced to the legendary gallery owner Alfred Stieglitz.

At first Stieglitz resisted the meeting; the exhibition season at his Little Galleries of the Photo-Secession, or 291, was over, and he had recently turned down a show by Max Weber. But after seeing Hartley's work, Stieglitz changed his mind and granted the thirty-two-year-old artist the first solo exhibition of an American painter in 291's history. The show, *Exhibition of Paintings in Oil by Mr. Marsden Hartley, of Maine*, garnered strong reviews and established Hartley as a member of Stieglitz's celebrated circle, which included Edward Steichen, Paul Strand, Charles Demuth, Arthur Dove, John Marin, Max Weber, and Georgia O'Keeffe, whom Stieglitz eventually married.

With support from Stieglitz, Hartley was off to Europe in 1912, which furthered his exposure to European modernism. In Paris, Gertrude Stein saw his work and exclaimed, "at last, an original American." Hartley then moved to Berlin, where his style became increasingly abstract. Soon he was creating some of his best work, but not all was well. He fell in love with a German military officer named Karl von Freyburg, who was subsequently killed in World War I. Hartley's mourning inspired a series of abstract portraits of Freyburg that are considered some of his greatest works. Writing about these paintings in 2003, art critic Peter Schjeldahl stated, "In Berlin, Hartley did something new that has stayed new." Hartley was soon forced home by the mounting unrest of World War I.

From 1915 to 1920, Hartley lived an increasingly peripatetic life, moving from New York to Provincetown, Bermuda, New Mexico, and points in between, never occupying a single residence for more than ten months at a time. He also began to publish his poems and criticism in the *Nation*, the *New Republic*, the *Dial*, *Poetry*, *Vanity Fair*, and elsewhere. (Hartley would go on to publish books of poetry and critical essays.) By the summer of 1920 he was painting in Gloucester, where Edward Hopper, John Sloan, and Elie Nadelman also were making art. That summer, Hartley claimed he "meant to go for a look" in Dogtown, which he may have heard about from John Sloan, who painted the area in 1916. Nonetheless, by the end of the year, Hartley was back in Europe where he was to spend most of the next decade in southern France. Though Hartley never set foot in Dogtown that year, in 1931 he wrote Stieglitz and said that he had "carried the memory . . . [of Dogtown] everywhere."

In 1924, the critic Paul Rosenfeld established Hartley's importance by celebrating his expertise in "record[ing] the genius of a place." Nonetheless, Rosenfeld was concerned with what he saw as Hartley's inability to truly connect and "lose himself in his object." He suggested that only when Hartley started to paint his native New England would a deeper intuitive association be conveyed in his work.

New England was the last place Hartley wanted to go. He associated the region with little more than his Dickensian childhood, the pain of which haunted him throughout much of his life. He once confided in a letter to Stieglitz that whenever he heard a New England accent "a sad recollection rushed into my very flesh like sharpened knives." But in 1929, the powerful critic Henry McBride accused Hartley of being unfaithful to his native land by painting foreign landscapes. The American art market, which had developed a taste for regional, American subjects, reflected these criticisms. That year, a few of Hartley's friends purchased four of his European landscape paintings to help him out of his financial straits—these were the only paintings he sold. His career was seriously faltering. Hartley returned to the United States, then entering the Great Depression.

Prompted by McBride's criticism, Stieglitz convinced Hartley to try to put his painful memories aside and paint New England.

In the summer of 1930, Hartley traveled to the New Hampshire White Mountains to paint. In Hartley's own estimation, the attempt was a complete failure and depressed him so much he stopped painting altogether. "[I] lost most of my will power and moral courage for what remains to me of the thing called life," he confided to Rebecca Strand, photographer Paul Strand's wife. Before returning to New York that fall, Hartley declared somewhat histrionically, "I've learned one thing— Never never never to turn north again as long as I live."

While he was in this major depressive episode, Hartley's physical health began to suffer, too. By the winter of 1931 he was kept bedridden with severe bronchitis and mastoiditis, an infection of the skull's bony protuberances behind the ears that can quickly and easily develop into meningitis, a potentially fatal infection of the membranes that surround and protect the brain and the spinal cord. Hartley's doctor was not only concerned that the fifty-four-year-old painter would suffer permanent hearing loss, more urgently, as he told Hartley's friend Adelaide Kuntz, his condition was so severe he was likely to live for only another couple more years at most. Kuntz, in deference to Hartley's delicate psychological state, never told him the prognosis.

Though he was physically weak, suffering from persistent bouts of pain, and nearly deaf, the receipt of a Solomon R. Guggenheim grant to paint in Mexico the following year buoyed Hartley's spirits. To prepare, he decided to break his vow against New England and travel to Gloucester to paint Dogtown.

NOT A SINGLE Dogtown painting was included in the Portland Museum exhibit. The Hartley I wanted to know—the man who had staked everything on a wasteland—was nowhere in sight.

THAT IS HOW, like Dante's Virgil, Marsden Hartley had led me to the edge of these woods, where the air smelled of thousands of crisping autumn leaves. The sky was oceanic with clouds as light and foamy as cresting waves. Wind stirred the treetops, ruffling the heavy silence. The map identified a shooting range immediately south of Dogtown, but sounds of gunfire ricocheted from all around. It seemed as if the wind had grabbed this sound and was tossing it back and forth, and occasionally dropping it like a ball. Whenever the wind stopped, the gunfire rang out only from the shooting range's direction. The effect was disconcerting, but I trusted that the noise came from the shooting range alone. If not, I had hiked elsewhere in hunting season and believed my purple backpack would keep me from being mistaken for a deer.

Past a small bend, a gate blocked the road, presumably Dogtown's official entrance. Several bags of yard clippings sat below a NO DUMPING sign. This was it: the place I had wondered about for five years. I looked

around for something to reflect the importance of this moment—
perhaps a knot in a tree resembling the faces of Janus peering into the
past and the future, civilization and the wilds—but saw no such indica-
tor. Soon after I slipped past the gate, the asphalt road gave way to
gravel, then dirt. The path narrowed and rose gently. Thick shrubs
crowded among the few trees lining the way. Pebbles upgraded to rocks.
Ruts in the path took on greater relief.

The landscape before me opened to resemble Hartley's *Blueberry
Highway, Dogtown*, a painting that flows with energy, beckoning the
viewer to enter via a river of paint. The image is fraught with hopeful
anticipation; there is no way of knowing where the road may lead as it
spills forth for the viewer to follow.

The road climbed steadily, into a landscape of flax-colored meadows and brittle trees, as though autumn had drained all the life and
color of Hartley's vision from the scene. I did not know if this, the Dogtown Road, was the path Hartley painted and that had appeared so vibrant and alive, but I knew the road in *Blueberry Highway* led to a
vanishing point. Only by journeying beyond the reach of Hartley's
brush could I learn Dogtown's story, its mysterious ways.

Wispy trees and gnarled shrubs grew over an old, low stone wall
running intermittently alongside the path, which dated back to the colonial settlement's earliest days. It was easy to imagine seventeenth-
century neighbors leaning against the wall and gossiping. Elsewhere the
wall had been completely swallowed by brush and briar, as if it had
never existed. The scene was vaguely reminiscent of Hartley's *The Old
Bars, Dogtown*. In the painting, looping, twisted fence wire hangs between towerlike fence posts above a deteriorating stone wall enclosing
a field in such vibrant shades of green one can almost smell the grass.
The posts look as if they might collapse, but Hartley secured them in
place with a heavy application of paint. This image of a neglected, broken fence corralling an empty space is surprisingly lively, as though a
spirit were trapped between the posts and suspended in paint. Perhaps
that is why after seeing *The Old Bars* in 1939 at the Whitney Museum,
where it is now in the permanent collection, critic Alfred Frankfurter
praised it for its "new Druidism."

As I walked on, various Hartley images continued to emerge from
the landscape, but Dogtown also began to seem familiar in an altogether different way, as if I had stumbled upon some long-forgotten,

collective memory waiting to be rediscovered. Perhaps that is why I felt as though Dogtown was older than other places I had traveled to, that it knew something and was watching me. Maybe because I grew up in Georgia next to a Civil War battlefield and played in antebellum mansions where I was always convinced the eyes of ancestral portraits were following me as I ran by, such ideas are not unusual to me. That is how I came to think that if I could listen to Dogtown's spirit, I might learn something essential, some sort of wisdom that I craved but did not yet know how to seek. And in a strange, comforting way, I felt as if Dogtown's ancient ghosts began to rise up and greet me.

I passed through an opening in the wall into a meadow where tall grasses lay flat, as though cattle had recently laid down their heft, but there were no signs of livestock. The sound of a woman's laughter drifted by in the wind. I stopped to look around, but the only traces of people I could see were rectangular pits lined with stones that appeared to be caving in on themselves.

According to my map these pits were cellar holes, the last remaining vestiges of colonists' homes. They could be traced to their individual pre-Revolutionary owners by small stones carved with numbers poking out of the grass alongside each cellar, but there was no reference or guide to the numbers, nor was anything posted to explain their purpose. That someone had taken the time to identify these ruins made the numbered rocks seem even more peculiar, as if they were remnants of a forgotten museum. It was easier to look across this landscape and envision the original forest primeval that Gloucester's settlers had first discovered in 1623 than to picture intact the modest dwellings colonists built sometime thereafter. But there among the ruins, the spectral presence of these people was inescapable. I wondered if Dogtown had absorbed something of the burdens of those who had been here before, as if places, like people, can be scarred by events and retain these wounds through the years.

The wind moved over the woods in powerful gusts, raking across distant treetops, sometimes spiraling in close, carrying the smells of woodsmoke and burning leaves, and leaving a salty taste in my mouth. Then the trees went suddenly still, the woods silent, until the wind worked across the highland again, spinning leaves into dust devils as they fell.

Unlike the landscape I had encountered along the path, Hartley's

painted Dogtown was nearly unrecognizable in this meadow surrounded by a burgeoning forest, as though he had been rubbed out of
the picture. The large rocks he had painted and *Mountains in Stone*, the
painting I most wanted to see, seemed far away and perhaps unreach-
able by foot on this day—or ever.

Trails laced through the woods in a variety of directions. I tried several of these, but they ended abruptly. One disappeared at a blueberry
thicket. Another terminated at a large boulder. A third stopped at no
place in particular. The next one I explored tracked several hundred
yards through the woods to a small fire pit filled with empty Budweiser
bottles with seared labels. Smoke drifted off a smoldering cigarette
butt, as if someone had departed mere moments before I arrived. I
turned and quickly walked away. My palms had started to sweat.

Reaching a trail juncture, I consulted the map, hoping to trace my
route back to the meadow with the cellar holes, but I could not figure
out where I was. I continued down the widest, seemingly more trafficked path. A strong gust of wind arose. Leaves tumbled. The wind
dropped suddenly, uncannily, replaced by a draft of silence, which is
how I noticed that something heavy was rustling through nearby leaves.
Struck by the sense that someone was following me, I froze. Blood
rushed through my head audibly. My heart pounded loudly. I peered
through the trees and up the path and back, but saw nothing and no
one. I continued on.

The sound of cracking leaves grew louder and closer. As soon as I
stopped, it stopped, too. A chill slid across the back of my neck. Sweat
webbed my forehead. I stood as motionless and quiet as possible. Whoever or whatever was there could see me and hear my breathing. There
was no place to hide, nothing I could do.

I tried not to let my imagination and some rustling leaves get the
best of me. The noises were just a deer or a squirrel foraging nearby—
nothing else, I reasoned. But I could not calm myself down. Gravel
crunched loudly under my feet as I started to run until the air was still
and eerily quiet except for the sounds of my breath and apprehensive
footfalls landing hard and fast upon the earth.

I came upon two tombstones standing in the shadows of some tall
pines. One was inscribed "Rayne Adams 1880–1931." I wondered if
Hartley met Rayne Adams before he died. The other, marked "Leila

Norwood Adams 1887," did not list a date of death. In my anxious state, I assumed she had vanished in Dogtown.

Catching my breath, I worried that if I went any farther I would simply disappear into Dogtown, never to return. I wanted to retrace my footsteps and find my way back to Hartley's landscape, to step back into his frame where his images, for all of their peculiarities, felt comforting; but nothing looked familiar. There were no mountains in stone in sight. Just me standing alone and scared in some strange woods in the outskirts of a town where I knew no one and no one knew me.

I stared at the map. All I could focus on were the blank white spaces between the skinny black lines of the paths and the fat green bulges of the land's contours. Their emptiness absorbed me.

I kept walking, trying to find my way back to the gate. Eventually the trees parted, opening onto a wide path; according to the map, this had to be the Commons Road. I felt momentarily relieved, but soon realized that the crumbling stone wall and ancient road in front of me looked the same as the Dogtown Road where my journey had begun. But unless I had walked some circuitous route through the woods, that could not have been possible. I worried that I was completely lost. To get my bearings I looked for the sun, which had started draining into the horizon.

I headed north, following a route into the darkening woods, and hoping eventually to intersect the Dogtown Road. A crow stood in the path and pecked at the ground, then made its way down the trail behind me as though out for a nice little dusktime stroll. I had read about Old Peg Wesson, a Gloucester witch who cursed a group of soldiers that had insulted her before they headed off to fight the French and Indians at Louisburg on Cape Breton Island in 1745. When the soldiers saw a crow hovering above their Louisburg camp, they shot at it repeatedly, missing each time. The soldiers believed that Old Peg had flown hundreds of miles to taunt them. Recalling that the base metals in their shot could not kill witches, one of the soldiers plucked a silver button from his sleeve and shot the crow in its leg. The bird fell from the sky to its death. After the men returned to Gloucester, they learned that Old Peg had fallen, broken her leg, and died. A doctor examined her and discovered a silver button matching those on a military uniform in her leg. In his account of Old Peg, John J. Babson, Gloucester's most trusted historian, commented on the tale's improbability, but remarked that it was widely believed at the time. With the strange way Dogtown was making me feel—disoriented, tired, afraid, and a little ridiculous— I could not fault anyone for harboring suspicions about crows, particularly when one was following me at a close clip. I turned to shoo the bird away, but it was no longer there.

Dusk was quickly settling in among the trees. The woods around me were coming to life. Large shapes I assumed were giant rocks held a vague glowing cast. Hartley had been deeply interested in mysticism, but he never mentioned Old Peg or witches in any of his Dogtown writings. Maybe he had been in cahoots with them and drank potion from their bubbling vats. That was what brought on the big life-changing epiphany he experienced. That was why the pool flamed and the stones rose into mountains and the rocks surged like Leviathans and the paths flowed like so many rivers.

That is how I almost scared myself to death while walking alone in these dark, unfamiliar woods. I was lost inside my imaginings and had no idea how to get out.

The path eventually rounded a corner and intersected with what had to be the Dogtown Road. In the shadows lining the road the colonists' walls appeared familiar and comforting. It was possible I had simply circled back to the Commons Road, but I felt certain I was on the right path. The gate soon appeared.

I turned around for one last look into Dogtown. Blackness was seeping into the woods like freshly drawn India ink, bleeding from the outlines of the trees. I could no longer see the edges of things.

Chapter Three

Cynomancy

L INDA RYAN BUSIED HERSELF in her old Victorian house. Even on the rainiest days, the house, with its floor-to-ceiling windows and brightly painted floors, was cheerful. It had a wood-burning cookstove and a zinc tub, and Linda's two horses corralled out back. When Anne came over, the two women talked, played piano, and sang as merrily as when they had lived together.

Earlier that morning, Anne had told Linda that she would arrive by eleven. When Anne did not show up, Linda called the trailer, but no one answered. She called again at noon, then tried Anne's brother-in-law John Tuck. He and his wife, Isabel Natti, Erik's sister, a print-maker, lived with their thirteen-month-old son Nathaniel in Tuck's family's old candy factory, a large house with Victorian gingerbreading. Anne would have passed their house soon after exiting the woods on her way to Linda's. John and Isabel, adamant about only eating animals they could raise themselves, always came home from work for their midday "dinner." Linda thought they might have invited Anne in for a meal.

As soon as Linda explained why she was calling, Tuck, who had introduced Anne to Erik, began to worry. "I thought there was a logical explanation," Linda later recalled thinking at the time. Anne and Woofer couldn't be very far away; it was about three miles from the Nattis' place to Rockport through the woods and five over roads. But the woods were thick and the trails were not properly maintained. Sections of these ancient paths got washed out in heavy rains. Deadfall blown down in the storm could have blocked a trail and forced Anne to go another way. She could have fallen and injured herself.

After lunch, Isabel drove Tuck to a quarry in the woods, rather than back to the Ralph Waldo Emerson Inn, where he worked. John walked part of Anne's regular route to the trailer while Isabel drove to the camp with Nathaniel and looked for Anne around there. Linda searched Rockport.

Anne and Woofer were nowhere to be found. Tuck called Erik at Marblehead High School. It was two o'clock. Four hours had passed since Anne Natti had been assaulted.

Erik arrived home just before 4:00 P.M. As he drove up Quarry Street, two teenage boys approached and asked if he had seen their neighbor's dog. It had followed them into the woods earlier that day and gotten lost. Erik asked if they had seen Anne or Woofer, but they had not seen a soul.

Once in the trailer, Erik started making phone calls. No one had seen Anne. He left her a note, as was their custom, saying he was walking to Rockport and to call Tuck or Linda as soon as she arrived. He wrote down the time: 4:00 P.M.

Erik's senses sharpened as he walked deeper into the woods. The sounds of the forest settling into itself after the rain were amplified. Water dripping from trees sounded louder than before. Birds rustled heavily. The sound of a swaying branch could have been Anne. Or someone else. He called for Anne and Woofer, but there was no response.

Most people would not notice the distinguishing traits of a forest, but Erik had both a scientist's eye for detail and a complete familiarity with this terrain; he recognized even the slightest variations in the land. He had known Dogtown when it was barren, its contours exposed, and could recall which trees had been only as big as his arm when he was a child. He knew white pine (five needles growing in a cluster) from red (two five-inch-long needles per bundle) and what different trees revealed about the soils in which they grew. A paper birch from a gray birch. A marsh from a bog. A blueberry bog from sphagnum. He understood that plants and trees reveal as much about human or wildlife traffic as the ground does. He studied the landscape, taking in details that might be important, watching and hoping for signs of Anne.

Erik followed her usual route, which yielded clear and fresh prints made by men's shoes—these would belong to John Tuck—and two sets of smaller prints—the boys'—but no real clues. He took the same path home and confirmed that Anne's boots were still gone. He called Tuck, notified the police, crossed out "4:00 P.M." on his note, wrote "6:00 P.M.," and set out again.

Erik sloshed through puddles, calling Anne's name and noticing how the path changed from large-grain sand to fine and how certain muds, depending on their clay content, take a better impression of a shoe than others. That was how he recognized the distinctive footprint of his wife's boots. He followed the prints, but they disappeared. He scanned the area but found no trace of Anne.

Climbing a hill to better survey the area, he spotted a single knobbly motorbike track and a set of especially large men's footprints. He followed these until they, too, suddenly ended. It was as though whoever he was tracking had simply vanished into the shadows now gently streaming into Dogtown's shallow vales.

As the sun began to drop, he heard a faint sound coming straight at him through the rising darkness. Woofer suddenly sprang from the shadows, prancing playfully, landing muddy paws on Erik's pants.

Woofer's surprise appearance made Erik's heart skip a beat. But where was Anne? She must have heard him calling and sent Woofer. She must be around the bend. She was there waiting for him with her broken leg, her twisted ankle. She would be cold, but fine. Erik scratched the pup behind his ears and stroked his thick fur.

Woofer ran off, came trotting back, ran off again, and returned. He did this anxious back-and-forth when Anne and Erik were walking together and one got ahead of the other on the trail. Suddenly Woofer stopped. He began to tremble.

A motorbike whined in the distance. Woofer tucked his tail and whimpered. It was out of character for the pup to shrink in fear. He had heard motorbikes in the woods before and knew not to be afraid.

Linda had saddled one of her horses and set out into the woods, eventually crossing paths with Erik. Together they paced the forest corridors for a while until reaching a trail juncture. Linda took the path that led to Eden Farm, where she planned to stable her horse. Erik went the other way, taking a trail he had not yet investigated.

Like a creature from the *Kalevala*, in which animals are often, if not always messengers, Woofer stepped in front of Erik, leading him down the path. The air was quiet. So still. There were no sounds except Woofer's gentle padding and the ground sponging up Erik's footsteps. If Erik strayed the slightest bit, Woofer hovered close and waited. Woofer's behavior was an ancient form of cynomancy, the art of divination based on canine activity. He was telling Erik to follow. But to where?

Slowly, gingerly, Woofer turned down the road to Johnson's Quarry. On hot, carefree summer days, kids jump from high rocks into the cool water that has filled in the quarry since it was abandoned during the Depression. Maybe Anne was waiting there, but instead, Woofer walked toward Professor Norton's tree farm, which Erik had previously overlooked.

The puppy entered the stand of young dwarf saplings and rooted around the matted undergrowth with his nose. A pile of clothing became visible: tan turtleneck, dark green chamois shirt, and blue sweater lying together, inside out and covered in blood, now dried. Striped, knitted vest. Tights and dungarees, also turned inside out. Rubber boots with socks standing in them. Yellow slicker zipped to the neck as though Anne had evaporated, all but for the blood that caked Erik's blue bandanna and the inside of the hood. The Ziploc bag with her bra, underwear, and the red-handled dog leash sat nearby. *Where was Anne?*

Nose to the ground, Woofer carried on for another thirty feet, looking back fearfully, making sure Erik followed. The flora was so dense it was hard to walk. Eric didn't see her body until he was almost on top of it. The bright yellow rain pants glowed through the thick mat of green. He stepped in to see Anne's arms pulled behind her body, her face half buried, hair matted with leaves and blood that had streamed from her ears, her exposed skin shining in the fading light. He untied the rain pants from around her neck, to make it easier for her to breathe. He reached out his hand. Felt a shock as soon as he touched her cold skin. He opened his mouth. Before even realizing that he had let out a scream, Erik Natti had started to run.

Suddenly he stopped. Hands trembling, he took some twigs, and arranged them on the path, marking the way. Shadows began to lengthen around him, coiling themselves around the trunks of trees, spreading a rich layer of dusk across the ground. He kept running through more woods, past the trailer to the nearest house.

The O'Hanleys opened their door to see their quiet neighbor, breathless and wild-eyed, tears brining his face. His wife was dead in the woods, the same woods that surrounded the O'Hanleys' home.

Erik called the police, then John Tuck, who broke out in sobs as soon as Erik told him the news.

Police cruisers arrived and blocked off the street in this area that was so far from the heart of Gloucester and hidden in the woods, the cops considered it to be "pretty much the boonies." Erik led them and the medical examiner into the forest.

The Tucks and Linda waited at the O'Hanleys'. Hours passed, but they stayed, searching the furry night for flashes of search beams coming through the trees.

It was nearly eleven o'clock when Mr. Pike, the undertaker, drove his hearse through Quarry Street's potholes and mud. He emerged in a suit, tie, and dress shoes, as if he had been summoned to retrieve a body from an old sea captain's parlor, not from deep in the woods. Mr. Pike could not carry the body out on his own so the policemen grudgingly placed the corpse on a stretcher and carried it through the trees to the hearse.

The remaining police investigators studied the crime scene. With bulbs flashing into the blackness, their cameras recorded the deep imprint where Anne's face had been pushed into the earth.

Chapter Four

The Painter of Dogtown

A FTER THAT FIRST TRIP to Dogtown, I convinced myself that the sound of my own walking was all that had followed me that day. Soon I was tingling with what Virginia Woolf called "the strange human craving for the pleasure of feeling afraid." The only thing to fear in Dogtown, I told myself, was how easily I had let myself become frightened. The place already had me in its grip. I was convinced that Dogtown was part of the hidden America I had wondered about since childhood.

I grew up regularly hearing a certain type of story: my maternal grandparents' tales of Revolutionary and Civil War heroes and of plantation noblesse oblige. Once my parents divorced and my immediate family essentially dissolved, I came to depend on these stories as a source of familiar, if distant comfort. Throughout my childhood, I yearned to belong to this history and become part of its proud lineage, but every character in these tales was so polished, so refined, so unlike me. In spite of my best efforts, it was altogether obvious that I was cut from a different cloth. I felt cast out, as if I did not and would never belong.

As I grew a bit older, began to learn about the pieces of bygone America that my grandparents had never told me about and that were also excluded from my school history lessons, I suspected that there were whole other collections of tales somewhere, perhaps lost. I fantasized about finding these alternate, unsung stories, this forgotten America. It was out there somewhere, waiting to take me in. This yearning held sway over most of my life choices and eventually became an enduring part of me. The more I learned about Dogtown, the more I became convinced that it was one of the places where this secret America had been hiding. Centuries of stories were there anticipating the moment when they would be awakened from their stone sleep.

Searching for clues, I again turned to Hartley.

MARSDEN HARTLEY HAD almost canceled his 1931 trip to Cape Ann. The day before his ship was scheduled to sail from New York to Boston in late June, he panicked. Sick with anxiety, and still ailing from his numerous illnesses, Hartley rushed to his doctor. He had expected to hear that he was not well enough to travel, but the doctor convinced Hartley that he was merely suffering from a severe case of "New York–itis." There was only one cure for this condition: leave town as soon as possible.

The travel exhausted him. After arriving at the guesthouse on Rocky Neck where he had resided in the summer of 1920, Hartley slept almost continuously for nearly two weeks. Though he had journeyed all this way to paint, Hartley was too weak to travel the five miles from his boardinghouse into Dogtown. His slow recovery from the mastoiditis—he was still hard of hearing—and nervous exhaustion discouraged him, as did the prospect of making art. But Hartley, who had not painted in nine months, told Adelaide Kuntz, "I must see if I can work again." His career and emotional well-being depended upon it.

Three lines from T. S. Eliot's poem "Ash Wednesday" eventually inspired him to get out of bed: "Teach us to care and not to care / Teach us to sit still / Even among these rocks." To the rocks he went.

By mid-July, Hartley was going to Dogtown every day, walking "alone and empty-handed," and covering at least five miles each day. Once he found a place he liked, Hartley "did as I always have to do about a place—look at it—see it—and think of nothing else."

For weeks Hartley sat still among Dogtown's rocks in this manner, learning to care and not to care, and memorizing as much of the landscape as he could. Artistic and spiritual practices were one and the same to Hartley, who believed in the Emersonian notion that God can be found by looking closely at nature.

Ten weeks after arriving in Gloucester, Hartley's health had improved enough for him "to pull through and get some decent work done." He confided in Alfred Stieglitz that he hoped to undergo a "general resurrection—revelation—evolution out of revolution" and to become "the" painter of Dogtown.

IN THE YEAR that lapsed between my first foray into Dogtown and the following autumn, I thought often of returning to the area, but the thrill and dark pleasure I had basked in after that first trip gave way to moments of reason. What if Dogtown was truly dangerous?

But danger increased the possibility of magic. Whales breaching from the earth. Flaming pools. Women transformed into witches, who then took wing in the form of crows. Mountains rising from stones. Hartley's ghost waiting to teach me the enigmatic ways of this secret place.

That initial trip to Dogtown had also piqued my curiosity about the area. Why had people left the coast to build a thriving settlement there and then left it for good, never to be resettled or developed again? How had this ghost town continued to exist seemingly unchanged so close to a major metropolis in the country's third most densely populated state? Judging by the close-set homes, both old and new, that I had passed in town, it seemed inevitable that Boston's sprawl would slowly extend runners out to the island and sprout new houses on any available land. After watching a tract of land near my then home in Portland, Maine, turn into a large subdivision seemingly overnight, I deepened my resolve to return to Cape Ann. To prepare, I immersed myself in Dogtown's stories until I felt emboldened, fearless, inspired.

I returned in late October. This time I arrived better prepared and carried a compass, a map, a flashlight, some granola bars, water, and several books of Hartley's paintings, as if they, too, could help me find my way in the woods.

A gentle pumpkin hue tinged Dogtown's morning light. A lazy breeze picked itself up every once in a while and then set itself down as if to rest. Leaves skittered by as though they were running from something.

I could have been following one of the many routes I had taken the previous year, but I had gotten completely turned around that day. Now I was on a mission to get to the Whale's Jaw, which Hartley had sketched and painted various times and was clearly identified on my map. Like an oracle, the monolith would lead me to *Mountains in Stone* and nothing would distract me from finding it.

It was not long before I had stumbled upon one of Roger W. Babson's large carved rocks. This boulder, which could have filled the entirety of my apartment bedroom, was carved with the words NEVER TRY NEVER WIN. According to my map, the Whale's Jaw was in the opposite direction of this and Babson's other inscribed rocks. Taking the boulder's advice, I turned around and continued on.

I wandered down another trail until I arrived at a boulder that stood at least twenty feet tall and looked like a friendly, mythical beast turned to stone. It was immediately apparent that this rock, which was identified on my map as Peter's Pulpit, was the subject of Hartley's painting *Altar Boulder*, an ungainly composition of a similarly giant, flat-topped rock with exaggerated round, bulging sides and a skinny cairn leaning against it. The rock dominates a buttery orange–hued landscape, as if everything were insignificant in comparison. Peter's Pulpit must have been one of the rocks Hartley was thinking about when he wrote that Dogtown is "essentially druidic in its appearance." Seeing it meant that the Whale's Jaw and the other large, dolmen-like rocks he described were not that much farther ahead. I carried on.

AS THE SUMMER of 1931 ripened to autumn, Hartley began to feel as though he was "casting off a wearisome chrysalis." He arranged to extend his stay in Gloucester until Christmas. After moving to a house on Rocky Neck Avenue where seagulls gathered outside the window, he fell into a rhythm of writing in the morning, walking in Dogtown almost every afternoon, and painting at night. He told Stieglitz, "I think I have set the pace now for the rest of my life."

In October, Hartley wrote Kuntz an elated letter and said, "I think I am succeeding in giving my entire being to this extraordinary stretch of almost metaphysical landscape . . . and while my pictures are small— they are more intense than ever before." He was finally beginning to produce the kind of paintings he had longed to create in New Hampshire the preceding summer. The change so inspired Hartley that he also began writing prolifically. He hoped to complete enough poems to fill a volume that he planned to title *Pressing Foot*.

Writing in his autobiography years later, Hartley would describe Dogtown in evocative tones: "A sense of eeriness pervades all the place therefore and the white shirts of those huge boulders, mostly granite, stand like sentinels guarding nothing but shore—sea gulls fly over it on their way from the marshes to the sea—otherwise the place is forsaken and majestically lonely, as if nature had at last formed one spot where she can live for herself alone." What Hartley had discovered was the one place where he could paint and write for himself alone.

Dogtown gave Hartley the New England homecoming that had eluded him in New Hampshire. Though the year before coming to Gloucester he had vowed never to return to the region, by November he wrote Rebecca Strand and said that Dogtown had given him "a real connection with my native soil. . . . It is a place . . . of psychic clarity." He composed a poem titled "Return of the Native," which included this telltale line: "He who finds will / to come home / will surely find old faith / made new again, / and lavish welcome."

The native had at last returned and had undergone a complete physical, mental, and creative transformation. By December he wrote Strand to say, "Dogtown is mine and as far as I know I have put it on the esthetic map . . . I must do some more Dogtown pictures—it is so in my system now." The ability to paint the unseen, most notably the sensation that a place is not merely alive but also knowing, had taken root inside him and would continue to grow throughout the remainder of his career. He would eventually fully embrace his New England identity and move to Maine, where the inspiration he found in Dogtown would serve as a springboard for some of his most celebrated works.

EVENTUALLY I CAME UPON a tepee and some wooden tripods filling a clearing just off the Commons Road. Leaves crunched underfoot as I started away from the road for a closer look. A squirrel sat on a nearby rock feverishly chewing away at an acorn and watching me with intent as though I were trespassing on its land.

The tripods had been constructed from slender branches stripped of their bark and lashed together with rope. They appeared to be waiting for canvas to transform them into tepees, but for the fact that bundles of twigs hung from ropes inside them. The scene reminded me of *The Blair Witch Project*, a horror film in which three students go into the woods to investigate a local legend, come across similar tripods, and never return. It was an eerie sight, but I was not going to turn back because of something that reminded me of a creepy film.

I sat on the ground and kicked off my boots to shake out the pebbles that had worked their way inside. The squirrel froze. The twig bundles began to spin inside the tripods, but I didn't feel a breeze; in fact, there was next to no wind that day. It was so quiet it seemed as if I could hear every branch snap, leaf rustle, and a bit of gravel crunch for miles—all punctuated by a rhythmic tapping sound.

A man dressed in a black hooded cloak struck the ground with a long wooden walking stick as he came up the Commons Road, then disappeared around a bend with his cloak billowing behind him. I could feel my heart beating so hard I worried that the man could hear it even though he was already gone. Soon another man in a similar hooded cape made his way up the road. I crouched down lower, afraid to move. I had broken out in a cold sweat. The squirrel scampered away.

The men had startled me, but I wondered if they were just some harmless guys who were on their way to a Society for Creative Anachronism meet-up where they would make chain mail with their friends and brew a giant vat of mead. Alternatively, something else might have been going on nearby; Hartley once wrote that Dogtown "gives the feeling that an ancient race might turn up at any moment and renew an ageless rite there." Maybe there was some truth to this. Witches were not just part of the past in this part of Massachusetts; Salem was a mere sixteen miles down the road and contemporary witches congregated there for a giant convention-cum-party every Halloween, which was less than a week away. Plus, Dogtown had reputedly once been the home of witches; maybe these men were gathering in homage to them. I wanted to know what the men were up to. I got up and started in their direction, but didn't make it very far. The sight of a huge pair of odd-looking boulders stopped me in my tracks.

A pointy stone with a smooth, diagonal underside that stood at least twenty feet tall towered over two smaller, flat boulders. According to my map, this was the Whale's Jaw, but the boulder did not rise from the earth with all the force of a great mammal, as Hartley had painted it. Its lower jaw was broken in two.

I felt stricken. Shocked. How could this have happened?

"I want to paint the livingness of appearances," Hartley once said, and one of his Whale's Jaw pastel drawings from 1931 shows how thoroughly he succeeded in this endeavor. As art historian Gail Scott has pointed out, in this particular work Hartley made the rock's top jaw dark and the lower one lighter to take after the coloring of a real whale. He then added a mark on the rock's surface to resemble an eye. The rock's edges are curvilinear, mammalian. Hartley's whale evoked the permanence of stone and the energy of a living spirit. It is strong and soulful, as though the stonelike depression Hartley had suffered through had softened while drawing it.

The broken Whale's Jaw was hard for me to bear. That a rock could be cleft along a nearly perfect forty-five-degree angle and stand upright for tens of thousands of years seemed miraculous. That it also strongly resembled the greatest, most mythical creature of the sea made it that much more magical.

I turned around and left, wishing that there were someone with whom I could share my disappointment, someone who, without my having to do much explaining, would understand.

I had hoped that seeing the Whale's Jaw would confirm my belief that Dogtown's landscape had encouraged Hartley's personal transformation, but it seemed that I had come too late.

Chapter Five

Le Beauport

O N TUESDAY, June 26, 1984, news of Anne Natti's murder flew from the *Gloucester Daily Times'* delivery cars, landed in mailboxes and on doorsteps in snug villages with charming names—Riverdale, Annisquam, Bay View, Lanesville, Folly Cove, Pigeon Cove, Rocky Neck, Eastern Point—that fit the distinctive coves, inlets, and promontories of the island's irregular coastline. In these little communities, each of which has its own unique character, colonial homes and small businesses huddle together as though bracing themselves against the sea and whoever may live in the next village over. When people this side of the Cut say they are part of the landscape, as they often do, they mean it somewhat literally. Here social boundaries on island Cape Ann often conform to geographic ones. Finns settled in Lanesville, Swedes in Pigeon Cove. Sicilians made their homes in Fort Square. Portuguese fishermen dominate "Portugee" Hill. Lebanese and Syrians settled on Maplewood Avenue, while the WASPs took to the edges of the place, Eastern Point in one direction and the Annisquam peninsula to the west.

While a few old-timers boast to have never crossed the Cut, some also claim to have never set foot in other Cape Ann villages, either. "It may as well be the end of the earth out there," said a Maplewood Avenue resident who purports to have never been to Lanesville and Folly Cove, which are on the northern side of the island. Whether these statements are true or an exaggeration is less important than the pride of place and provincialism that Cape Anners seek to convey with such remarks. In any given Cape Ann neighborhood, residents may know one another's business but know nothing of what goes on beyond their own village or block. That is why news of Anne Natti's murder traveled quickly in some places but not in others. It was like the ocean's unequal displays of power, crashing and pounding incessantly against jagged rocks in one spot and gently lapping back and forth in another—each force changing the shape of the land in its own way.

Tourists appeared immune to the news, if they had even heard it. They never went near the woods anyway; in fact, most of them did not even know Dogtown existed. They milled about Gloucester's most famous landmark, a bronze statue of a man in oilskins at the wheel of a fishing boat gazing intently toward the horizon. Though the Gloucester Fisherman's Memorial is actually a cenotaph honoring centuries of local fishermen lost at sea, most out of towners recognize the "Man at the Wheel" in a more profane context: boxes of Gloucester-based Gorton's fish sticks. Beneath the statue's gaze, the blue and green sea fills Gloucester Harbor, and is as enchanting as on the 1606 day when Samuel de Champlain explored the coast and named Gloucester "Le Beauport." That name was dropped after Captain John Smith sailed through in 1614 and called the promontory "Tragabigzanda," in honor of a Turkish princess who helped him escape slavery. (All of this took place before another exotic maiden, Pocahontas, saved Smith's life in Virginia.) People here are ever grateful that England's seventeenth-century Prince Charles put an end to Smith's romantic gesture by naming the place in honor of his mother, Queen Ann.

If there were any proof that Champlain got the name right the first time, Tuesday morning, June 26, 1984, was it. On this bright summer day painters stood at their easels along the Rocky Neck peninsula, sketching harbor scenes, and hoping to capture the town's weary beauty, as generations of artists have done ever since Fitz Henry Lane first painted the region in the 1800s. Artists such as Winslow Homer, William Morris Hunt, John Henry Twachtman, Childe Hassam, Charles and Maurice Prendergast, Stuart Davis, John Sloan, Edward Hopper, Hartley, Milton Avery, Paul Manship, and many others have followed in Lane's footsteps by drawing inspiration from Cape Ann's land and sea ever since.

But on this June Tuesday, Gloucester's residents were still in shock over a different sight: the Main Street fire. One of them, a young letter carrier named Jack Chase, passed the building's charred remains as he walked his mail route. Chase, who had watched the blaze from his second-story window, worried about the ash and ruin so close to his home. Chase knew his Gloucester history and was fully aware of the fact that fire had destroyed downtown Gloucester more than once before, consuming buildings and people. This time the flames had burned eight buildings but was extinguished before anyone got injured. It was a miracle that registered lightly on no one, not the business owners who lost their livelihoods, the residents who lost their homes, or the neighborhood's mailman.

Chase turned his back on this scene and continued into the gleaming day, but thoughts of the fire weighed on him. Chase, like many Gloucester residents, felt an especially strong passion for this olden island city. Any affront or tragedy that befell the community pained him deeply, as it did others; it was part of an unwritten code of sentiment that was embedded in the fabric of this historic seaport.

Gloucester has long been referred to as a "suburb of the sea." For more than three hundred years, from the 1600s until the early 1950s, most traffic in and out of this place came and went by water. In 1984 many residents were still continuing in their ancestors' ways by earning a living from the sea. This long-standing maritime tradition intensifies Gloucester's insular, island character. It has created a self-reliant, egalitarian community with what Chase calls "four hundred years of tensile strength" and a corresponding social network that is so strong, he claims, "it's like girders holding up the community—but it can be equally destructive."

If anyone Chase passed along his route this morning knew about Anne Natti or was concerned about a murderer at large, he did not see it reflected in their faces. St. Peter's Fiesta—or Fiesta, as locals call it— was scheduled to open the following evening. Workmen had spent weeks pinning pieces of colored aluminum foil into an altar that towered forty-five feet tall and stretched eighty feet wide. They painted trompe l'oeil colonnades and scallop-shaped niches inspired by St. Peter's Basilica and village churches across Sicily (Gloucester's Italian American population is predominantly Sicilian and nearly always distinguishes the island from the country's mainland), Italy, and Greece. They tested lightbulbs and generators while children climbed scaffolding and watched carnival hawkers unload cotton candy machines, mid-way games, and rides with metallic limbs done up in bright paint and colored neon lights.

As the bearer of news both good and bad, Chase did not take his job lightly. Each time he handed over the mail, he watched for fluctuations in people's moods, sometimes taking the brunt of their emotions, such as the time when a man who had lost his job ran after Chase and threatened him. Chase's supervisors told him to "use dog spray on the man," who was a known arsonist and "general nut case," but instead Chase simply told the man that if he didn't calm down, he wouldn't be getting his mail. This is just how things are in Gloucester, Chase concedes. "We tolerate each other's weirdness, make room for it, and get out of the way when we can tell someone is going to snap. People here are well informed on a ground level. It's an animal thing." The man continued to cause trouble until he attempted to hold up the post office with a toy gun and was taken away.

One person whom Chase knew he might need to steer clear of on this particular day was the owner of a small grocery store on the corner of Washington and Beacon Streets. Letters stamped "urgent," "private," or "confidential" quietly revealed that the man's business was failing. This morning, as Chase walked into the shop, the proprietor, an older Italian man who was fairly new to town, sat behind the counter, brooding, as per usual. When Chase handed over the mail, he caught the *Gloucester Daily Times*' headline out of the corner of his eye: "Slain Woman Found in Woods." Chase stared at the paper, trying to absorb the scant details of the story, including the "severe injuries" to Anne Natti's face and head. Looking up, Chase searched the proprietor's face for a reaction, but the man stared impassively out the window, watching cars roll by, as if waiting for the day to move along with them.

"This is unbelievable," Chase said, his face blanched in shock. He stared at the shopkeeper, imploring him with his eyes. "This kind of thing just does not happen here. Who could do such a thing? Why?"

"Yeah, yeah, yeah," The proprietor said, turning to look at Chase like he was an idiot; then he began thumbing through the mail.

Chase stepped outside, where things appeared just as they had moments before. The sunlight was so clear as to be crystalline, but suddenly "nothing was the same." Chase did not know Erik or Anne Natti personally, but he had played in the band at their wedding. Anne was so friendly; whenever he saw her afterward, she always said hello, but that was the extent of their acquaintance with each other. And Dogtown: Chase had taken his children there many times. He wanted to talk to someone and "break the shock somehow," to do something. But nothing could be done, which made him feel stricken and helpless.

As news of Anne Natti's murder spread, Chase recalled, people "went around with their eyes glazed over." A pair of Rockport residents remembered that it was simply "a shattering experience." "Of all the nice ladies who walked across these woods, she was the best of us," a Folly Cove resident stated years later. "Why was she the one to die?"

It was not as if no one had ever been attacked in Gloucester or Dogtown before. The preceding Saturday night on Dogtown's western edge, two teenage boys who were on their way to a party in the woods happened upon an unconscious man who was lying next to a car and bleeding while another victim lay sprawled across the driver's seat. They were going to the same party, but had gotten into a fight with an acquaintance who was later arrested and charged with attempted murder. And in 1982, Donald Pinkham, a forty-seven-year-old homeless man, was found beaten to death near Dogtown's Babson Reservoir. But these crimes did not register the same response as Anne Natti's death. In these incidents, as in most violent crimes, the perpetrators knew their victims, who were from the same social milieu as their assailants. None of them were perfectly innocent, nor were they anything like Anne Natti, that well-loved schoolteacher who regularly marveled over the pictures in her dog-eared copy of *The Family of Man*, the catalogue for Edward Steichen's landmark 1955 Museum of Modern Art photography exhibit that presented a portrait of humanity in all its myriad forms. Anne had found something profoundly stirring in each and every image. She was someone "who had that rare gift," as her brother-in-law John Tuck put it years later. "She didn't judge others, she embraced them and gave them confidence, without ever losing her patience or showing any scorn." Nor were these other victims well-respected locals like Anne Natti's in-laws.

People called the extended Natti family "Lanesville royalty," and the Nattis had an artistic and educational legacy worthy of the title. Before his death in 1966, Erik's grandfather, sculptor Paul Manship, threw parties where famous artists mixed with locals—everyone from professors to fishermen to quarry workers. Erik's uncle Robert, an affable, widely

liked man, was superintendent of the Gloucester school system, and
Lee Kingman Natti, Robert's wife, was a Caldecott Award–winning
children's book author and editor. Then there was Erik's uncle Eino,
who was a member of the Folly Cove Designers, a design cooperative
started by another Caldecott Award–winning children's book author,
Virginia Lee Burton, who wrote the classic children's books *Mike Mul-
ligan and His Steam Shovel* and *The Little House*. Sculptor Walker Hancock, whose presidential busts decorate the U.S. Capitol rotunda and
whose bas-reliefs adorn Washington, D.C.'s National Cathedral and
Georgia's Stone Mountain, was also one of Erik's uncles by marriage.
These Natti family members were part of a larger year-round artists'
community based in Lanesville and Folly Cove (the northernmost part
of Lanesville). Unlike the artists who came for the summer and mixed
almost exclusively with other "summer people" or members of Gloucester's and Rockport's arts associations, the Nattis were invested in the
community; it was their home.

They also were admired for being good Finns. Erik's father, Ilmari
"Jimo" Natti, devoted his free time to translating the *Kalevala* into English. And Erik's uncles Bob and Bill led a singing group that wore traditional Finnish costumes and welcomed the summer solstice with a
concert of Finnish folk songs atop Drumlin Street each year. Every Saturday Bob's wife, Lee, baked *nisu*, a sweet cardamom-scented bread,
and invited family and friends to take saunas in the traditional bath-
house Bob had constructed. Each spring Bob harvested silver birch saplings he had planted to make traditional leafy whisks for beating the
skin while taking a sauna.

When people from the motherland came to visit extended relatives
on Cape Ann, they discovered a community "more Finnish than people
in Finland." And being Finnish means having *sisu*, a quiet, stoic tough-
ness that enables one to endure life's difficulties, no matter how hard
they may be. Now, with a heretofore unthinkable family tragedy suddenly in their midst, the Nattis called upon this inner strength and
sealed their borders around Erik and his children, sheltering them as
best they could.

Elsewhere across Cape Ann, Jack Chase and others considered Anne
Natti's death to be "an event of epic consequence"; not only did people
lose a gifted teacher, whom they embraced as one of their own, in Dogtown, they had also lost their "sacred place."

Here where hardworking fishermen, corporate executives, and impoverished artists might be next-door neighbors, people reveled in the fact that Dogtown's colonial common is not a manicured jewel box lined with expensive real estate, as the commons in Salem and Boston are, but a place shared by many, from the homeless to the most refined WASPs who came searching for the ruins of their ancestors' homes. The area affirmed the ideals of tolerance and socioeconomic diversity that are so central to Gloucester's idea of itself even today. That Cape Anners' expression of these democratic values go back well before the founding fathers committed them to parchment added to the area's sanctity. And people didn't just think these things about their old common, they attempted to live them.

The culture of the 1960s was still alive on Cape Ann in the 1980s, and in Dogtown in particular. Come Memorial Day weekend, when landlords raised rents for the summer tourist season, some of the artists, musicians, and free spirits living in these homes packed up their belongings and drove their VW vans to the periphery of Dogtown, not unlike the Nattis with their summer camp. A woman named Lee Steel, who resided in a house just on the forest edge, allowed people living in the woods to use her shower and washing machine. Once Labor Day rolled around and landlords slashed rents back to off-season rates, those individuals returned to their rental properties. Many say that a commune was attempted at one point or that most of the time it simply seemed like one was already there.

But Dogtown was not just some free-spirited place spun out of the era of hippies and free love. For more than a hundred years, the area had sheltered a certain drifting America. Hobos rolled in on the commuter rail or floated in from the sea and set up camp. Every so often Erik Natti's aunt, Lee Kingman Natti, would find one peering through her windows. In a history of Cape Ann published in 1955, the authors reported seeing an old woman in a ragged dress secured with a piece of rope come "stivering" along the Commons Road, as if one of the area's old witches had come back to life. As mysteriously as these dust-caked, road-weary individuals appeared, they disappeared, as though they had walked straight out of the refrain of a Depression-era folk song and were on their way back to the chorus. While this unofficial population was an annoyance to some, it was not altogether menacing. If anything, it was tolerated as part of that colonial ideal of an egalitarian commons.

Years after Anne Natti died, Bill Noble, a seventy-six-year-old retired fireman who has spent most of his life at the top of Gee Avenue,
on Dogtown's western edge, reminisced about what it was like growing
up "on the Common" in the 1930s and 1940s:

"It was so open if you climbed a hill you could see straight through
to Maine. You did not know where Dogtown began or ended and it did
not matter.

"After the colonials cleared away the trees, cattle ate the shoots of
everything that grew but the junipers and blueberries. There were so
many cows roaming all over the place they would poke their heads in
kitchen windows and so many blueberries the Common was a carpet of
blue come summer. If it hadn't been for the berries people would not
have made it through the Depression.

"Our grandparents took us up for picnics at the Whale's Jaw like
their grandparents had done. They wore high-collared dresses and suits
and top hats and climbed all over the place. We did the same, wearing
out our sneakers in a matter of weeks.

"I was so wild my mother had to trap me to send me to school. All
I learned there was professional clock-watching, waiting for that last
bell so I could go back to the Common.

"My mother would call my name and I would hear it go by on the
wind. There was a tremendous echo when the land was still all open,
but if we kids went down to 'Judy Millett's parlor,' we never heard our
mothers calling us to come home. There was a field atop Millett Street
where the lumpers [longshoremen] shot craps all weekend long. The
men didn't trust each other enough to roll the dice, but if we were
lucky, they let us do it. The Lebanese were there, too. They came here
in the '30s and '40s, and would bring a lamb to roast, and shine made
from raisins to drink. When the cops raided everyone out, the lumpers
took off running into the woods with the paper money. We kids got to
clean up all the coins they left behind. For a long time after that you
could see where the ground was all beat down from where they had
played.

"It was Sunday afternoon entertainment to go see what was going
on up at the Common. We would take a big kettle and fry clams up
there. Or take an old glue barrel from the LePage's factory and build a
bonfire. We could really raise some hell driving around up there and

screaming out the back of the rumble seat. Some individuals had binoculars and would go up there watching the younger people.

"We got around by knowing the names of all the [colonial] cellar holes' [owners]. That was how we gave directions. I wandered all over the place, but never went up the Hoot Owl Trail, where all the drunks went. An old Finn everybody called King Tut would round them up every so often and take them down to Willows Rest and let them dry out for a bit."

Bob Quinn, another old-timer and nearby neighbor, had similar recollections, but added, "Sometimes it was spooky, especially down near James Merry's field," where Merry had been gored to death by a bull in the late 1800s. "There are stories that people tell about some of those fields that can start to work on your mind, especially if you were up there when it started getting dark."

Twenty years after Anne Natti had been killed, when people from all walks of Gloucester life talked about this place—"the soul of Cape Ann," as many of them called it; "a paradise," others said—they slapped their knees and wiped bittersweet tears from their eyes because though the region's eerie notoriety was never far from their memories, they believed that at its heart Dogtown was good and wholesome, a reflection of what they saw in themselves.

But when Anne Natti died and was suddenly ferried across to that mystic, distant underworld of memory, she took Dogtown with her; it became a setting no one could get back to. In its place stood a land of unknown wilds and lore filled with loss and suffering.

THE EVENING AFTER Anne Natti's death, more than one hundred fishermen's wives and mothers gathered on the third floor of the harborside St. Peter's Club for the penultimate night of the novena. They sang and prayed in their Sicilian dialect, working their fingers over rosary beads, and thanking St. Peter for bringing their men home safely from the sea.

Though the northern Cape Ann community that had embraced Anne Natti rarely crossed paths with the Sicilians down in Fort Square, these women read the paper and kept their eyes on the goings-on about town. It was part of their devotional, an extension of their idea of grace, and also that "four hundred years of tensile strength." Knowing that death is hardest on the living, they called out Anne Natti's name and prayed for her loved ones.

The women then sang of how St. Peter was the only apostle who, like Jesus, could walk on water, until he momentarily questioned his faith. Down he fell, sinking to an unknown but recoverable depth.

Chapter Six

The Baron in the Trees

N EARLY A YEAR after my second visit to Dogtown, I moved to
New York City for graduate school. Less than two weeks
later, the World Trade Center was attacked. I felt desperate to
escape to a place that could shelter me from the sudden, overwhelm-
ing anxiety that permeated New York. Going back to Maine, which I had
just left, would have felt like some form of defeat. It had been hard
enough for me to leave the community that I had loved so dearly there.
Georgia, where my family lived, was off-limits, too. My family filled my
head with vivid scenarios of future terrorist attacks that only made me
more anxious. I had no idea where to go or what to do. Around this time,
I came across a line from *The Confessions of St. Augustine*, which Hartley
had read closely and meditated on when he was in Dogtown during the
summer of 1931—"And the people went there and admired the high
mountains, the wide wastes of the sea, and the mighty downward-
rushing streams, and the ocean, and the course of the stars, and forgot
themselves." That was what I wanted: to go back to Dogtown, where I
hoped to get over my own case of "New York–itis."

Unfortunately I could not go just yet. Stuck in the city because of
school and work commitments, I began searching for Dogtown on the
Internet and discovered a Gloucester arts organization called Fishtown
Artspace, whose director, a visual artist named Shep Abbott, happened
to sell poster-size illustrated maps he had made of the area. I ordered
one immediately.

The map was in the style of a children's-book fantasyscape. Flora (white pine, red pine, hemlock, oak, lady slipper, cranberry) and fauna (short-eared owl, otter, raccoon, wood duck, crow, chickadee, skunk, spotted salamander, painted turtle, yellow-bellied sapsucker, belted kingfisher, fishercat, and coyote) decorated hills rendered in delicate strokes of green and brown. Washes of yellow portrayed pastures and lowlands. Blue streams and orange trails laced through the land like veins. Tidy grids of black lines stood in for the city of Gloucester and the town of Rockport. A turquoise ocean surrounded this elaborately rendered cheerful place. Abbott's attention to detail was extended to the title, which read like an old-fashioned broadsheet: "THE DOG-TOWN MURAL MAP Being a Complete and Accurate Depiction of Roads, Trails, Brooks, Ponds, Vernal Pools, Quarries and Swamps PLUS Historical and Geographical, Geological, and Natural History Information." It reminded me of Narnia, only better because Dogtown was real.

The flip side of this colorful map was rendered in black and white. Here Abbott had reproduced a guide to the Commons Settlement ruins that an artist named George T. Odum Jr. had drawn in the 1970s. Colonial walls and cellar holes zigzagged across the landscape in tiny loops like links in a delicate chain. Odum's map looked as if it had been copied from an ancient original that might have lined an old sea chest. It seemed as if it would lead to the treasure Dogtown's witches had allegedly buried there. Cartoonish drawings of a wild-eyed dog bordered this side of the map, appearing comically out of place.

I would eventually come to understand that Shep's map accurately captured Dogtown's two natures: a mythical, reclaimed wilderness full of life and color on one side, and a brittle, haunted ruin on the other. At the time, though, I focused on the colorful, fantastic portrait, which made Dogtown seem to be the perfect place to escape to. I called Artspace and made arrangements to travel to Gloucester and meet Shep Abbott during my school's fall break.

I WAS HALF ASLEEP at a Gloucester bed-and-breakfast when Shep's voice trailed up the stairs along with the smell of fresh coffee. It was eight o'clock on a Sunday morning, time for our meeting, but too early in the morning for me. The windows had rattled and the house had settled audibly through the night, keeping me awake along with the insomnia I had developed that fall. I peeled away the covers, crawled out of bed, and scampered around frantically, attempting to get dressed, pack a daypack, and brush my teeth all at the same time.

Shep appeared well slept, well caffeinated, and seemingly well acquainted with Rick, one of the B and B owners, with whom he was chatting at the base of a large central staircase.

From our phone conversation, I had placed Shep in that netherland between the late thirties and midforties, but his solid head of gunmetal-gray hair that came into view as I made my way down the stairs surprised me. Shep turned out to be an extraordinarily youthful fifty-seven.

My stomach grumbled audibly. The smell of a bagel being toasted was tempting, but Shep had already been waiting for more than fifteen minutes. As soon as I introduced myself and apologized for being late, he zipped up his wool jacket and cocked his head toward the door with a gleam in his eyes. He was ready to go to Dogtown.

When Shep opened the door of the B and B, a blast of cold wind blew through the house. It was the first sign that winter was ready to blow the long Indian summer into the lower latitudes.

"Have a good time with Mr. Dogtown," Rick yelled out, as the heavy Victorian door closed behind us.

"Mr. Dogtown?" I asked, turning to Shep.

He shot me a "What are you looking at me for, kid?" look and ducked his six-foot frame into his gray Honda Civic hatchback.

I climbed into the car, which smelled of coffee both fresh and stale, and accidentally stepped on a paper bag on the passenger-side floor. Coffee seeped from the sack. "Oh, those are for you," Shep exclaimed, overlooking the coffee spill. "Thanks," I said excitedly, reaching for a soggy and squished croissant that sat in the bag along with a cup of milky joe.

Each time we hit one of Gloucester's numerous potholes, I dribbled coffee on my jacket and the car. If Shep noticed, he did not seem to mind. He was busy driving and asking me all sorts of questions about Hartley's Dogtown experience and New York—Shep had lived there during his former career as a documentary filmmaker.

Looking for a place to set my beverage, I noticed that every available surface in the car was covered with things. Miniature Peppermint Patties, a vendor-size packet of Fig Newtons, a Sonic Youth tape, and an assortment of road maps covered his dashboard. Buckets, fishing line, a net, and assorted art supplies were strewn across the backseat. Judging from Shep's taste in junk to tote around in a car, I could tell we were going to get along just fine.

Gloucester's bumpy roads were quiet this Sunday morning, as if the town were still asleep. We made our way up Dennison Street, where modest cottages lining Goose Cove gave way to larger homes on expansive lots. The road ascended steeply and suddenly leveled out, ending at an unmarked gate with a path surrounded by mature evergreen trees. Something about how high up we seemed from the rest of town, the lack of signage, and the way the path disappeared into the trees made this Dogtown entrance feel especially secret; I am not sure I would have found it on my own.

A bitter wind threaded through my jacket as I exited the car, giving me a chill and quickly drawing a flush to Shep's cheeks. Appearing trail-ready and positively toasty in his wool pants and sturdy boots, and with his glasses and gray goatee providing good cover for his face, Shep tucked his hands into his snug, woolly pockets and slipped around the gate and into Dogtown.

Evergreens swayed as we skirted the Norton Memorial Forest, Professor Norton's woods. A nearby stand of deciduous trees, with leaves turned to a russet brown, shivered in the cold gusts of wind. Shep stepped lively and told me how he became Mr. Dogtown.

Born in 1943 and raised in the nearby town of Wenham, Shep often came to Cape Ann's beaches in the summer with his family as a child, but had never visited Dogtown. "I was told that Dogtown was bad," he said. "I remember people saying there were killings up here or that someone had been killed." The notion that a place could be fundamentally bad haunted Shep. Years later, when he returned to Cape Ann for a vacation, he recalled how frightened he had been of Dogtown in his youth.

Shep did not strike me as the sort of person to be much afraid of anything. After graduating from the University of Pennsylvania, attending naval officer school, and serving in the navy during the Vietnam War, he went to Africa and made a documentary film about cheetahs in Tanzania. Though New York City became his home, Shep spent extended periods of time in Africa, where he and his anthropologist wife lived with Kenya's Masai tribe. He continued to make films, which led him to live with a Navajo tribe in New Mexico for a while. Sometime thereafter, he wrote a horror movie screenplay about homeless New

Yorkers living in underground Manhattan. In the film, *C.H.U.D.*, which
stands for Cannibalistic Humanoid Underground Dwellers, exposure to
toxic chemicals transforms these subterranean New Yorkers into mu-
tant cannibals. The movie, which is decidedly more schlocky than scary,
became a cult favorite.

Despite being so worldly, and so conversant in horror films, Shep
was still afraid of Dogtown. When a freelance video project brought
him back to Cape Ann in the late 1980s, he set out to overcome this
fear. He started to explore Dogtown, first with people familiar with the
region, then alone.

Learning Dogtown on foot and in print, Shep began to feel as if he
were "puncturing an old myth." Soon he was climbing its trees, including one particularly sturdy oak that grew above a large boulder on the
edge of Briar Swamp. From its heights, a northeasterly vista of the region's hummocky topography stretched seemingly to the sea. Each
time Shep visited Gloucester, he climbed the oak and watched how the
shape of the land revealed itself through the changing seasons. He felt
there was something special about the location—not just the view, but
the place itself. Linda Crane, a local Gloucester shaman he met, agreed.
Crane told Shep that Native Americans believed the large rocks such as
the one by the oak on Briar Swamp's edge were sacred. "There is something powerful in the combination of hard rock and soft swamp; those
two elements so close together like that," Shep explained. He gathered
pieces of oak from the surrounding woods and, using skills from another of his former jobs as a high-rope tree pruner, he rigged a platform
high in the tree so he could watch the woods change and possibly film
them one day.

After Shep and his wife divorced, he felt as if Dogtown were calling
him. He relocated to Gloucester and started Artspace. Soon he was
spending much of his time atop the platform in the oak tree, where he
felt an unparalleled sense of freedom that made me think of Italo Cal-
vino's *Baron in the Trees*, a story in which a young man leaves society to
live in the treetops. In time, Shep's mind and emotions traveled to a lost
part of himself: his childhood. He began writing a screenplay about a
boy who meets a Native American living in some forbidden woods similar to Dogtown. Writing this story so high up in the trees, Shep said,
"felt like a rebirth . . . a new beginning."

I followed Shep along the trail, listening and thinking that his story was similar to Hartley's, only more idiosyncratic. Did Dogtown have this kind of life-changing effect on others? Would it have one on me? Dogtown seemed vast and full of possibilities.

Nothing around us looked familiar from my two preceding trips, which prompted me to ask Shep why he made his map. "People have been getting lost in here for centuries," he replied. Even after Shep became pretty familiar with the area he still managed to get lost. Plus, he added, he had heard rumors about people who "simply disappeared."

Was Dogtown some woodland Bermuda Triangle or something altogether different? The area seemed to exist according to its own set of principles, as if the most likely thing one would ever meet here was the mesmerizing experience of the place itself. This was no distant wilderness, but there were times when it felt like one.

Within moments we had reached the Whale's Jaw, which looked pathetic and forlorn. A case of empty Budweiser cans filled a makeshift fire ring underneath the monolith, the breaking of which, Shep explained, was blamed on some teenagers and drifters who had built a similar but much larger fire. "Dogtown was and still is a commons," Shep said, meaning that it belonged to everyone. It was not a park with signs and lights where people jogged on paved trails with baby strollers, though there had been a lot of mountain bikers as of late. People came here to let themselves "off society's leash," adding to the true wildness of the place. "It is anarchy," he exclaimed, tossing his head back and nodding repeatedly.

I told Shep how much the broken Whale's Jaw saddened me. "I know," he said wistfully, "it was magical. When that thing broke, it was like a dark omen."

Clearly people imposed their own narratives onto this place, but something about Dogtown made it seem hard not to do so. I told Shep about the tripods and how I had assumed they were related to neo-pagan rituals.

"Those were put here by the Boy Scouts," Shep replied, suppressing a laugh, "getting their shelter badge."

"Right," I said, feeling embarrassed.

"Dogtown really feeds the imagination," he replied.

Obviously mine had been gorging on it.

I had expected Shep to fall over laughing when I mentioned the men in black capes whom I had thought were warlocks. But he replied,

"Oh, yeah. There are witches here in Dogtown. In fact, I know a war-lock that you should meet." Shep's response was so matter-of-fact and earnest—as if every town had a warlock available for consultation in some street corner booth—that I initially thought he was joking. After a minute he said, "They also could have been teenagers who are really into Goth. They used to hang around the Route 128 bridge and upset a minister in town who talked about them as if she had seen vampires." What was going to be next, I wondered, werewolves?

According to Shep, Dogtown attracted people who were different, misunderstood: misfits. He then told me about this "militaristic old guy" named Joe Orange, Dogtown's constable, who "likes to come crashing through the woods," threatening to arrest people. Shep thought that Joe Orange might have followed me on my first visit here and "was probably waiting for you to pull out a joint so he could arrest you." I was astounded that someone had been appointed to patrol Dogtown.

We had been walking off-trail for a while when we reached a boul-der and climbed a stack of smaller rocks to its top. A flimsy-looking ladder made of skinny branches rested against the tree—Shep's oak—towering above. I followed him up the ladder to the platform, made of slender, twiggy branches that looked like another Boy Scout shelter badge project. A smaller platform, accessible by a rope tied with loop-ing rungs, stood farther up in the tree. I was relieved that Shep did not want to climb any higher.

Shep stretched out along the platform edge, making a picture of comfort and ease, and produced a thermos of tea and a small picnic from his bag. Worried that the platform would go crashing down through the tree or that a stiff wind would send me flying off the edge and into Briar Swamp, which was just below, I sat as close to the tree trunk as possible.

Shep sliced into a green apple, handed me a quarter, and said, "Dog-town is bad." He poured some tea. "There are five thousand acres of woods here, but people who live here don't come here." He cut a wedge of cheese, tore off pieces of a baguette, and offered them to me.

Shep's characterization of Dogtown shocked me. The area had seemed uncanny, but I had no prior inkling that it was as bad as he made it out to be. I wondered if I had missed something glaringly obvi-ous, as if approaching this place through Hartley's paintings and story were akin to looking at it through a Lorrain glass, a lens that nineteenth-century landscape painters looked through to make a natural setting more pleasing to the eye by sharpening its shapes and heightening the contrast in its colors. Hartley's paintings did have a gloomy cast, but I liked that about them. It made them seem honest, raw, and emotionally unflinching, qualities that intensify the yearning that surges through them, making them all the more compelling.

Shep focused his dark blue eyes straight onto mine and said, "A young woman like you shouldn't come here by yourself." I flinched. I hated it when people, especially men, tried to tell me where I should or should not go, but I was curious to hear Shep's explanation. This was when I first heard about Anne Natti, though Shep's account of her death was brief and he didn't refer to her by name. "Twentysomething years ago a teacher was murdered here. She walked these trails alone, kind of like you. People told me her killer thought she was Satan. Nobody talks about it and nobody asks about it, but it has had a tremendous impact on this place."

While Shep told me this story, the feeling that I had been utterly foolhardy socked me in the gut. Perhaps it was the "kind of like you," or the realization that my hope that I could come here and escape all the darkness of that particular 2001 autumn was utterly naive, but I began to feel as if the platform were going to collapse beneath me, though it was holding firm.

"People fear what they don't understand," Shep continued. "I can't really explain how powerful this place is."

The wind stretched and pulled clouds across the sky as if they were giant pieces of taffy. Beneath them, Briar Swamp glimmered. To my eyes, the swamp looked more like a large pond than the swamps I had known in Georgia, where the stumps of giant tupelo and bald cypress trees resembled stalagmites. Shep pointed out some red maples that actually grew in the swamp, beyond its stretch of open water. Slowly my eyes adjusted, and I made out a slight depression among the trees. The red maples' leaves were crimson, as though they had been drinking the life force out of this place, while the leaves of other nearby trees were so dazzling yellow, they appeared to belong to the sun. The longer I stared at the swamp and the trees, the more the landscape appeared to vibrate, like a color-field painting. If I looked away and turned back again, the swamp's far edges seemed to vanish. After a moment I could again see the heavily forested part of the swamp, as if there were another world that was visible beneath the surface of things.

SHEP'S STATEMENT THAT Anne Natti's killer thought that she was the devil sounded more like a Nathaniel Hawthorne story than something someone could have believed a mere twenty years ago. I wanted to know if it were actually true and to learn more about what had in fact happened. Plus, the things Shep had said about the kinds of people who were attracted to Dogtown made me wonder if the murderer was an outcast.

The following day I went to the library to research this crime. The librarian recalled the incident. "It seems like yesterday," he said as if it were still fresh in his mind. "Oh, we used to go up blueberrying in Dogtown all the time come summer but not since then. Now it just gives me a creepy feeling. That girl that got killed up there was a sweet girl. The place just isn't the same anymore." He handed me my microfilm and said, "Be careful up there."

While scrolling through the newspaper accounts, I began to wonder if this brutal act of violence had altered Dogtown's character, or if bad seeds had sprouted there all along. Was there something truly different and dark about Dogtown? Why had the land been abandoned in the first place? Did some places have a propensity for tragedy in the way that others brew their own dust storms? Did the murder account for why the place always seemed empty?

The next day, as my train pulled away, I sat facing backward so I could watch Dogtown and Gloucester recede from view. Barren trees and brittle marsh grass flashed by, making the land look as if it were drying itself out for winter storage like all of the boats in dry dock that I saw outside my train window. I mentally began arranging a return trip as soon as possible. Until I could come back to Cape Ann I planned to go to the library for some armchair travel back to Dogtown's earliest days, when colonists arrived fleeing Indians and pirates.

Chapter Seven

Ghost Dog

ANNE NATTI'S DEATH left the police with large bootprints, a motorbike track, and a victim who had been bludgeoned to death and possibly raped. The perpetrator could have drifted in and washed back out with the tides, as strangers on Cape Ann often do. Or he could have remained in the woods or in town, hiding under a semblance of normalcy, lying in wait for his next victim.

The police strung evidence tape around the trunks of trees, but outdoor crime scenes are the hardest to secure. In the Natti case there were no latent fingerprints. Rain had washed away most of the blood, except for what had caked the victim's body, bandanna, and the interior of her rain slicker's hood. They were fortunate, at least, to have an intact corpse. Weather, animals, and insects pose risks to the integrity of outdoor crime scenes that are not an issue indoors. Anne Natti's body had been so well hidden that if Woofer had not led Erik there, it might not have been discovered for years.

Authorities urged people to stay out of the woods. Parents living close to Dogtown were discouraged from letting their children play outside. Police questioned nearby residents and advised them to lock their windows and doors. For many, it was the first time they had done so in their lives. Women were afraid to be home alone; some found other places to stay. A neighbor came through the woods to the Norton Farm carrying a shotgun for self-protection and pleaded for Professor Norton to leave, but the professor refused to budge.

Parts of Dogtown had become a locus for petty crime by 1984, especially near the colonial ruins, which were easily accessible to motor vehicles via the Cherry Street entrance. Large groups of teenagers went there to party and drink, while vandals spray painted the Babson Boulders or used them for target practice. People also dumped large household items such as broken appliances and old mattresses in addition to cars that were part of an increasingly popular insurance scam. In this con, people would drive into the colonial pastures, strip their cars for parts, douse them with gasoline, and set them on fire. They would then report the "theft" to their insurance companies and wait for their settlement checks to come in the mail. In 1984 alone, this practice was responsible for six Dogtown wildfires.

The police set their priority on reviewing dirt bike registrations and sex offender records, and cross-referenced these to their list of offenders and squatters who were known to hang out in the area. Most of these unofficial Dogtown residents were a little odd or down on their luck—part of an "older, weirder America," to borrow Greil Marcus's turn of phrase—but police did not consider most of them to be capable of the kind of brutality inflicted on Anne Natti.

Consider Bernard Taylor, a supposed genius who would disappear into the woods for months, then suddenly materialize in town wearing a ragged trench coat and a long, grizzled beard, eager to discuss algorithms or scientific theories. Taylor, who lived in a VW bus, once represented himself in a Cambridge court to contest a parking ticket. He argued that because the parking meter measured time, not space, and he lived in his car, it was illegal for the municipality to use such a mechanism to charge him rent, a form of blackmail dating back to feudal times when one was expected to pay the lord of a manor for protection from marauding bandits. Taylor then explained the difference between white rents (paid in silver and coin of the realm) and black rents (paid in cattle, grain, and things not easily convertible into currency) in an effort to wheedle his way out of the charge. Taylor did not get out of paying the fine, but the judge was reportedly impressed by his erudition. Most others were, too. Gloucester people did not think Taylor was crazy. To the contrary, they accepted that he was differently abled and respected him for adhering to an unwritten Gloucester code: working the system.

Gloucester's flair for circumventing the rules goes all the way back to the 1600s, when goods were regularly smuggled to get around British tariffs. In one incident, local shipping magnate Colonel Joseph Foster hatched a plan to thwart a British customs inspector who was on his way to assess tariffs on cargo that Foster was unloading that day. Foster enlisted the aid of Gloucester watchman John McKean, who waylaid the inspector by confining him to the watchhouse under the ruse that he needed to fumigate the inspector against smallpox. McKean commenced blowing smoke at the inspector for the remainder of the day and into the night, only releasing him well after Foster and his men had successfully unloaded his entire haul.

People across Cape Ann routinely turned a blind eye to most minor infractions, but on one occasion they also looked the other way when a major crime was committed. Around midday on a busy spring Saturday in 1932, a tailor named Arthur Oker was found dead in his Main Street, Rockport, shop. Residents did not report seeing anything suspicious and speculated that the killer came and went via one of the tunnels leading from town to the beach that rum smugglers had used during Prohibition. A year and a half later, at a Congregational church Halloween social in Rockport's predominantly Swedish village of Pigeon Cove, a woman named Augusta Johnson told people she knew the killer's identity. The next morning, a neighbor saw flames coming out of a second-story window in Johnson's home. The neighbor entered the house to find a half-naked Johnson, tied to a flaming bed, burned beyond recognition. State and local authorities questioned each of Rockport's then two thousand inhabitants and received only false leads. Some of Pigeon Cove's old Swedes reportedly told police, "The leprechauns did it." Even as recently as 2005, an eighty-one-year-old Rockport barber named Walter Julian told a *Boston Globe* reporter, "I could tell you who killed them, but I won't."

Though this story suggests that Cape Ann was not necessarily an easy place to conduct a serious murder investigation, in the Natti case police tip lines began ringing off the hook. Meanwhile, detectives focused their attention on a 1980 incident in Dogtown involving a woman named Linda Crane.

THOUGH PEOPLE REFERRED to Crane, who had been poet Charles Olson's caregiver and lover near the end of his life, as "one of Dogtown's tending spirits," Crane might have said that it was Dogtown that tended to her. Born in the same year as Anne Natti, Crane wrote nature poetry and earned her living by plying her trade as a healer, harvesting edible seaweed, and foraging among the five thousand different species of wild plants that grew in Dogtown's exceptionally botanically diverse landscape.

With her thick brown hair and solid build, Linda Crane had a powerful, down-to-earth presence that attracted people from university professors to the town chimney sweep. Even those who did not consider themselves to be of an alternative or spiritual bent were clients or friends of Crane. She was not misty-eyed and vague about the homespun shamanism she practiced, which was gleaned from anthroposophy, polarity, astrology, tarot, poetry—especially the *Kalevala*—and a variety of indigenous beliefs. Jack Chase, the mailman, liked to poke fun at Crane for "oddball things" such as feeling auras by "doing some hand jive" and saying "booga, booga." But when Chase and his wife moved into a new house where they felt something was a little off, they called Crane, who arrived with a rosemary smudge stick and managed to snuff the chill that Chase had described as a black cloud. Chase claims the house has felt normal ever since.

Crane's guiding passion, however, was teaching people how to connect with nature; Dogtown was often her classroom. Whenever Crane went there with friends she would ask, "Do you feel it?" meaning the spirits in the place, which she felt were especially palpable in Dogtown because of its rich biodiversity and ancient boulders. Crane taught that nature was constantly broadcasting across a frequency that only a few knew how to tune in to; Dogtown happened to be one of the places where the signal was strongest. And when people listened to the earth, it listened back. Dogtown, in particular, was all whispers and ears.

Likewise, Crane did not merely teach people how to identify and pluck berries, wintergreen, sassafras, hen-of-the-woods mushrooms, and chanterelles; the way she explained it, the spirits of these plants were giving themselves to her and her students, who were thereby participating in a larger spiritual exchange and restoring balance to the earth's harmony. One of Crane's former students, who had a particularly strong connection with owls, would go to Dogtown, lie upon a rock, and wait for them to appear. In time, the birds would fly into nearby trees and commune with her through the night.

On a 1980 April day, Crane, then thirty-five, was drawing water from a Dogtown spring with her golden retriever/collie mix, Ghost Dog. Crane and her ex-husband, a painter named Thorpe Feidt, had named Ghost Dog for his plumelike tail that "whooshed by like a ghost." After Crane and Feidt's divorce, people marveled at how they remained such good friends. They claimed it was because of Ghost Dog, "a wonderful, radiant being, equally devoted to each of us," as Feidt said, and whose custody they shared as though he were a child.

This particular April day Ghost Dog went bounding off while Crane was filling some jugs with springwater. It was quiet but for the sound of water gurgling peacefully. Bottles filled, Crane turned away from the spring to find an exceedingly tall, naked man standing in front of her, holding his erect penis, and pointing it at her "as though it were a weapon."

"If you scream, I'll kill you!" he said, and pushed her to the ground.

As Crane fell backward, screaming, she noticed a large stick "that glowed yellow." She thrashed at the man with the stick and continued to yell.

Ghost Dog, who heard her cries, came running. He leapt at the naked man and tore into his flesh. The assailant ran away, clutching his crotch and screaming, with Ghost Dog giving chase.

When police asked Crane if she could pick a suspect out of a mug shot book, she worried that she would not remember the man's face; the attack happened so quickly. But police claimed she said she would have no problem recognizing his member, which, she told them, was huge. In the end, Crane was able to pick out a face. When the suspect, a local man named Peter C. Hodgkins Jr., was brought into the police station for questioning, he confessed to the crime and was charged with assault with intent to rape and open and gross lewdness.

When it came time to try Hodgkins, a repeated petty sex offender, the assault with intent to rape charge was dismissed. Hodgkins was found guilty of assault and battery and served a six-month prison term at the Essex House of Corrections in Lawrence.

Four years later, when police phone lines began ringing with the many calls from people offering tips on Anne Natti's murder, Peter Hodgkins's name was spoken more than any other.

Chapter Eight

Rollicking Apparitions

ONE JULY 1692 EVENING, Ebenezer Babson, a twenty-five-year-old fisherman and farmer, was at his home at the Farms, a "remote and lonely spot" two miles inland from Gloucester's main settlement, when he heard strange voices and the sounds of people running coming from outside. Babson cocked his ear to the wall of his modest cabin and listened carefully. Peering out of his window into the night, Ebenezer might have seen tree branches shift in the breeze, or his scarecrow, the only figure in sight, standing watch over his corn. Babson sat down by the smoldering coals of the evening's cook fire and gathered his wife and children around him to pray.

That summer, many of Gloucester's men were off serving in King William's War, the North American theater of the Nine Years' War that was being fought in Europe at the time. In America, the English colonists were fighting the French, while various Indian tribes aligned themselves with these opposing sides.

Thus far, the town of Gloucester and its four hundred residents had been spared from the violence, but by summer, the war had escalated. Raids of nearby mainland towns left residents in a state of increasing unease, a fact that might account for the peculiar events that were about to take place.

For weeks, Ebenezer Babson listened to these and other strange noises work their way across his land. And though each time he heard these sounds Babson peered into the shadows and saw no one, he still believed that something was out there. Puritans interpreted spiritual meaning from everything around them: landscapes, weather, ordinary occurrences, and human behavior, which they believed had the power to inspire good or to spread the contagions of evil. Devout and self-sacrificing human thoughts, words, and deeds disseminated saintliness; selfish and impious ones perpetuated wickedness. The former granted God's rewards, which were meted out with bumper crops, good health, and sound minds; the latter brought on his punishments, which included war. All were the extension of a larger invisible spirit world in which God and his angels were continually at war with the devil and his forces of evil. These forces included the Catholic French and pagan Indians, with whom the colonists were at war, and the unseen wild spirits that proliferated in the woods.

One night as Babson was coming home, he saw two men run from his door and into his corn patch. "The man of the house is come now, else we might have taken the house," Babson heard one of them say as leafy stalks folded in to conceal where they had fled. He ran home and flung open the door to find his wife and children spending a typical evening. They had not heard a sound, which convinced Babson that his family had come within moments of a stealth Indian attack of the most severe violence.

Such attacks were common throughout the Bay Colony. One story that was well known in Gloucester dated from the 1675 King Philip's War, which colonists had fought against forces led by Metacom, sachem, or chief, of the Wampanoag tribe. (To this day historians consider King Philip's War to be one of the deadliest conflicts in American history.) Gloucester native Lieutenant George Ingersoll, who had moved to Falmouth, Maine (present-day Portland), heard shots from his neighbor's farm. Investigating, he discovered "an house burnt down, and six persons killed, and three of the same family could not be found. An old man and a woman were halfe in, and halfe out of the house neer halfe burnt. Their owne Son was shot through the body, and also his head dashed in pieces. The young mans Wife was dead, her head skinned." The wife was "bigg with Child," and two of her children had "their heads dashed in pieces." Three others were missing and believed to have been taken captive. Ingersoll would later lose a son and his home to similar brutality.

Babson grabbed his musket and chased after the men, but to no avail. He ran home, gathered his family, and fled down a dusky, moonlit path to the town garrison, half a mile away. Like other New England garrisons, Gloucester's was most likely a house that had been fortified with timbers at least one foot thick and a surrounding external wall at least eight feet high.

Soon other families on the run from similar sightings arrived at the garrison. They exchanged reports of Indians and Frenchmen who were gathering in number and readying for attack. The garrison dwellers might have had strength in numbers, but they were isolated from the rest of the town, the heart of which was located two miles away at the confluence of the Little and Annisquam Rivers. This village, known as the Green, was home to the First Parish Church, Gloucester's first and only church and the center of colonial life. The majority of Cape Ann's seventeenth-century population resided at the Green, which was perfectly situated between two natural harbors, Annisquam and Gloucester Harbors. In 1658, Ebenezer's father, James Babson, a cooper, was the first to settle the Farms, an area far from the Green and surrounded by wilderness, which the Puritans considered especially dangerous. "Some affirm that they have seen a lion at Cape Ann . . . ," a man named William Wood wrote in the 1600s. "Some, likewise, being lost in the woods, have heard such terrible roarings as have made them much aghast, which must be either devils or lions." Puritans believed that wilderness and wild creatures were malevolent, while all things cultivated under white man's aegis were good.

Yet these woods, as terrifying as they might have seemed, also were home to Gloucester's first industry: logging. Soon after the town was incorporated in 1642, a sawmill was constructed near the edge of the highland forest along the Alewife Brook. Colonists cleared the land of this evil with such fervor, Gloucester's shipbuilding and cordwood industries soon thrived. It was later said that an entire fleet of the British Royal Navy was constructed from Cape Ann hardwoods.

After a week in confinement at the garrison, the Babsons and the other families continued to hear voices and noises, as if rocks were being thrown against their stronghold, leading them to believe that enemy forces were gathering outside their reinforced walls. Every so often, the men summoned the courage to go out and assess the situation. Such was the case when Ebenezer Babson and a man named Isaac

Prince saw an Indian just beyond their redoubt. Prince fired his gun at the man as he ran off, escaping into a nearby swamp. Babson decided to make a break for town and alert people to the crisis.

Running through Cape Ann's antediluvian forest, Babson looked over his shoulder and saw four men, French and Indians, chasing after him. He most likely worried that there were more enemies nearby. In a then well known story from King Philip's War, a small group of injured Wampanoag Indians called out for help from a clearing in a forest near present-day Cumberland, Rhode Island. When eighty-three colonial and Indian-allied soldiers entered the clearing, five hundred Wampanoag warriors suddenly appeared as if out of nowhere. Eventually an additional four hundred Wampanoag arrived. The majority of the colonial soldiers and their Indian allies were killed.

Ebenezer heard a shot and felt a bullet fly within a hairsbreadth of his head, lodging itself in the trunk of a hemlock tree. The men began closing in on Babson, who dove into some bushes and fired back with his musket. Racing off toward town, he peered over his shoulder one last time and noticed that the men had vanished.

Babson arrived in town unharmed. Returning to the woods with six men to search for his assailants, Babson located the hemlock and dislodged the bullet. Seeing no other trace of his pursuers, they hurried to the garrison, where they came upon several sets of footprints running in a variety of directions. They then noticed an Indian watching them from a nearby tree. Upon seeing the colonials, the man ran off, his blue coat flashing through the forest. They started in pursuit when a Frenchman raced by in another direction. Confused and terrified, the Gloucester men rushed back to the security of the garrison.

Two days later, Benjamin Ellery and Richard Dolliver departed the stronghold to check on fellow garrison dweller John Rowe Jr.'s abandoned home. Cotton Mather described the bizarre scene they encountered in his 1702 book *Magnalia Christi Americana*. Dolliver and Ellery "saw several men come out of an orchard, walking backward and forward, and striking with a stick upon John Row's [sic] deserted house, the noise of which was heard by others at a considerable distance." Dolliver fired at the men, who immediately "dispersed themselves, and were quickly gone out of sight. People far away heard the commotion."

Town officials sent for help. A company of sixty soldiers, all experienced Indian-fighters from nearby Ipswich, arrived to search the spirit-filled woods. The soldiers most likely fanned out across the Cape Ann promontory, with torches lit, ready to smoke out the enemy. They would have come upon Briar Swamp, which fed a brook with suspiciously red water that coursed through the highland forest. Nathaniel Hawthorne wrote that according to "gray tradition," swamps "were once the resort of a Power of Evil and his plighted subjects." Come "midnight or on the dim verge of evening" they gathered around the swamps' "putrid waters in the performance of an impious baptismal rite." But no power of evil, Indian or French, appeared, only the inhospitable wilderness, made all the more menacing by the giant boulders strewn about the land.

According to seventeenth-century belief, the large boulders the soldiers would have seen were deposited as the waters of the great Old Testament flood receded. In actuality, the Laurentide ice sheet, the continent-size Pleistocene Epoch glacier that had covered half of North America, had left them behind. This giant river of ice crept along, picking up whatever debris was in its way, from dust-size particles called rock flour to house-size boulders called erratics—some of Dogtown's came from as far away as what is now Jackman, Maine, more than two hundred miles to the north. The Laurentide planed down the Cambrian mountain that was once island Cape Ann to its bedrock, then molded and pinched the land into shape, scooping away softer rock to form rivers, and heaping up debris to create hills and ridges of rock and soil called moraines. Where the rocky surface of the outer layer of the Earth's crust was exposed, the glacier marked it with long scratches. This activity happened all over Cape Ann, but when the Ice Age ended, much of the affected land was submerged. The Dogtown highland, where the glacier's terminal moraine left a giant rock pile and many of these erratics, is one place that remained above sea level.

Across this forsaken, boulder-strewn earth, the Ipswich soldiers searched for an enemy that existed only in the minds of a handful of Gloucester men: there were no French or Indian attackers on Cape Ann that 1692 summer. Nor have there been any since. Ebenezer Babson and his neighbors were all suffering from a collective delusion that historians believe was an extension of the hysteria that consumed the nearby town of Salem with its witchcraft trials that very same year.

In the incident's aftermath, Babson and six additional Gloucester residents, all of sound seventeenth-century Puritan minds, were called to testify to the General Court about their hallucinations of enemy sightings. All were convinced their imaginary attackers had been real. "Village scolds, misfits, and poor widows," the same type of people who would later populate Dogtown, were rounded up in connection with the visions, but no one could account for an earthly source of these sightings. And there was no explanation for the bullet lodged in the hemlock tree.

After the incident, Gloucester's Rev. John Emerson penned a letter to Rev. Cotton Mather, who later included the story of Ebenezer Babson in *Magnalia Christi*. Describing these "rollicking apparitions" and their "diabolical revelry," Emerson concluded "that the devil and his agents were the cause of all molestation which at this time befell the town," and asked Rev. Mather to pray "that those apparitions may not prove the sad omens of some future and more horrible molestations."

THAT DOGTOWN WAS originally settled by colonists fleeing Indian attacks is a widely held belief, yet this bit of delusional lore is the only recorded incident involving Indian violence on Cape Ann. The confusion over Dogtown's origins most likely originated from a misreading of the historical record: people did in fact leave nearby villages that had been ravaged by Indian attacks and relocated to Gloucester, but not to the highland area that would later become Dogtown. The area's true settlement would not occur until "the time of the pirates," as Hartley called the 1720s when, according to my Cape Ann guidebook, pirate attacks inspired the village's creation.

Chapter Nine

Taking Care of Its Own

A TOP PORTUGEE HILL, on the Wednesday after Anne Natti's murder, sunlight gleamed off the twin blue domes of Our Lady of Good Voyage Church. The patron saint of Gloucester's Portuguese fishermen, Our Lady of Good Voyage, is a Madonna whose likeness stands between the church's domes as though presiding over Gloucester. In her left hand the Madonna holds a boat; her right is raised in benediction, as though eternally blessing the town and its surrounding waters. Her back, as always, is turned to Dogtown.

A few blocks away from the Madonna's feet, an investigative team sat in a Gloucester police station office and discussed the Natti case. The bums known to hang around Dogtown, a few known and suspected sex offenders, and area dirt bike riders had all checked out okay but for one. Police continued to receive multiple reports that Peter Hodgkins Jr. had been seen riding a motorized dirt bike through Dogtown over the weekend.

In the years preceding Anne Natti's murder, most Cape Ann women knew that "there was a creep in the woods," as one Rockport woman later recalled. "Lots of times we'd get a report about an exposure in the woods, and the first person to come to mind would be Peter Hodgkins," police sergeant David Reardon remarked at the time. "But it would be only a report, no name, no assault . . . just an individual who exposed himself."

People said that Peter Charles Hodgkins Jr., a thirty-one-year-old dockworker, "haunted" Dogtown's woods and quarries. Many assumed he lived there, as though from his earliest days he had been raised by a pack of Dogtown wolves. Hodgkins had in fact grown up in Riverdale, a predominantly working-class village between the edge of Dogtown and a thumb-shaped peninsula called Wheeler's Point, where pride was as deeply rooted as insularity.

Hodgkins has been a well-established Gloucester name since the 1600s, and Peter's particular branch of the Hodgkins family tree was hardworking, respected, and, in the words of one Gloucester resident, "completely Gloucester normal." That is, except the son, who had long preferred the company of the woods to people. Horace Edward Hodgkins Jr., Peter's father (who went by the name Pete), was a World War II U.S. Army Air Force veteran who had worked various jobs at Elliott Stevedoring until his retirement in 1980. But Mr. Hodgkins did not take to retirement very well. A teamster, he went back to work at a local trucking outfit called Gloucester Supply. He was also employed by a construction equipment outlet in the nearby town of Rowley. Peter's mother had worked as a waitress at a restaurant called Dexter's Hearthside in the neighboring town of Essex until 1975 when she died from heart disease. But for as long as anyone could remember, young Peter had always stood apart. A former neighbor said, "You would look at Peter and know he was different. The kids knew he was different." Another commented, "He was strange, but he was a neighborhood kid and we knew him. We were used to overlooking what he was doing."

Disappearing: that's what he had been doing ever since he was six and a neighborhood boy showed him the forest and meadows and rocks that seemed to go on endlessly beyond the top of his street. That first trip was memorable. Peter Hodgkins claimed he "disappeared for the entire day," and did not arrive home until late, upsetting his parents. Yet Hodgkins went back again and again, until he was soon disappearing in Dogtown daily. Eventually he had all but memorized every inch of the place, and claimed its creatures got to know him, too. "Snakes, birds, hawks, coyotes," Hodgkins once said, "I was never afraid of them, they considered me part of the area." He claimed to have become so familiar to one particular hawk that he was able to get close to the nest where it sat with a recently hatched fledgling. Once he even showed it to a group of bird-watchers passing through the area. It did not take long for Hodgkins to need Dogtown the way some people need the ocean or mountains or gardening or exercise; it settled him and gave him a sense

of place. But there was more to how Peter Hodgkins felt about Dogtown. It was the one place where he felt safe. "Every year I ran away, so
to speak, to the woods," he once said. "Any fears, I'd go there and forget
them." When asked what he needed to feel safe from, though, he was
unable to say.

Others seemed to know. One childhood classmate remembered
how "the kids would beat him up on the [school] bus. . . . I don't remember anyone defending him. He used to walk home a lot [to avoid
it]." Schoolyard bullies seized upon Hodgkins's unusual physique with
alacrity. They called him animal-like names, as if he were not fully
human: "the Boar," for his buck teeth; "Daddy Longlegs," for his dispro-
portionately long legs; and "Chicken," for his heart-shaped chest. "Your
heart just broke" watching him get beaten up, one of his former classmates recalled.

Even into adulthood, people commented on Hodgkins's unique appearance. "He was odd-looking," his former landlord Joe Walsh said,
adding that the six-foot-eight Hodgkins was "one long drink of water."
Detective Reardon, the lead investigator in the Natti case, observed
that down on the waterfront where Hodgkins worked, "people always
said they could tell Peter was driving the jitterbug [forklift] because his
knees would stick out above the steering wheel." After the Linda Crane
incident, Hodgkins's coworkers were shocked to learn that he had exposed himself to and attacked a woman. One of them said, laughing,
"Who would have liked to see him with no clothes on?" The cops made
their own jokes about how Hodgkins's exposure victims referenced the
size of his member when describing their assailant. Hodgkins's crystalline pale blue eyes, which lightened near his irises, also set him apart.
One acquaintance commented, "There are times when you know nobody's home behind those eyes." Another said that he had "a way of
looking at you but not looking at you at the same time." "He was one
strange duck," said policeman Kenneth Ryan, repeating an oft-stated
sentiment. Most everyone claimed that Peter Hodgkins was simply
"strange," as if he came from some faraway place beyond known, nor-
mative boundaries.

But for many, Peter Hodgkins, whom even the police had described
as "a likable guy," was as familiar as he was unusual. One childhood
neighbor said, "He always gave me the creeps—but he didn't, really,
because I'd say, 'Oh, that's just Peter.' I didn't want to be the one to

point a finger at him just because he was a little odd." That was the issue. Much of Hodgkins's childhood behavior walked the line between boyishly aggressive antics and true deviance. He once nearly strangled a kitten to death; in another incident he blew up a large firework called a Barrel Ball in his dog's face. Peter also invited harm on himself by repeatedly crashing his bicycle into moving cars. A neighbor recalled that out of all the kids on Hodgkins's street, Peter alone "required constant vigilance." He was nearly always testing some limit. One childhood classmate remembered how "kids would say, 'I hear you can get hit on the chest and it doesn't hurt.' He'd say 'yes,' and they'd hit him as hard as they could." Hodgkins never fought back.

School was not only socially fraught for Hodgkins, it was academically taxing, too. Peter repeated the first and seventh grades, and by the time he entered Gloucester High School, he was sixteen. When the high school kids held keg parties in Dogtown, he would sometimes show up, but was "always off to the side." Hodgkins, who was not much of a drinker, later claimed that "once in a great while" these revelers would invite him to join them, offer him a beer, and ask what he was doing in the woods. It seems unlikely that he would have told them the truth: that on certain Gloucester nights he liked to walk through the woods. Oftentimes he would climb to the top of the rock that had been inscribed with the words KEEP OUT OF DEBT, where he would lie down and watch the woods and the stars. It was one of his favorite things to do.

Though many people believed that Hodgkins lived in Dogtown—he did spend most of his free time there—he claimed to have spent only a few nights in the woods. On these evenings he would "make a bed out of a few feet of padded-down leaves," and watch the sky. "It's real pretty at night," he mused, which was part of why the parties with all the garbage the kids left behind upset him. "The beer cans, the beer bottles—all it did was mess it [Dogtown] up." Sometimes he gathered these bottles and took them down to Gronblat's Pit, a gravel pit near the Cherry Street entrance, where he would line them up and shoot at them with his BB pistol.

But back at school, Peter Hodgkins held two advantages over his fellow ninth graders: a driver's license and a car that he had purchased with money he earned from working on the waterfront. And like other Gloucester teenagers, he would sometimes take "a certain girl" to Dogtown to make out. "You could back your car into the bushes and be totally out of sight . . . and alone," he recollected.

Ultimately, work proved to be more gratifying for Hodgkins than school. "Peter was a pretty good worker," claimed Jim O'Neill, Hodgkins's Elliott Stevedoring coworker. "He would do anything you asked. He was always helpful; in fact, more than helpful—he wanted to be your friend." By the end of his freshman year, Hodgkins dropped out of school and began working full time.

With a good job and enough money to buy grown-up toys, Peter Hodgkins was starting to achieve some young adult stability. Yet even into adulthood, Hodgkins remained a loner. "He played his cards close to him," said O'Neill, who was also one of Hodgkins's two friends at work. They never spent time together socially, but O'Neill would see Hodgkins most every day. Even after Hodgkins changed jobs, he would come around. "He would say hello, but didn't get into conversations with people—just a yup, no, maybe."

When Hodgkins did talk, he rarely, if ever, mentioned Dogtown. Instead, he told people about the big-engine hydroplane boat that he had purchased and in which he sped around Gloucester Harbor. Or he would say how much he wanted to race his car at the New England Dragway in Epping, New Hampshire. A solid mechanic, Hodgkins had stripped the interior of his Ford Pinto, remounted the engine, and painted the car candy apple green. But after putting a significant amount of time and money into the vehicle, Hodgkins couldn't get the car to start and "tried to teach it a lesson with a tire iron." O'Neill managed to keep Hodgkins from destroying the car, but this was only one of Hodgkins's numerous out-of-control rages that he had observed. Like others who tried to help Hodgkins, O'Neill was careful and respectful of how he talked about the younger man. "I'm not saying he did anything wild," he said of these episodes, "but his father would help him calm down." Hodgkins's issue with anger aside, O'Neill "always thought he was a nice kid, but he was very confused." And this confusion only seemed to worsen after Hodgkins's mother died.

By all accounts, Peter Hodgkins's mother was a warm, loving presence in her son's life. After her death, "Peter was pretty well distraught," O'Neill said. "I don't think he could quite fathom the situation." It was an oft-repeated observation. Though Hodgkins had been ostracized as a child and into adulthood, his mother was extremely protective of him. "He didn't know who to turn to after she died," O'Neill believed. Peter, who was twenty-four at the time, attempted suicide. Hodgkins's father's remarriage a year and a half later, on July 4, 1976— the Bicentennial—deepened the trauma of his loss. "I had *one* mother," he said with conviction thirty years after her death. "Nobody can replace her." And while Hodgkins believed that his stepmother understood how he felt, he also claims they never got along. Family friends believed that she feared the powerful young man. Others did, too. It all started with a series of incidents that Hodgkins referred to as "sunbathing."

While some Cape Anners indulged in nude sunbathing, especially around the quarries or at the oceanfront Flat Ledge Rocks, those who did not partake tolerated the practice without complaint. But when Peter Hodgkins began exposing himself to women near the quarries and in the woods and was confronted about these incidents, his claims to merely be "sunbathing" did not hold up. In one ocurrence, a woman named Terry Rubin, who lived in a VW van atop Woodbury Street during the summers, was outside sunning herself while her vanmate, Ira Levine, was inside reading. Levine looked up from his book and saw Hodgkins—naked and masturbating—come running out of the woods toward Rubin. Levine flew out of the van and chased Hodgkins, who disappeared through the trees. There were many such stories. Some were attributed to Hodgkins, others never ascribed to any particular person. And people believe that there were additional incidents that victims simply kept to themselves. But preceding the attack on Linda Crane, the frequency with which Hodgkins had harassed women far exceeded the number of times he was arrested.

Peter Hodgkins's arrest record began in 1972, when he was twenty and was charged with annoying and accosting a woman. This charge was reduced to disturbing the peace. In 1975, the same year his mother died, Hodgkins exposed himself to a female bicyclist and pushed her to the ground. He was indicted for open and gross lewdness and assault and battery. By 1977, another open and gross lewdness accusation was filed against him. This time he had grabbed a female acquaintance. He let her go and ran away, but returned without any clothes on and masturbated in front of her. Two years later, similar charges of disorderly conduct and public masturbation were levied against Hodgkins. He pleaded guilty to all of these incidents and was charged with additional sexually predatory infractions, including indecent exposure, obscene phone calls, and an incident described on his arrest sheet as a "near-nude chase." On one of his arrest reports Hodgkins is quoted as saying, "I did it. I did it. I can't help myself, I need help, please help me." In each of these cases he received a light sentence and complied with his probation officers. When required, his father made sure that he also saw a court-appointed psychiatrist and paid his punitive fines.

Most Cape Anners were unaware of the full extent of Peter Hodgkins's transgressions and tolerated the wayward, apple-cheeked boy who had grown into a troubled man. They believed that Hodgkins had an emotional, not a criminal, problem, and thought that he seemed "tormented." Moreover, he was from a good family; he was one of Gloucester's own. One woman who had filed a complaint against Hodgkins did not think his behavior was that extreme. At the time she said, "A community can absorb a certain amount of that. It's okay here to be a little crazy; the community will take care of you. . . . It's the way a community should be."

Though residents acknowledged Dogtown's ability to "comfort strange people," Cape Ann, not just Dogtown, took care of many eccentrics back in the day. One town character named Dan Ruberti marched into traffic while blowing a bugle in local election years to announce his mayoral run. (Ruberti continues to run for office and always finishes in advance of last place.) Then there was Eino Leino, who, though named after a famous Finnish poet, preferred his nickname, "Yksi" (pronounced *irksy*), meaning "Number One" in Finnish. People said that if Yksi had an itch on his knee, he would drop his pants in public and give it a scratch. Every so often he would barge in through the backdoor of writer Gregory Gibson's house and say, "This is my house. The Indians gave it to me." Still, Cape Anners maintained that Yksi was not crazy, just that he liked to get bent pretty hard. There were many other characters about the place, especially in the decades leading up to 1984—"Doctor Pet," "Catnip Bill," "Skippy Cream," "Mary the Duck," "Rosie Crud," and "Sweet Pea"—but the spectrum of Gloucester eccentrics was not limited to the working class or barflies. Inventor John Hays Hammond Jr., who counts the radio transmitter among his more than four hundred patents—making him second only to Thomas Edison in the number of patented inventions to his name—was a descendant of one of Cape Ann's most aristocratic families. Prior to World

War I, Hammond steered an unmanned yacht around Gloucester Harbor via remote control and got a kick out of spooking people with this "ghost ship." Eventually it was widely understood that Hammond was testing out his new invention, the Gyrad, which incorporated the gyroscope into the radio wave–receiving technology he had developed and sold to the U.S. War Department. With all of his riches, Hammond later built a waterfront replica medieval castle with a moat, drawbridge, towers, catacombs, and an inner courtyard where he installed an artificial rain system.

"Like any seaport," as one former policeman put it, "we had the characters." Some "were a pain in the ass, but we knew what to expect from them."

Knowing what to expect was the very crux of the matter.

In any other place, people like Ruberti and Yksi might have been shunned. But sending someone to the loony bin or a treatment center just because he was a little peculiar would violate that Gloucester ethos of tolerance and support that was a source of town pride. If these individuals proved to be harmful to either themselves or others, such as the man who chased after Jack Chase, they would indeed be institutionalized. But most of Gloucester's characters were harmless and amused the rest of the town, some of who looked out for them, like Yksi's neighbors who tended to him in his final years. If anything, the kinds of people Gloucester residents find intolerable are finger-wagging, judgmental goody-two-shoes and know-it-all outsiders who think that this (or any other) aspect of the Gloucester way of life needs to change. People here like Gloucester the way it is, for better or worse. And it was in this same spirit that Gloucester residents excused or accepted Peter Hodgkins's behavior because, as one woman put it, "I knew the family, I had no reason to be afraid." And as another said, "I don't want us to overreact to this. I don't want to lock up every neighborhood drunk in town; I don't want to live in that kind of place." No self-respecting Gloucester resident did.

But when does eccentricity mask a serious problem? And when does tolerating it become dangerous? "Peter was strange," Detective David Reardon claimed, "but not what I consider to be strange from a law enforcement perspective." In other words, and as Gloucester reporter Wendy Quiñones noted at the time, no one expected Peter Hodgkins to turn dangerous. Hodgkins may have pushed the limits repeatedly, but officials observed that his sex offenses were consistently more perverted than violent until his encounter with Linda Crane on that April 1980 day.

After his 1980 release from the Essex House of Corrections, Hodgkins returned to Gloucester and to worsening tensions with his stepmother. Joe Walsh, who owned a boardinghouse in downtown Gloucester and knew the Hodgkins family, intervened. Walsh offered to let Peter clean the boardinghouse halls and bathroom and take care of the garbage in exchange for free rent. "I know your father and I know your mother so if you give me any trouble I'm going to go to them," Walsh told Hodgkins. It was what he said to all of his residents, and it worked especially well on Peter.

Hodgkins got along well with Walsh and the other boardinghouse inhabitants, particularly Hazel Harris, the building's residential manager, who claimed she could not "say anything but good about him." He brought her wildflowers picked fresh from Dogtown and tended to her when she was ill. Mrs. Harris trusted Peter so much she allowed him to babysit her kindergarten-age granddaughter, who affectionately called him "Jolly Green Giant."

Frank Elliott, who owned Elliott Stevedoring, where Hodgkins and his father had both worked, also tried to help. Noticing that the younger Hodgkins did not know how to handle his money, Elliott opened a savings account for Peter and taught him how to manage his finances. "Frank did a lot for him," Hodgkins's Elliott Stevedoring coworker Jim O'Neill said. Peter obligingly followed his advice. He was always eager to please.

In the years after the Linda Crane incident, some felt that Hodgkins was beginning to pull his life together. Perhaps this came in part from the quasi-familial relationship and maternal trust he received from Mrs. Harris and the assistance from Walsh and Elliott. Hodgkins told people he had a steady girlfriend and that they were considering marriage. Even the police noticed his change for the better.

But other Cape Anners found themselves feeling afraid of the man they had long tolerated. A neighbor who had previously excused Peter's behavior saw him near Dogtown's Vivian Spring and realized that she had experienced a change of heart: "He ceased to be the small child of a Peter I used to know; he began to look sinister to me."

One of the female tellers at the bank also began to fear him. When

Hodgkins found out, he promptly withdrew all his money. Another neighbor who watched him grow up now claimed, "We were scared of him in the neighborhood." The woman who had watched him get beat up on the bus felt differently, too. She saw Hodgkins while blueberrying in Dogtown one day and immediately packed up her things and left.

PETER HODGKINS QUICKLY became the prime suspect in Anne Natti's murder, but the police had trouble finding him. He had no known, fixed address—Walsh had sold the boardinghouse by 1984—and Hodgkins's grandfather, with whom he had also lived, had passed away in April of that year. Sometime thereafter, people occasionally saw Hodgkins going around with all of his clothes in his car, but by late June, he had somehow lost his car, too. When Detective Reardon called Peter's father, Mr. Hodgkins didn't know where his son was either. But someone came forward and tipped off the police to Hodgkins's possible whereabouts.

When the policeman knocked at the door of Wilma Upham's home, she was there to greet them. Upham, an employee at one of the businesses that had burned in the Main Street fire, was suddenly without a job. The police did not say why they were looking for Hodgkins, just that they wanted to ask a few questions. Upham was not at all shy about her affection and concern for Hodgkins. "Oh, he had been living here, all right. Just about six weeks," she said later, and recalled, "He had some fight with his girlfriend. She threw him out and he was living in his car. I always felt very bad for Peter. He was a sweet man, a very sweet man. He'd come home stinking and smelling like fish and I would tell him to take a shower before having supper. He had an appetite like an elephant. He was just like a little boy. He even had a teddy bear he kept on the dresser. 'Course, he was so tall he always smacked his head on the light in the living room. Then his feet poked through the end of [the] wrought iron bed frame. He was a good old slob and hard on his luck. He was just like a twelve-year-old. I was looking out for him."

After six weeks, Upham's husband grew wary that the arrangement would never end. Hodgkins had already left by the time the police came looking for him. Upham had no idea where he went.

AFTER POLICE CARS pulled away from Wilma Upham's house without any strong leads, a neighbor called her and yelled into the phone receiver, "Don't you know you're harboring a murderer?"

"No!" she replied. "Peter does not have that in him. I would stay locked in a room with him and feel safe!" She slammed down the receiver.

Unbeknownst to the police, Peter Hodgkins was actually living in the shadow of Our Lady of Good Voyage on a slender little street with a gregarious friend from the docks who was known to frequent the town's rougher bars: Brian Langley. When not at Langley's, he was in Dogtown, whiling away the hours.

The Tuesday evening after Anne Natti's murder, Hodgkins asked Langley to give him a ride to an overpass on Route 133, just beyond where island Cape Ann begins. He claimed he was heading out of town to see a friend. Langley obliged the unusual request.

En route, Hodgkins was jittery, nervous, and scrunched down in the front passenger seat. Langley asked Hodgkins why he was acting so weird. An anxious Hodgkins said that his girlfriend had pressed charges against him for assault and battery and that the police were looking for him. He was just a little out of sorts over it all.

When the two men reached the overpass, Hodgkins began to exit the car but then suddenly hopped back in and ducked down toward the passenger side floor again. The sound of sirens had scared him, he said. But there were no sirens, just a semitruck speeding by.

Hodgkins eventually left the car. Langley watched him walk down the road and into the woods.

Chapter Ten

In the Time of Pirates

T HE MORNING OF April 14, 1724, Gloucester Captain Andrew Haraden embarked upon a brief fishing voyage aboard his unfinished sloop, the *Squirrel*. Bound for Cape Sable, Haraden and his crew must have anticipated the Nova Scotia island's most ominous sight: the giant skeletal ribs of shattered hulls strewn across its shores. Though the conflict between the English colonists and the French and Indians had momentarily ceased close to home, the French and Indians continued to "make fearful depredations" upon Gloucester fishermen in Nova Scotia. Haraden's grandfather, an accomplished mariner, had lost a ship to French forces on Cape Sable in 1711. The harsh North Atlantic conditions were ever present, too. In 1716 five Gloucester vessels were lost during a violent storm, but by the spring of 1724, Captain Haraden could count a new hazard among these: the notorious pirate John Phillips, who had taken to cruising the waters between Cape Ann and Newfoundland in search of bounty.

Unlike other pirates such as Blackbeard, Barbarossa (a.k.a. Red Beard), and Black Bart, whose dreaded exploits also filled the pages of eighteenth-century London broadsheets, John Phillips had a perfectly milquetoast name, though he was no less feared. From August 1723 until April 1724, the month the *Squirrel* set sail, Phillips had seized more than thirty ships while "prosecuting his intended Rogueries," as Daniel Defoe, who covered piratical (and other criminal) activities for *Mist's Weekly-Journal* and the *Original Weekly Journal*, reported and committed to posterity in his 1726 volume *General History of the Py-*

Phillips, whose ship bore down on the *Squirrel* until it was but a cannon-shot distant.

The *Squirrel* had not made its way very far from home. As the sloop rounded the Isles of Shoals, a group of nine rocky islands located ten miles offshore from the Maine and New Hampshire coast, Phillips's vessel opened fire, striking the water less than a hundred feet from the *Squirrel*'s bow. Phillips's ship showed "death's head," the pirates' signature black flag. With no armaments on board, Haraden had no choice but to surrender.

Phillips and his crew boarded the *Squirrel* and admired the brand-new sloop's four square sails—all rigged from a single, center mast—and her clean hull. On the second day of the *Squirrel*'s capture, Phillips's men moved their cannons, ammunition, and supplies to the new ship. The pirates then forced Haraden's crew onto their old vessel, lashed them to her mast, and cut her lines. Haraden, now a prisoner, watched his men drift off until they disappeared.

That night, as the *Squirrel* sailed for Newfoundland, two of Phillips's crew, Edward Cheeseman and John Philmore, kept watch over Haraden. Above decks, men on the graveyard watch observed the starfall and the moonrise. Wind played in the sloop's rigging. The sea roiled beneath the gunwales, drowning out the voice of Cheeseman, "a modest sober young Man" from Virginia, as he "broke his mind" to Haraden about their plan to overthrow Phillips. Cheeseman and Philmore, a seaman from Ipswich, whose great-grandson, Millard Fillmore, would become the thirteenth (and by some accounts the worst) president of the United States, had been forced into piracy by Phillips along with half of the crew. With Haraden and the broadax and adze that his crew had brought along to work on the unfinished ship, they now had enough men and weapons to execute their mutiny.

The following day Cheeseman, Philmore, and Haraden worked their tools over the *Squirrel*'s deck and planed down their plan of action to a smooth finish, leveling its burrs and easing the worry out of its knots and their men's concerns. Phillips, who had a gash across his forehead from a blow with a handspike, cut a moderately less intimidating figure than the navigator, John Nutt. A thick, "long-armed" man sunbaked to the red sturdiness of a brick, Nutt swaggered fore and aft giving off an air of one who would not easily be overcome. Cheeseman volunteered to be the one to take him.

On the third day, the mutineers busied themselves with their ship-wright's chores in hopeful anticipation of noon, when they had agreed to execute their plan. At the appointed time, only Nutt and Burrell, the boatswain, were on deck. The remaining pirates, including Captain Phillips, were belowdecks. Cheeseman set down his adze and walked aft to retrieve his brandy. He poured Haraden a dram, then raised his glass to Nutt and Burrell and toasted "to their next merry meeting." Cheeseman then turned to Nutt and engaged in talk about the weather. Philmore idly spun his ax around on its point, which was the agreed-upon signal to the other mutineers that the time had come to act. Cheeseman immediately seized Nutt and heaved him overboard as Philmore swung his ax onto Burrell's head, splitting it in two. Hearing the commotion, Captain Phillips came running on deck, where Ha-raden struck him with his adze. Sparks, the gunner, attempted to inter-cede, but Cheeseman tripped him and flung him into the arms of two other mutineers, who tossed him overboard as Haraden bludgeoned Phillips to death.

There were shouts and heaving sounds of exertion, of living flesh meeting its violent end, a head rolling across the deck, then another. The splashing sound of bodies tossed to the sea. The metallic smell of warm blood mixed with the cool, salty breeze. Within minutes the struggle was over. The remaining pirates surrendered.

Haraden set their course for Annisquam Harbor, with Phillips's and Burrell's heads hanging from the *Squirrel's* mast.

One month later, Captain Haraden, Cheeseman, Philmore, and oth-ers who were forced to join Phillips's crew stood trial in Boston for pi-racy and were acquitted. John Rose Archer, the quartermaster who had previously sailed with Blackbeard, and William White, who was one of the first to sail with Phillips, were found guilty and executed in front of "a multitude of spectators." Archer's body was hung in the gallows on Bird Island, where the creatures who gave this place its name tore at his lifeless flesh.

WHILE READING THIS I expected to then learn that people who moved inland seeking protection from additional pirate attacks created the village that would become Dogtown. But as with the specious story of Indian attacks, the oft-repeated notion that people fleeing early-eighteenth-century rogues settled the area did not hold up to the historical record. With the exception of some pirates who had been apprehended in Gloucester twenty years before, Phillips's April 1724 attacks against these captains were Cape Ann's only pirate tales from the era. Perhaps the confusion lies in the fact that the village that would become Dogtown did in fact begin "in the time of pirates." What's more, two of the Gloucester captains whose ships were taken by Phillips, Samuel Elwell and Joshua Elwell, happened to lived there. These captains' stories of mistreatment at the hands of Phillips would have undoubtedly been well known in their day, but the Elwells were only two out of forty-one residents in a village that began three years before Phillips's attacks. Records are scarce, but I was able to piece together a different, far less dramatic account of the beginnings of the village that would one day become Dogtown.

By the early 1700s, Cape Ann was so thoroughly deforested, "the rocky surface of the town" was fully exposed "with scarcely a tree or bush to relieve the eye." The protean woods that had so terrified Ebenezer Babson had been cleared. Abundant highland common land was now available for settlement. It happened to be the worst land on this rocky promontory, but the town's selectmen looked toward the future and pictured snug cabins to house families whose men could plant crops, drive nails, mend sails, and work nets to help grow the town's fledgling maritime industries. Hoping to attract a much-needed workforce, the town passed a vote to offer land grants to new settlers.

In 1721, the year that Ipswich's Rev. Wise had looked to Gloucester for inspiration, officials measured forty-three lots across the highland and laid out a village that later historians would call the Commons Settlement. This village was just over the Alewife Brook and up a hill from the Green, early-eighteenth-century Gloucester's social and commercial center. Proximity to the Green was undoubtedly part of the area's appeal, along with the numerous mills then located along the eponymous Mill River, into which the Alewife Brook flowed.

Descendants of Gloucester's oldest families—not the intended newcomers—soon congregated to break this land, build their homes, and create a village. They planted fields, built fences, and made neighbors while the giant boulders stood nearby, casting a funereal air over their activity.

In 1729, a mere eight years after the Commons Settlement's inception, a parish dispute would begin. This quarrel, which hinged upon one man's desire to maintain the status quo, fractured the community, and hastened the Commons Settlement's decline into the ramshackle hamlet known as Dogtown.

Chapter Eleven

The Green Man

J UST AS QUICKLY AS Peter Hodgkins had disappeared, he could suddenly materialize as he had with Terry Rubin and Linda Crane. On Wednesday morning, he turned up on Dennison Street near where he had lived with his grandfather. That day, Stephen Amaral, an off-duty police detective, came up the street and noticed that Peter was standing in the road, staring off into the middle distance. When Amaral asked Hodgkins what he was doing, Peter said that he was waiting for his grandfather. This struck Amaral as odd; Hodgkins's grandfather had died in April of that year. Amaral, who was just coming back from vacation and was not aware that the police were looking for Hodgkins, stood and watched as the prime suspect in Anne Natti's murder walked away.

Later that day, Hodgkins picked up the message that Detective Reardon had left with his father and called the sergeant at the station. Reardon, who had dealt with Hodgkins since the early 1970s, when he first got into trouble with the law, grew up a third of a mile down the street from Hodgkins and knew his family. While he was one of many officers on the Gloucester police force from Riverdale, the same working-class neighborhood where Peter Hodgkins grew up, Reardon and Hodgkins had a special rapport. When Reardon asked Hodgkins to come to the station for routine questioning, Hodgkins told the detective to meet him in the woods along the Dogtown Road that afternoon. He insisted that Reardon come alone.

Reardon knew how Hodgkins felt: Dogtown was "his castle," as the detective later put it. He was also aware of the fact that most of Hodg-kins's violations against women had taken place in the area's woods. Now Hodgkins wanted to meet a few miles from where Anne Natti's body had been found. Reardon's suspicions were piqued. Was he re-turning to the scene of the crime like a telltale criminal? Did he have other motives?

That afternoon, Reardon's unmarked cruiser began the steep climb up Reynard and Cherry Streets. Additional police waited nearby, but Reardon, who kept his police radio mike open, peeled off the macadam onto a dirt road, entering Dogtown on his own.

Reardon drove to Gronblat's Pit, the gravel pit not far from Dog-town's entrance where Hodgkins sometimes shot cans and bottles with his BB pistol, and waited. Hodgkins didn't show.

The detective decided to look over by the Vivian Spring, where Hodgkins had attacked Linda Crane four years earlier. As he started turning the car around, Hodgkins emerged from behind a rock on a nearby hilltop, like some American equivalent of the English Green Man, a wood-dwelling pagan deity with a human face that materializes from a tangle of leaves. The Green Man is often depicted carved in stone or wood on the outside of buildings or painted in the margins of medieval illuminated manuscripts—liminal realms that are neither of one world nor another in medieval iconography. Similarly, Hodgkins regularly crossed the boundary between civilization and the wild and seemed incapable of finding his place in either setting.

Reardon told Hodgkins that the police wanted to ask him some routine questions since he had been in the area over the weekend be-fore Anne Natti was killed; that was all. Peter agreed to ride to the sta-tion if they could stop at a few places so he could look for his girlfriend.

Reardon obliged Hodgkins's request. Though Peter had told Lang-ley that his girlfriend had pressed charges against him, he had appar-ently lied. When they could not find the young woman, Hodgkins told Reardon they had actually broken up.

At the station, Hodgkins told Reardon and Massachusetts state po-lice sergeant John J. O'Rourke how he had spent the past several days: he had been in the woods riding a motorized dirt bike on Saturday and Sunday but had not seen anyone or anything suspicious. On Monday morning, the day of Anne Natti's murder, he left Langley's house, where he had spent the night, and took off on Langley's ten-speed bicycle. It was sometime between 8:30 and 9:00 A.M. Hodgkins rode around town for a while, then made his way to the unemployment office. At about two-thirty in the afternoon he returned to Langley's, where he stayed for the rest of the day. He was home all day on Tuesday, too, but for a trip to a nearby store to buy cigarettes. Then Langley gave him a ride to West Gloucester where he had planned on staying with a friend, but the friend was not home. He spent the night and the following morning in the woods.

Reardon told Hodgkins that Detective Amaral had seen him on Dennison Street that morning. Hodgkins insisted he had not been anywhere near Dennison Street or seen Amaral. But Reardon informed Hodgkins that Amaral had described his clothes. Hodgkins continued to deny all of it.

"Why didn't you get in touch with me when you first heard I was looking for you?" Reardon asked.

"I thought you wanted to talk to me about the murder," Hodgkins replied, saying that he was afraid.

Reardon bore down: "I think you know something you're not telling me, Peter." Hodgkins, stone-faced, claimed he had no knowledge about or involvement in the murder.

Unable to elicit any information from their suspect, Reardon and O'Rourke had to let Hodgkins go. They had one way to confirm their suspicions: checking his alibi, Brian Langley. Before releasing Hodgkins, Reardon got a search warrant approved and sent a group of detectives and state police chemist Robert Pino over to Langley's. He then called Hodgkins's father and arranged for him to be picked up from the station.

IT WAS JUST after 5:30 P.M. Langley, who worked at Flex Key Corporation assembling computer keyboards, was unwinding at home with his friend Brian Cunha when a knock unexpectedly rattled the front door of the Oak Street duplex where he lived with his two sons. Detective Kenneth Ryan and state trooper Mark Lynch told Langley they wanted to ask him some questions about Peter Hodgkins. Langley said he had not seen Peter since that ride to the overpass. But Hodgkins was erratic; he could show up at any minute.

Langley told the authorities how Hodgkins had been staying with him for a week, during which he devoted his time to fixing Langley's red and black Honda XL 250 trail bike. With its proboscis-like front fork shocks, high front fender, gas tank decorated with Honda's signature wing, and high-pitched whine, the XL 250 is a mosquito rendered in metal, plastic, and vinyl. It is light and fast, good for popping wheelies and catching steep air, but Langley's bike had sat rusting away the seasons in a corner of the garage until Hodgkins came along. Hodgkins lovingly worked it down, WD-40 in hand, clearing salt from the gas tank and coaxing the engine back to working condition. The bike may have appeared dwarf and squat under Hodgkins's giant frame, but he rode it every day without fail, buzzing through the quiet, imprinting miles upon miles of Dogtown trails with waffle tread, and crosshatching the air with hazy exhaust.

Peter had spent the entire weekend on the bike, for all Langley knew. And Monday, too.

That day, Langley got up with his alarm clock in time for his shift. Hodgkins stirred, too, anxious as ever to ride. Langley opened the garage door combination padlock and let Hodgkins take the bike. The rain, fog, and commotion from the Main Street fire would have kept most bikers off the road, but Hodgkins took to his ride as soon as possible. He pulled the choke, set the kill switch to run, squeezed the clutch, depressed the starter until the engine fired, and let the bike idle to life. The wheels started to turn beneath him. He released the clutch and leaned into the ride. It was 6:45 A.M.

After a stop at the package store, Langley arrived home from his shift with his friend Brian Cunha at around 4:45 P.M., but Hodgkins was not there. Neither man looked to see if the motor bike was in the garage. A soaking wet Hodgkins arrived soon thereafter.

"Don't use the bike," Hodgkins said as soon as he walked in the door. A policeman had stopped him and threatened him with arrest because it was unregistered.

Perhaps Langley or Cunha thought about this for a minute: wouldn't the police just issue a ticket or a summons? Why threaten an arrest, unless Hodgkins was riding like a madman, which would not have been a surprise; he was well known for being a speed freak.

The police listened to Hodgkins's alibi fall apart. Now they needed evidence: the bike.

Cunha stayed upstairs and watched TV, while Langley led the detectives and Pino down to the garage. There was nothing visibly unusual about the Honda, just some mud, as would be expected on a dirt bike. Then there were details that only a trained specialist would know how to detect: wear patterns, discoloration, tears, scratches, fibers, and blood.

The phone rang. Cunha yelled out the window. Hodgkins was on the line, wanting to speak to Langley. Lynch asked if he could listen in on the call. Langley agreed.

Lynch and Langley went upstairs, while Pino continued examining the bike and Detective Ryan went through Hodgkins's other belongings that were stored in the garage. Lynch set his hand on a phone receiver in the kitchen and peered through the doorway at Langley, who watched him from the bedroom where there was a second phone. They picked up the receivers in tandem. Hodgkins started in.

"Have the police been there?"

"Yes," Langley said while watching Lynch, who had placed one hand over the receiver so as not to make a sound. Lynch was scribbling furiously on a Kleenex box near the phone.

"Did you tell the police I used the motorcycle Monday?"

"Yes," Langley replied.

"Shit, that's one hole they got me on," Peter said. "They are trying to pin a murder on me."

"Well, I couldn't lie to the police," Langley explained. "I had to tell them."

Hodgkins was growing audibly distressed and speaking quickly, as if he were short of breath.

"This is serious," Peter replied. "Did they find the green bags in the room? Hide the green bags in the garage."

"This *is* serious," Langley repeated.

"You ain't kiddin'," Hodgkins quipped. "I'm scared shit. Did they check for the green box in the room?"

"Yes," Langley replied.

"Make sure you hide it, because it has a BB pistol in it that I haven't fired in two years and I don't have a permit for it. I don't care where you hide it, just hide it."

"If I can," Langley said.

"Are they looking at the bike?"

"They are looking at it right now."

"Don't let them take the motorbike," Hodgkins pleaded. "If I have to, I'll come down and take it and hide it somewhere, keep it out of sight."

"It's too late," Langley replied. The police were actually taking the bike as he spoke.

"I have to go visit a friend out of town," Hodgkins replied, stating he was calling from Addison Gilbert Hospital. "Don't tell them where I am and that you heard from me. They are trying to pin a murder on me," he said, and quickly hung up.

THERE WERE A few pay phones that Hodgkins could have walked or ridden a bike to from the woods or his father's house, but he happened to call Langley from a phone at Addison Gilbert, Cape Ann's only hospital, where Anne Natti's body lay in the blue chill of the morgue.

The medical examiner had determined that a severe blow to Anne Natti's head by a blunt instrument had been the principal cause of death. This blow created a "massive skull fracture that progressed from back to front, almost the entire length of the skull" and pressed against her brain, causing substantial bleeding into her scalp and hair. Blows to her face, delivered with "substantial and severe force," contributed to the "massive" amounts of soft-tissue bleeding that had already begun. Her jaw had been broken, her nose deformed, her left eye marked with "very severe" contusions. Her chest and stomach were scraped and bruised from being dragged thirty feet. Blood on the front of her body had dried with dirt and leaves and concealed a chest wound just below her breasts. This wound most likely had been caused when she was dragged. She bled from her scalp, eyes, and mouth. Her nose and ears were lined with a similar film of bloody dirt from her face having been pushed into the ground. She had remained alive throughout much of the attack.

Moments after hanging up the receiver with Langley, Peter Hodgkins took off.

Chapter Twelve

Dooming the Seats

O NE 1737 AUTUMN SUNDAY Nathaniel Coit, a sharp-minded seventy-eight-year-old town oligarch, shifted his weight in his seat as he listened to Gloucester's Rev. White intone from the Book of Matthew, "Ye are the light of the world. A city that is set upon a hill cannot be hid." But something hidden was at work that would contribute to the eventual demise of Gloucester's village upon a hill, the Commons Settlement.

Like most others across colonial New England, Gloucester's First Parish meetinghouse—a creaking edifice in a desperate need of repair—was the center of the town's colonial life. Meetinghouses served civic as well as religious purposes. Town authorities posted marriage banns, property sales, and violations of colonial law by their entrances, and sometimes hung the heads of slain wolves that had preyed upon colonists' livestock. The buildings doubled as powder magazines and went unheated to reduce the risk of fire or explosion. In many communities, townsmen were obligated to bring their firearms to services in case of a surprise attack by French and/or Indians; pirates had effectively been eliminated from the North Atlantic by this time. But for eight years, the conflict that posed the biggest threat to Gloucester's community silently raged inside the overcrowded building, adding to the heat and thickening the air: a protracted argument over where to build a new meetinghouse and how to pay for it.

For motives that might seem quaint today but were a matter of serious business to Puritans, relocating a meetinghouse was no simple matter for one reason above all others: it was always accompanied by a change in a parish's assigned seating chart. "Perhaps no duty was more important and more difficult of satisfactory performance in the church work in early New England than 'seating the meeting-house,'" nineteenth-century historian Alice Morse Earle observed. Parish committees were created to "dignify" or "doom" the meetinghouse seats based on a matrix of age, family lineage (descendants of the town's earliest settlers had higher rankings than newcomers), public service, and wealth that reflected one's standing in the community.

Whenever opportunity arose for a new assignment—communities varied in the frequency with which they changed their seating charts—townspeople either immediately began jockeying for a better seat or labored to maintain the status quo. Nathaniel Coit was of the latter sort. To prevent the outcry that usually accompanied reassignments, seating committee members were granted unquestioned authority and demanded that "there be no Grumbling at them." This did not stop parishioners from quarreling, however. Earle tells of two women, sisters-in-law, who were assigned seats next to each other and regularly fought over who happened to be sitting in the more "dignified" locale. The sisters-in-law's dispute grew so heated, it had to be settled in a town meeting. Other arguments lasted for decades. So it was in Gloucester, too. Not only did Nathaniel Coit strongly oppose relocating the First Parish meetinghouse from the moment the issue was raised—he was so against the new seating policy that was part of the relocation plan, he was willing to risk dividing the town to prevent the change.

Change had already arrived in Gloucester and affected its First Parish by 1729, the year this dispute began. For most of the town's first century, the First Parish at the Green had served all of Cape Ann. But starting in the early 1700s, the town's population was in the process of quadrupling from 700 residents in 1704 to 2,745 by 1755. Encouraged by this growth and tired of the arduous weekly travel from their homes to the Green, parishioners living in two outlying villages broke off to form their own parishes. Even after these divisions, the First Parish meetinghouse continued to swell with worshippers from the influx of newcomers drawn by the town's growing maritime economy; Gloucester's much-anticipated boom had finally arrived. Though these newcomers and some locals settled around Gloucester Harbor, the First

Parish meetinghouse continued to keep the town's spiritual and civic life anchored to the Green.

In 1734, however, First Parish members voted in favor of abandoning the old meetinghouse at the Green and building a new one closer to Gloucester Harbor one mile away. A proposal to pay for the new meetinghouse by selling pews was rejected by a slender four-vote margin. Arguments broke out. Under such a plan, the parish seating chart and, therefore, the town's social hierarchy would no longer be determined by its century-old method that valued age, family lineage, and public service over wealth. Wealth—first and foremost—would determine rank. A stalemate ensued for three years until the autumn of 1737, when a group of wealthy harbor leaders forced the issue.

That autumn, a new meetinghouse went up near the harbor. Plank by plank. Nail to stud. In less than a week, a new building, twice the size of the old, was complete. Yet the harbor leaders' privately constructed edifice sat empty for an entire year as if it did not exist. The First Parish continued to hold services in the dank old building until the fall of 1738, when parish members finally addressed the matter. They voted in favor of relocating to the new meetinghouse and requiring parishioners to purchase pews to reimburse the men's construction costs. The harborside meetinghouse became the parish's official home.

A significant amount of "Grumbling" followed. Nathaniel Coit, who lived at the Green, took up the opposition's lead. Money was not an issue for Coit, who was one of the town's wealthier men and could afford one of the best pews. But Coit had created animosity with the harbor leaders by always opposing the First Parish move. That some of these men had previously brought a General Court suit against him over an unrelated issue probably didn't help matters, either. And with a new seating committee composed of harbor leaders, Coit was almost certainly guaranteed a less venerable seat. Thus, for Coit, there was no turning back.

In response to the vote, Coit and his supporters started to foment dissent and pushed for the parish to split. Families became divided over the issue. Yet harbor leaders wanted the parish to remain intact. That they had laid out a considerable sum for the new building's construction most likely fed their resolve. The recalcitrant Coit began going from house to house "Up in Town"—the villages at the Green and the

Commons Settlement—to garner support and collect signatures on a petition to the Massachusetts' General Court to formally separate.

Coit entered the highland Commons Settlement, where multiple generations of a family lived in wood-framed houses that typically measured fifteen by thirty-five feet. According to colonial New England custom, the front doors on these houses faced south and were often built in line with the noonday sun. (Numbers were carved around the south-facing entrances of some New England homes to enable the facade to be used as a time-telling device similar to a sundial.) Colonists ground clamshells and mixed them with salt hay and animal hair to make plaster for walls. Only a few homes had glass windows; the material was quite expensive. Some thresholds, doorposts, and fieldstones may have been engraved with signs to keep away evil spirits, as was customary throughout colonial Essex County. Under their homes, residents had constructed fifteen-foot cellars from granite blocks, which, along with their granite doorsteps, are all that remain of these houses today.

Men toiling in their various workshops near the Alewife Brook and Mill River made barrels, wheelbarrows, drags, sledges, plows, chairs, tables, rods, rails, posts, poles, masts, doors, shutters, booms, buckets, gun handles, yokes, and more. The blacksmith forged their knives, fishhooks, keys, nails, oxshoes, and horseshoes from iron. Thimbles, buttons, buckles for shoes and belts, and sailmakers' palms (a device with a leather strap that wraps around the thumb to secure a metal plate in the palm to help drive needles through thick layers of canvas) were made from copper. Settlers could grind the corn they grew in gardens adjacent to their homes, felt their woolens, and cut their timber at the various mills for which the area's river was named. They could walk to the village at the Green to purchase dry goods, woolen fabrics, boots, and fishing gear. Some ventured in the opposite direction, toward Annisquam, to have their pick of the four different brands of rum George Dennison sold out of his store (Professor Norton's future home). A schoolhouse operated in the highland. A tannery, too.

Commoners, or landholders, came to the highlands from all across Gloucester to tend their pastures, graze their livestock, and cut wood for fuel and building materials on the area's common land. The commons system, which was derived from an old English tradition, enabled every landowner to hold rights to the town's common lands, hence the name Commons Settlement. The town granted these rights, which could be bought and sold like real estate, and governed them closely. Occasionally Gloucester would also grant its propertyless residents rights to tracts of land for wood cutting.

Though most of the highland common land served an agricultural purpose, it was a difficult place for growing much of anything. While settlers could dress their fields in peat and rich organic matter from the area swamps, the land was nearly carpeted in rocks. Livestock roamed freely to graze, while crops were fenced. The town employed a "fence viewer," an elected official who made certain that these fences were in good order.

As elsewhere on Cape Ann, the Commons settlers subsisted by simple means. They ate boiled dinners—pease porridge (a mush of boiled peas), "Injun and rye" (a porridge of cornmeal and rye), baked beans, fish, and whatever wild plants Providence offered for harvest—served in wooden trenchers or English earthenware. Their furnishings were likewise minimal. Upon his death, the belongings of a settler named Benjamin Allen consisted of a house, a barn, an adjoining eight-acre pasture, one bed, one quilt, three "good" sheets, five additional sheets of unspecified quality, two blankets, a round table, a case of bottles, a bedstand, a cow, a swine, and a hammer. Allen's possessions were meticulously divided among his widow and their six grown children. One daughter received "the Western lower Room and one fourth part of the cellar under it," along with one and a quarter acres of land. Descendants sold shares within the family and sometimes lived between two dwellings.

Nathaniel Coit did not need to labor his point with the Commons settlers. Though they did not have much in the way of money or worldly possessions, under the old meetinghouse's seating plan these descendants of some of Gloucester's earliest settlers had the honor of rank. Under the new plan, most could not afford to maintain their status. And while no one could waltz into town and simply buy the best seat in the harborside meetinghouse—harbor leaders vowed not to grant pews to newcomers until they had resided in Gloucester for at least six months—this assurance did not appease the vast majority of the Commons settlers.

By November, Coit had gathered eighty-four signatures in support of his petition. "Ye major part of your petitioners," Coit wrote, were not only incapable of affording a pew, "many of them seafaring men and have no convenance [*sic*] for going to meeting but by going a foot which is verry uncomfortable for elderly people, women, and children."

Town selectmen and the First Parish harbor leaders were called upon to answer Coit's claims. Life everywhere on Cape Ann was difficult, the selectmen replied. The soil was "fit for little else but pasturing and a great deal not even fit for that." And thanks to the Upper Towners who were using "all Art to dissuade" people against reconciliation, life was getting harder. The meetinghouse debate had so divided the community, the selectmen believed that Coit's plan would "Confound, Ruin, and Destroy the Whole," meaning all of Cape Ann, not just the First Parish.

The harbor leaders did their part to weaken the Upper Towners' appeal by complaining about the numbers of transient seamen who paid nothing in taxes or ministerial support but "Sail with every Wind and Will Cast Anchor in any Harbour that will best Suit them," creating the impression that these itinerants dominated the Upper Town's population, even though the majority of them resided near Gloucester Harbor.

In May 1739, the General Court dismissed Coit's petition. Additional arguments followed. Parish meetings ended abruptly after the Upper Towners became disruptive. Others dragged on past dusk, the "candle-lighting" hour, when curfew began. Being out after curfew, or "nightwalking," was considered an evil, punishable crime.

Unwilling to give in, Coit filed a second petition for separation. Parish and harbor leaders again refuted Coit's position. They claimed that in addition to the pews, other, less expensive seating options were available in the new meetinghouse. What's more, the distances the Upper Towners had to travel were "not great for a country town." If the Upper Towners were going to complain that they had "no conveniences to carry their families to meeting," they averred, "they have as little to detain them in that part of the Parish; and must remove to some other place where they may get their bread on shore." The harbor parishioners saw the writing on the wall: there was no future in the Upper Town, either at the Green or in the Commons Settlement. Gloucester's economy was shifting to the harbor; its population was following.

In an effort to settle the dispute as judiciously as possible, the General Court called in a surveyor named Josiah Batchelder, who was sworn under oath to calculate distances. Batchelder determined that the average Commons Settlement home was approximately two miles from the old meetinghouse. To the General Court, the additional mile to the harborside building substantiated a legitimate complaint. But the harbor contingency contested the survey's accuracy. They griped that Upper Town parishioners who had assisted Batchelder by carrying his surveyor's chain had not been sworn under oath. As an appeasement, the General Court ruled that the Upper Towners could hold services in their old meetinghouse during the winter.

Both sides dug in their heels. Coit and company continued to reject every possible conciliation until 1743, when the First Parish formally agreed to allow the Upper Towners to separate and form their own parish. This Fourth Parish served the Green and the Commons Settlement and held services in the old meetinghouse. Nathaniel Coit had finally won, but the status quo he had sought to maintain was lost.

That same year, eighty-four-year-old Nathaniel Coit lay down from the fight for the last time. Parents would have forced their children to stare into the abyss of Coit's grave, as was customary in Puritan culture. Presumably Coit's visage bore a peaceful expression, but townspeople were not wholly content with the new division. Without a large parish population that came to worship from various points across Cape Ann, the Upper Town became increasingly socially isolated. Extended families that had attended worship services together when the parish was intact were now separated. Upper Town residents wishing to be reunited with their families now had yet another reason to relocate to the harbor.

A new meetinghouse was eventually constructed in 1752 to replace the old building at the Green, whose poor condition had sparked the debate fourteen years earlier. But it was as if dusk were rolling around to greet the Fourth Parish's dawn. Though the new parish kept enough people anchored to this place through the years leading up to the Revolutionary War, population losses sustained during that conflict would eventually force the Fourth Parish to close. The Green and the Commons Settlement would become a desolate, haunted place, a characterization that would endure long after the war's end.

Chapter Thirteen

Shadow Hunting

A FTER PETER HODGKINS hung up the receiver at Addison Gilbert Hospital, he walked past rows of homes where smells of supper filled the air. An employee at the Richdale Farms convenience store let him charge doughnuts and a Coke to a store account. From there, Hodgkins climbed the backside of Fox Hill, where the Dogtown witches Tammy Younger and her aunt Luce George had once cursed passersby. Through the woods near Strangman's Pond, men were removing shells from their firearms as the Cape Ann Sportsmen's Club, the shooting range just south of Dogtown, began closing down for the night.

Dressed in camouflage pants, a tan hooded sweatshirt, brown corduroy jacket, and army-issue combat boots, Hodgkins was absorbed by the landscape. Although he did not leave town as he had told Langley, he had left Gloucester's civilization for its shadow self.

Hodgkins roamed the Dogtown highland, passing the boulders Roger W. Babson had carved. "STUDY," one of them commanded. Peter Hodgkins had dropped out of high school, but he had studied Dogtown throughout his lifetime of going there. "NEVER TRY NEVER WIN," another boulder declared. He was trying to get out of this fix. "COURAGE," a third instructed.

While Hodgkins was making his way farther into Dogtown, police chemist Robert Pino was examining the belongings police had taken from Langley's garage and duplex. Pino applied orthotolidine solution, which turns blue when in contact with blood, to the bike. Blood came to light in numerous places: on the left- and right-hand grips, the clutch, the left side of the gas tank, the ignition column, the fuel line shut-off valve, the foot gear shift, the left foot pedal, the right foot brake, the right foot pedal, the key, and the helmet. Pino discovered hairs on the gas tank and the right side of the engine, in addition to some fibers.

Eyes adjusted to the night, Peter Hodgkins continued making his way across the summer nighttime woods. After a rainfall such as Monday's, ephemeral puddles called vernal pools appear in parts of Dogtown. Eggs of the fairy shrimp, which have endured cryptobiosis during the dry winter, begin to hatch. Orange mole salamanders and wood frogs, whose quacklike calls fill the woods, arrive, too. By autumn, these pools will have dried out and their creatures will have disappeared, as if they were an illusion. Peter Hodgkins knew where he, too, could effectively disappear—in a copse of trees near Gronblat's Pit, where he found some old blankets and bedded down for the night.

Across Cape Ann, cars lay tucked into their bays. Lights glowed in the occasional window. Moths fluttered by window panes. Televisions flickered to snow. Headlights moved across the police station garage as Gloucester lieutenant Carl Churchill and state trooper John J. O'Rourke returned from the morgue with samples of Anne Natti's hair. It was between 1:00 and 2:00 A.M.

Pino prepared a slide and compared the hair samples from the bike to Anne Natti's under a four-hundred-power microscope. Though damaged, the samples made a clear, positive match. A police station typewriter hummed and pinged as Pino completed his report.

The police radio crackled to life with the sound of an officer reading a warrant for the arrest of Peter C. Hodgkins Jr., wanted for assault and battery with a weapon with intent to rob and murder in the first degree.

The early morning air was heavy, making for the kind of day when you could practically taste the rain that was about to fall. Down at the harbor, gulls dotted a gray sky. Hodgkins was scheduled to help unload a freighter at Quincy Market Cold Storage in East Gloucester that morning. The shift clock struck seven o'clock. Boots squeaked across the damp cement floor. The smells of fish, ice, salt, and the tide began to steep in the warming day. Reardon and his partner, Detective Kenneth Ryan, paced back and forth, watching the jitterbugs busy unloading the morning's catch, waiting for the moment a streak of light would cut through the dim, damp room, and Peter Hodgkins's tall frame would fill the door. Six other officers searched for him elsewhere along the docks.

Back at the police station, calls were going out to auxiliary officers and police in nearby towns to assemble at the O'Malley School, just south of Dogtown. The posse would begin searching the woods for Hodgkins at 9:00 A.M.

By noon, more than fifty policemen and state troopers were combing Dogtown's labyrinthine terrain with firearms, search beams, and dog teams. Treetops swayed under a state police helicopter's beating blades as it worked its way across the area. When the helicopter unknowingly nearly touched down on Hodgkins in a meadow, he slipped away effortlessly.

Hodgkins would later claim it was like being back in Vietnam. The throbbing, wet heat. The air's adhesive quality. Crouching small and trying not to breathe so no one could hear. Listening and feeling for the slightest pulse in the earth, for human or canine footfalls. The mosquitoes boring into his ears and face and hands. The heat at his back. Strange men—not members of the local police force, whom he knew and would recognize—walking by with loaded guns.

The late afternoon sky opened up, releasing leaden raindrops that turned Dogtown's trails to mud. The search was called off until the next morning. By evening Hodgkins's resolve had begun to wane. He made his way past an industrial park on Dogtown's southeastern edge to a pay phone outside of a sheet metal fabricating plant and called Langley.

Hodgkins told him he was afraid of getting shot. "Let me come to you," Langley replied. "We'll talk. If you're not guilty, I'll stay there and make sure there is not a shoot-out. I'll go down and stand between you and the police so they won't shoot you," he added, feeling emboldened. "Peter, did you do it?"

"No, I didn't," Hodgkins replied. Langley repeated that he would come see him, but Hodgkins changed the subject and asked if the police took his stuff. He sounded nervous and jittery. Langley again advised him to turn himself in.

Hodgkins hung up and called the police station. He would turn himself in within the hour, he said, but he walked back through the woods to the blankets near the gravel pit and tried to sleep in the rain.

The following morning between seven and seven thirty, a man named William H. Spinney was stepping between creosote-soaked railroad ties and listening to the rhythmic crunch of gravel underfoot. The fifty-eight-year-old freelance laborer regularly walked along the commuter railroad tracks that ran between Gloucester and Rockport through Dogtown's eastern edge. On good days, he found cans worth a nickel apiece that he turned in to the local redemption center. Spinney was just starting over a railroad bridge when Peter Hodgkins emerged from underneath. The shock of Hodgkins's sudden appearance stopped Spinney dead in his path.

Hodgkins was "dirty, soaking, wringing wet," but Spinney, who had been out of town and knew nothing about the murder charge, recognized him. Spinney had done some plastering work in Hodgkins's childhood home and knew his parents, especially his father. The two older men had worked together from time to time plowing snow and stevedoring. Over the years, Spinney had made small talk with Peter, too, but Peter didn't recognize him.

"You got a cigarette?" Hodgkins asked.

Spinney held out an open pack.

"Do you mind if I walk with you?" Hodgkins asked, as though talking to a complete stranger.

"No, it's perfectly all right," Spinney replied, still holding the cigarette pack out for Hodgkins, who took three. Spinney gave Hodgkins a light and reminded him who he was.

Hodgkins took a drag from his cigarette and told Spinney that he had been sleeping in the woods for a couple of days because the police thought he had killed a woman.

"I doubt it, Peter," Spinney replied. It was hard to believe his friend's son could do such a thing. "No, you couldn't do that," he said.

They walked "a good mile" toward the Babson Reservoir. Hodgkins "wasn't talking ragtime or anything like that," Spinney later recalled. They were just "gabbing back and forth," with Hodgkins seeming his usual self until he suddenly noticed a man in the distance and jumped behind a boulder to hide. Hodgkins peered out from behind the rock and told Spinney he recognized the person up ahead: Lawrence Davis, a retired machine shop foreman in his mid-seventies who often walked in the woods. Spinney also knew Davis, who collected cans in the same area.

Before Lawrence Davis had ducked under some large oak trees to get out of the rain that had started to fall, he noticed the two men coming along the train tracks and immediately recognized Hodgkins. Like many in Gloucester, Davis had watched Peter Hodgkins grow up. When Hodgkins worked at Empire Fish, Davis, a regular customer, saw him repeatedly. More recently, Davis knew him as the fellow on the motorbike who always stopped for a friendly chat whenever they ran into each other in the woods. Now Hodgkins was the man on the TV, in the paper, and on the minds of most everyone in town, and he was starting down the path in Davis's direction.

"I want to go home," Hodgkins said over his shoulder to Spinney.

"Mr. Davis will probably take you," Spinney yelled out, "but if you murdered a girl, why don't you have him take you down to the police station?"

Hodgkins walked on without saying a word.

"How are you, Pete?" Davis asked, feeling a little bit shaky but steeling himself against his nerves. He continued on his regular route around the Babson Reservoir, pretending that he knew nothing. Hodgkins accompanied him.

"Not so good. I'm in trouble and my father will be mad at me."

His father. Not the police or any mention of possibly going to jail, just Horace Edward Hodgkins Jr.

When Hodgkins asked Davis what he knew, Davis told him about the news coverage. "I'm scared," Hodgkins said. The police had been following him with guns. He was "tired, hungry, and didn't want to run anymore."

"Why don't you give yourself up?" Davis said calmly. But Hodgkins did not want to go to the station alone.

"Well then, let me give you a ride," Davis responded, as breezily as if he were offering the younger man a lift to the grocery store.

Hodgkins nodded. Davis started walking toward the car. Hodgkins followed.

As Davis pulled his Ford Grenada out of the Blackburn Industrial Park parking lot, Spinney drove by and honked his horn. Hodgkins scrunched down low in the front passenger seat as if to hide. He stayed like this for most of the ride until he told Davis that he wanted to go by his girlfriend's apartment; it was on the way to the police station. Davis hesitated. He worried that Hodgkins might get out of the car if he stopped, but he complied with Hodgkins's request. When they arrived at the apartment building, Hodgkins looked up and saw two men standing on the front steps and ducked down again. One of the men had disappeared inside, but Hodgkins remained crouched low, afraid to move.

Chapter Fourteen

God's Burning Finger

W HILE RESEARCHING DOGTOWN'S HISTORY, I sought out individuals the city archives staff had recommended for their
firsthand knowledge of the area. Each time I met one of
these people, I would mention my interest in Hartley, his paintings, and
his time in this place. They frequently responded with comments that
echoed Hartley's experience, such as "I feel a healing relationship with
Dogtown." After I told an older gentleman that Hartley claimed to have
been changed by Dogtown, he replied, "It has a tendency to do that."
Another told me, "It's a beautiful, magical property, but there's something very distinctive there. . . . There's a little vortex." Like others,
these people would then mention Anne Natti's murder, and my mental
picture of the area would darken as if a giant storm cloud were coming
over the land.

Nearly everyone assured me that Dogtown had changed since the
"time . . . when it was very dark," meaning the 1980s. But the manner
in which people such as Shep Abbott and these others told me about
those "dark" days made it seem as if they believed that Dogtown's eerie
history and peculiar atmosphere had deepened the pall of Anne Natti's
tragic death. Eventually I learned that the idea that Dogtown could cast
such a long metaphorical shadow was nothing new. The notion actually
dated back to the American Revolution and its aftermath, when the
Commons Settlement became a place characterized by absence, a negative space full of spirits.

IN 1777, TWO years into the American Revolution, David Pearce, Gloucester's wealthiest merchant, began building an extraordinary warship: a brigantine with eighteen carriage guns that he christened the *Gloucester*. Local historians claim that the *Gloucester*'s outfitting was "the most important enterprise of its kind," making it a source of pride and optimism for the town long before its construction was complete.

On July 1 of that year, just three days shy of the first anniversary of the adoption of the Declaration of Independence by the Continental Congress, the *Gloucester*'s crew crowded its deck for the first time and awaited command. Of its 130 crew members, 60 hailed from Gloucester. Like many Revolutionary War privateering vessels—private ships that were authorized by the Continental government to engage in wartime activities—no extant muster roll exists for this ship, but town historians claim that most Commons Settlement men went into privateering. The *Gloucester*'s ragtag crew, dressed in mismatched clothes their wives had made or tattered bits donated to the town's public stores by wealthier residents, comprised part of the original U.S. naval forces.

From the war's earliest days, the British Royal Navy was particularly intent on punishing the Massachusetts Bay region for fomenting revolution. And the Cape Ann promontory, so well positioned for maritime commerce, was sorely exposed to attack by sea. In August 1775, this reality came flying at Gloucester Harbor in the form of a surprise cannonade from the British warship *Falcon*. Gloucester men managed to save the town by capturing the *Falcon*'s crew as they were rowing ashore to set the harbor-front village on fire.

A militia was raised, breastworks were constructed, a bankrupt merchant's mansion became a barracks, and the town's fishing and trading vessels were modified to serve as privateers.

A few months after the *Falcon* incident, on November 1, 1775, the Massachusetts legislature officially sanctioned this form of legalized pirating, a practice that dated back to medieval Europe. Authorized to harass and plunder enemy merchant ships and take prisoners, privateers quickly formed the greater part of Continental naval might. Government-issued letters of marque and bonds held ship owners and crew to strict laws that regulated their enterprise. Once a privateer captured an enemy ship, a government court of admiralty had to approve the capture, or prize, before the spoils could be divided among the owner, captain, and crew. By 1776, privateering was so successful in Massachusetts, the Continental Congress legalized the practice in all thirteen colonies.

With most trade cut off because of the war, Gloucester privateers brought in both necessities and luxuries: oats, bacon, sugar, cotton, mahogany, coffee, fish, salt, porter, pipes, indigo, rum, Madeira wine, live tortoises, tortoiseshell, silver plate, gold dust, and elephants' teeth. A Gloucester privateer captured a British munitions ship whose cargo of arms, ammunition, and cannons included a new brass mortar; that was sent to General George Washington's army. Yet prizes did not always live up to their full potential. One haul of livestock came from French Canada, where settlers worked their oxen with yokes attached to their horns, rather than wooden ones that fit over the beasts' necks, which was the English custom. Because the beasts had not been trained using the English method, they were useless as work animals to the Gloucester farmers.

Without a doubt, privateering was a dangerous undertaking. A Cape Ann commander was shot in the throat with a musket ball during an attack on an English transport ship. Before dying, he swallowed some water and "could only prevent the liquid from taking a wrong direction by pinching his wound." When blown off course near the West Indies in 1779, a Gloucester ship "was driven about upon the ocean" for six months. The crew survived by eating "parched cocoa and West India rum 'burned down.'" Another privateer's crew swam ashore to safety after an attack and watched their former shipmates call out in desperation as they drowned. Captured crew members were either pressed into Royal Navy service or sent to prison ships where disease and malnutrition took their toll; dead sailors' bodies were promptly tossed overboard. When one group of freed prisoners returned to Gloucester in 1780, they were so weak they had to crawl into town on their hands and knees.

In spite of these hazards, Gloucester needed its privateers. Three-quarters of the town depended on income from the maritime industries that had been curtailed since the start of the war. Throughout the war's duration, Gloucester suffered deeply.

Though other privateers had sailed from Cape Ann to fight in the Revolutionary War, the *Gloucester* was the first private ship to be built expressly for this purpose. Thus on the day of her launch, townspeople celebrated with exuberance, wishing the men well and putting on a good face in spite of the hardships the men's absences would bring.

BY THIS POINT in Gloucester's history, townswomen had been waiting for their men to return from the sea for a century and a half. It was a hard enough life even under the best of circumstances, but the Revolution brought a new set of challenges. Individual towns had to meet quotas of soldiers, supplies, and salaries to raise the Continental Army. Women did their part by holding spinning bees, sewing uniforms, and more. To supply munitions, they made saltpeter and melted down candlesticks and other metal household goods. They cooked for militiamen, washed their clothes, darned their socks, and nursed injured soldiers, former prisoners, and victims of the recurring smallpox epidemics. Because Gloucester's gristmill had been neglected since the start of the war, women had to walk twenty-four miles to Ipswich's mill and back. An elderly woman once made the journey while carrying a peck (nineteen pounds) of corn. Wealthier women were relocated out of town. The most impoverished ones left to follow the army and supported battalions by cooking, laundering, nursing, sewing, and performing other services. Though these women offered the troops vital support, they were heavily scorned by military brass and foot soldiers alike.

Nearly a month after the *Gloucester* departed, a large fleet of enemy ships appeared off Cape Ann when "on a sudden the fleet vanished in a fogg and we have heard nothing of it since," William Whipple, brigadier general of the New Hampshire militia, wrote to Continental congressman James Lovell. Speculation over the activities and destination of "this invincible Armada" followed for weeks.

Much to everyone's relief and excitement, two weeks later, *Gloucester* crew member John McKean (the town watchman who had fumigated a certain British customs officer against smallpox) sailed into Gloucester Harbor aboard the prize *Two Friends*, carrying various botanicals ("balsam peru, jesuits bark, gum elemi, licorice root, balsam capivi"), spirits, and much-needed salt. The *Gloucester* had captured the

Two Friends in the middle of the ocean, due east of New York. On August 31, Captain Fisk, commander of the Boston-based *Massachusetts*, noted in his log that he was sailing with the *Gloucester* and three other Massachusetts privateers closer to home. Soon thereafter, *Gloucester* crew member and Commons settler Isaac Day arrived at the helm of the *Spark*, which the *Gloucester* had seized on Newfoundland's Grand Banks. The *Spark*'s holds were loaded with fish and more salt. It was an auspicious beginning.

As summer turned to fall, women pondered the fates of their men. They might have reassured themselves that the *Gloucester*'s crew would be able to navigate their way home by the *clethra alnifolia*, or summer sweet, a shrub with bottle brush–like spikes that blossom with delicate white or pink flowers. The old mariners said that even in the deepest fog, wafts of the plant's peppery scent signaled that they were off Cape Ann as if the clethra had the power of a homing device. But there was no sign or word from the *Gloucester*'s crew.

With no commerce, Gloucester was soon incapable of paying the salaries that supported its soldiers' wives and children. Many succumbed to smallpox and relied on donations from Cape Ann's wealthier citizens to fend off starvation, but the flow of goods into town was also hindered by the war. And with its lack of arable land, Gloucester depended on donated foodstuffs that came from as far away as Virginia and Pennsylvania. Anxiety about the town's lack of provisions, the encroaching winter, and further attacks ran high. The days grew shorter; the cold turned bitter. Soon the ground froze. Weeks accumulated with the snow into a seemingly endless winter of "unutterable grief."

The insurance companies that posted bonds for privateering vessels were legally required to publicly announce captured prizes. But after the *Two Friends* and the *Spark*, the *Gloucester*'s name never appeared on any insurance, newspaper, or government list. Newspapers also publicized descriptions of shipwrecks that captains reported seeing, but no wreckage detail matched that of the *Gloucester*. It was never heard from again. No trace of her was ever found.

The ocean had swallowed the celebrated vessel and nearly the entire story, but for a peculiar incident that soon followed.

"One dark night," as Gloucester historian John J. Babson wrote, "about the time it was supposed the ship was lost, a ball of light (called a corposant by seamen) was seen to move about the town in a mysterious manner, and approach successively the homes of all who were on board of her; remaining a few moments at each one of them, to indicate the melancholy fate that had befallen the ship and her unfortunate crew."

Scientific theory holds that these balls or flashes of light occur when a charged electrical field surrounding an extended object such as a mast creates a faint glow or flicker that can be seen in low light. But in the eighteenth century, "corposants" (named from the Italian *corpo santo*, meaning heavenly body, and also called St. Elmo's fire) were believed to be signs from God foretelling of death. In the 1790s, Samuel Taylor Coleridge described a corposant in "The Rime of the Ancient Mariner" as "death-fires" occurring over "water, like a witch's oils." Closer to home, but three-quarters of a century after the *Gloucester*'s disappearance, Herman Melville referred to the lights as "God's burning finger." Imbued with a similarly ominous, spiritual significance, the town's corposant went from house to house, deepening the *Gloucester*'s widows' anguish.

"The number and the names of those who were lost in her cannot now be ascertained," Babson concluded about the *Gloucester*'s fate, "but current tradition has always affirmed that sixty wives in Gloucester were made widows by the loss, and that the calamity overwhelmed the town with sadness and gloom."

The appearance of the corposant is where the story of the *Gloucester* ends, but the mourning had only just begun for the town's new widows and orphans. This was the negative space of American history— the hollow sound beneath the guns of war—a silence filling homes, sitting across from wives at the supper table, waiting in their beds at night, always by their sides. And once the *Gloucester* disappeared, it was a silence that stayed with sixty of the town's women and their families for the rest of their lives.

For the immediate future, though, these women still had to endure the war. In 1779, two years after the ship's disappearance, "a large troop of women . . . marched" to Colonel Foster's store and supplied themselves with provisions. John J. Babson claims that the colonel, the same man who had ordered McKean to detain the British customs inspector prior to the war's inception, was so moved by the women's plaintive "tale[s] of suffering and destitution" that he allowed them to take the items for free.

By this same year, the town had lost more than half of its ships and one-sixth of its residents were dependent on charity. Things seemed as if they were going to take another turn for the worse when another sign appeared. On May 19, 1780, people awoke to a gradually darkening sky. By noon it was pitch black. Birds had stopped singing, as if it were night. From northern New England to New Jersey, where General George Washington noted the daytime darkness in his diary, people reacted as if Judgment Day had arrived. Today scientists believe that extensive forest fires in eastern Canada caused New England's "dark day," but at the time, the end of all existence was believed to be well nigh. Preachers pounded their pulpits with renewed fervor. Americans began to panic. The British were defeating their troops in South Carolina. It seemed as if the war was never going to end. But a year and a half later, on October 19, 1781, Cornwallis surrendered at Yorktown. Independence was finally won.

More than 1,000 Gloucester residents—nearly a fifth of its pre-Revolutionary population—died during the war. Of its remaining 3,893 residents, 335 were now widowed. These widows resided in all of Gloucester's parishes, but every account of the Commons Settlement's demise mentions the area's Revolutionary War widows, as if theirs were a solitary realm of mourners. The *Gloucester*'s disappearance alone does not account for why the Commons Settlement became the mythic epicenter of Cape Ann's post-Revolutionary gloom, but at the very least it offers a plausible explanation for the region's enduring forlorn reputation. The First Parish rift and the town's gradual shift to a maritime economy influenced the highland village's decline and heightened its isolation, but the war dealt the Commons Settlement a blow from which it could not recover.

Though Gloucester, like many towns, was extremely impoverished immediately following the war, most of its villages eventually bounced back, but not the Commons Settlement. Residents who had the means left. Some moved their houses in their entirety or salvaged the materials for construction elsewhere. Others rented out their properties, which soon fell into neglect. With fewer economic resources, the widows had no choice but to stay in this place that was now abandoned and haunted by loss, just like them.

Chapter Fifteen

Confession

E ARLY THAT FRIDAY MORNING, four days after Anne Natti's murder, wind blew through St. Peter's Square. Puddles dotting the ground reflected the bright colors of the dormant Fiesta carnival rides. Every so often the wind distorted these reflections, wrinkling them up and ironing them out again, as if the carnival were a mirage. But tourists and locals would begin streaming through the midway in a matter of hours for Fiesta's much-anticipated weekend activities.

The week's unfortunate events continued to trouble city and state officials. Monday's conflagration had destroyed four buildings and severely damaged four others, leaving Main Street looking like its front teeth had been knocked out.

Over at the police station, officers from state and local forces had been discussing where to focus their manhunt since 6:30 A.M. They studied maps of Dogtown, paying particular attention to its densest terrain: the moraine, a massive pile of boulders shoved into place by the Pleistocene Epoch glacier that had covered the region tens of thousands of years ago. In 1888, Nathaniel Southgate Shaler, director of the U.S. Geological Survey's Atlantic Coast Division, observed that in this moraine "there is no fine material to fill their [the boulder's] interspaces; the result is that the heap remains open, presenting cavities which extend in many cases to the depth of twenty feet or more below the surface, the whole mass appearing in the landscape like the ruins of Cyclopean masonry." The detectives considered whether Hodgkins could have burrowed in between some of those rocks, right alongside the raccoons and snakes and whatever other creatures made their homes there. As they were plotting out the details of the second day of their search, Lawrence Davis was downstairs leading Peter Hodgkins through the police station backdoor. It was just before 9:00 A.M.

The sergeant on duty looked out of the station intake office window and stared in disbelief at the old man and a disheveled, wet Hodgkins. Two other officers turned and gawked at the pair, who just stood in the station foyer looking as if they didn't know why they were there. An officer finally came out and escorted Hodgkins into an office. No one said a word.

Davis hung around for a while, wondering if he should leave. Eventually an officer came and took a statement from him about the morning's events. The officers thanked Davis with handshakes and pats on the back. Lawrence Davis, now a hero, went home.

Upstairs, the detectives' secretary noticed an officer escorting a tall figure down the hall. "I think this is your suspect coming now," she told Detective Reardon, who had walked in the door less than a half hour before. Thinking that he didn't hear her correctly, Reardon looked up and saw Peter Hodgkins walk into the room.

Hodgkins stood before Reardon, looking like hell and stinking to high heaven. Reardon, who had hardly slept since Monday night, could not believe his eyes. The news quickly spread around the station. Other detectives who had been working on the case came in and gaped at Hodgkins, the prime suspect in the most shocking murder to hit town in recent memory. After fifty men, thirty search dogs, and a helicopter had tried to hunt him down, Peter Hodgkins just walked right in the door, as if he had been hiding in some back closet the whole time. And he wanted to talk.

Reardon sent his secretary out for coffee and doughnuts, then along with state policeman Carl Sjoberg, escorted Hodgkins down the hall to Lieutenant Churchill's office, where they could talk without any interruptions. Sjoberg produced a notebook and some forms, including a card printed with the full statement of the Miranda rights. Hodgkins read the Miranda aloud and waived his right to remain silent and refuse to answer any questions and his right to have an attorney present before he said anything. He signed the card "Peter C. Hodgkins, Jr."

"You okay, Peter?" Reardon asked, noticing the welts from the numerous mosquito bites that covered Hodgkins's hands; the stench wafting off of him from spending days as a hunted animal; and the dazed, wild look in his eyes.

"I'm okay," Hodgkins replied.

"You want to make a phone call?"

"No, not now."

Reardon was still trying to get over the fact that Hodgkins was not only sitting right in front of him, he was refusing an attorney. Reardon and Sjoberg didn't have to break Peter Hodgkins or offer him an out, such as the possibility of a plea bargain. Hodgkins had been through this drill before, but he wasn't hardened to it or savvy enough to insist on an attorney. That was unfortunate for Hodgkins, but a good thing for the detectives.

"We have been looking for you for a couple of days," Reardon said.

"I know."

"Peter, do you want to tell us a story?" Reardon asked. "What happened?"

All it took was a couple of questions, basic and routine. Before Reardon and Sjoberg knew it, the story was pouring right out of Peter Hodgkins and matching the evidence and crime scene details in a way that only the murderer or an extremely close witness would know. But Hodgkins's delivery was scattershot, befuddling. And he had a way of mumbling and garbling his words. As far as Reardon was concerned, it was classic Peter Hodgkins. He always seemed confused, but with a lot of patience the detectives managed to piece together a coherent statement from him.

"I first saw her walking while I was dirt bike riding," Hodgkins began. "I was parked off the path because it was pouring rain. . . . I saw a dog. The dog was checking the bike out. . . .

"I got off the bike and I don't know what happened. . . . I followed her. . . ."

Because it was early in the morning and raining and nobody else was around, he thought it seemed like a good time for a robbery.

"She never saw me. . . . I pushed her down and hit her with a rock. I hit her in the back of the head. . . .

"I didn't even know it was a woman when I hit her. . . . I don't know if she was knocked out. I never spoke to her. . . . I didn't punch her. I may have hit her in the face with a rock and don't remember, it was raining so hard."

The doughnuts arrived. Hodgkins started wolfing them down. Reardon realized that Hodgkins probably had not eaten since Wednesday, possibly longer, and asked what else he wanted to eat.

"A cheese-steak submarine sandwich." Hodgkins's answer was precise, as if he had been fantasizing about that exact meal for the past few days.

Reardon sent his secretary out again, this time to get two large subs, including one for himself, and some Cokes. Reardon also noticed that Hodgkins had on the same clothes that he had been wearing earlier that week when the detective brought him into the station for questioning. Reardon asked if Peter wanted some clean clothes, but Hodgkins, who was busy eating, never answered.

The detectives wanted to know where Hodgkins had been when he first saw Anne Natti and decided to pursue her. At the detectives' request, Hodgkins drew a map of his location. It was about a quarter of a mile from the Nattis' summer camp.

"After I hit her with the rock," Peter continued, "she was only half conscious. She half walked and I half carried her into the woods. I was looking for money. . . ."

"She didn't fight?" Reardon asked, redirecting him.

"No."

"She didn't scratch you?"

"No. . . . I checked her pockets. I slipped her clothes off. I saw a dog's leash wrapped up in a little plastic baggie."

"Do you remember what she was wearing?" Reardon asked.

"Yes. Rubber boots, rain gear, yellow pants, and a yellow rain slicker. They just slipped off."

"Was she conscious when you took her clothes off?" Reardon pressed.

"She moaned and started to move. . . . When I left, I booked. I just ran. I got lost after it happened. . . . I had to find the dirt bike. . . ."

"How long were you lost?"

"Maybe fifteen minutes. I was just running. When I found the bike, I drove off toward Norton's Pines. I don't remember having any blood on me. I didn't see anybody else up in the woods. I couldn't drive down the streets, so I stuck to the woods. This happened in the morning. I got home. I put the motorcycle away. I wiped myself off with the towel and then went upstairs and changed into these clothes, then I took the ten-speed and rode around for the day."

Hodgkins talked about the rest of the day that he had ended Anne Natti's life as if it were just an ordinary Monday with no work and little to do. He ran errands—the same ones he had told Reardon about on Wednesday. Then Hodgkins told the detectives about his nights of sleeping at Gronblat's Pit. He claimed that he would have turned himself in during the manhunt if he had recognized a Gloucester police officer. Then Hodgkins went back to talking about what happened that Monday morning in the woods.

"When I had slipped her clothes off, they just came off easily. She was groggyish when I ran, she was moving."

"Why did you take her clothes off?" Reardon pressed.

"I don't know. I didn't have any idea. . . . I did think about raping her, Mrs. Natti, when I took her clothes off, but I didn't rape her. . . . I guess I wanted to . . . see what she looked like. . . ."

Of all the things that Peter Hodgkins was saying, Reardon believed that four were bald-faced lies: that he didn't know Anne Natti was a woman from afar—she was so petite; that Anne Natti didn't put up a fight; that her clothes "just slipped off"; and that Hodgkins didn't rape her. Time and again Reardon had listened to suspects confess to killing a female victim in great detail and refuse to admit to any sexual violence until the rape tests came back positive. And though just about everyone who gets in trouble with the law lies, Reardon felt that Hodgkins's lies were different. Whenever Hodgkins had been called out on his mendacity in the past, he would not admit that he was wrong or cave in and tell the truth. Instead, he would simply continue to lie with greater conviction, as if he believed every word of what he was saying, even if what he was saying was glaringly false. Plus, given that most of Hodgkins's past offenses were sexual, it was hard for Reardon to believe that a guy like Hodgkins would go through such trouble merely to kill a woman.

Reardon and Sjoberg tried to press Hodgkins about the potential rape, but Hodgkins just said, "I didn't plan this. It just happened. I didn't know she was going to be in the woods that day. . . . I have sexual fantasies when I'm in the woods." The woods, as if they had something to do with his urges.

"I know how I feel," Hodgkins said. "I just don't know if she was married or had kids. How do they feel?" It was a question that Hodgkins did not try to answer.

The subs arrived, and Hodgkins ingested his food so quickly Reardon asked if he wanted something else. Another sub. Same thing.

The detectives reviewed Hodgkins's statement a few more times. Hodgkins crossed out the line that said he "had urges" and signed the transcription.

While the detectives checked Hodgkins's boots against the tread measurements and photographs from the crime scene, Hodgkins complained that his feet hurt. He thought that a thorn might have been lodged into his toe or that it was possibly broken. His feet were covered in blisters but otherwise looked fine to Reardon and Sjoberg, and Hodgkins could walk okay.

Reardon again asked if he wanted to make a phone call. Hodgkins shrugged. The detective suggested that he call his father, who could bring him clean clothes. Hodgkins made the call, ate his second sub, and was formally booked.

PETER HODGKINS'S FATHER lived out on Wheeler's Point, a thumb-shaped peninsula where many generations of the Hodgkins family have lived since Samuel Hodgkins settled there in 1684. Generations of the family have lived elsewhere on Cape Ann, including the Commons Settlement, but various eponymous Wheeler's Point place names attest to their strong presence there. Houses built by Hodgkins's forebears line a street that was named after the family. The surname is repeated on numerous headstones in a nearby cemetery. Hodgkins Cove is also just up the way.

Beginning in 1694, Samuel Hodgkins operated a ferry across the Annisquam River and carried people, goods, and livestock to and from the mainland. Individual passengers were transported to the island in a canoe for a penny; those on horseback paid twopence to be accommodated in a boat that held up to three beasts in good weather, two in foul. Another Hodgkins was a cabinetmaker who built the coffin of Dogtown witch Tammy Younger. Centuries of Hodgkinses had lived and worked in the footsteps of their ancestors, and there had not been a single bad apple in the bunch. They were not all perfect, but as far as anyone knew, none of them had ever done such a terrible thing, until now.

Horace Edward Hodgkins Jr., Peter Hodgkins's father, preferred the name Pete to his given one. In fact, he liked the name so much he gave it to his only son. But Pete Jr. had been exceptionally hard to discipline as a child. He was always in and out of trouble. But work seemed to help the boy. Mr. Hodgkins helped Peter get his Elliott Stevedoring job and, perhaps most important, helped him hold on to it.

While people who worked with the two Hodgkins men said how outwardly good Mr. Hodgkins was to his son, they still wondered what the family went through in private. Some ventured that Mr. Hodgkins might have lost patience with Pete Jr., who seemed "mentally challenged" by his mother's death and his father's remarriage. Nonetheless, Pete Jr.'s Friday morning phone call was terrible for Mr. Hodgkins, who had to respond to the devastating news that his son had confessed to a murder by gathering some clothes for him.

Mr. Hodgkins found a pair of his son's dungarees and a shirt, but the mud-soaked boots Pete Jr. was wearing that morning were his only shoes. Mr. Hodgkins went out to purchase new sneakers, socks, and underwear for him. These might as well have been the clothes Pete Jr. would be buried in, because after taking these articles down to the police station and talking to his son for roughly twenty minutes, Pete Sr. never saw his son again.

WHILE PETER HODGKINS changed into the clothes his father brought and his old ones were placed into evidence, Essex County assistant district attorney James Gribouski reviewed the transcription of Hodgkins's confession. The thirty-year-old Gribouski, who had graduated from law school a mere four years before and was admittedly "a little bit wet behind the ears," was astounded by the statement's contents. While the vast majority of murders take place either between people who know each other or in situations in which the victim is not without some blame, such as a drug deal gone bad, the unprovoked, cold-blooded, stranger-on-stranger violence to which Peter Hodgkins had just confessed is extremely rare. And the fact that Hodgkins had admitted to not just one but all three criteria of first-degree murder made it even more exceptional.

In the Commonwealth of Massachusetts, first-degree murder must be proven on one of three theories: that the murder was carried out with deliberate premeditation and malice aforethought; that it was

meted out with extreme atrocity or cruelty; or that it was committed
during the commissioning or attempted commission of another crime.
Less than a second of thinking about an act can qualify as premeditation. Peter Hodgkins had freely admitted to watching Anne Natti and
thinking about attacking her, supporting the theory of deliberate premeditation and malice aforethought. Killing her by crushing her skull
with a forty-pound rock, striking her again, dragging her naked body
over rocks and thorns through the rain, and leaving her for dead deep in
the woods far from the nearest house were undeniably atrocious and
cruel. And Hodgkins had also confessed to attempting to rob Anne
Natti, which proved the third theory. If convicted of first-degree murder, Hodgkins would face a mandatory sentence of life without parole.
An additional assault with attempt to rob conviction would add another
twenty years to this sentence and would virtually guarantee that Peter
Hodgkins would never set foot outside of a prison again. But this was
not an open-and-shut case. The possibility loomed that Hodgkins could
be found criminally irresponsible by reason of insanity and that further
lab tests would contradict his statements. But with a written statement
with all three theories in hand, Gribouski couldn't believe his luck.

The Gloucester District Court, which was just upstairs from the
police station, was buzzing with activity in anticipation of Peter Hodgkins's arraignment. Erik Natti, still reeling in shock, sat in a corner of
the courtroom with his family. Reporters from Boston and North Shore
newspapers and television stations filled the halls. The sight frightened
Hodgkins, who asked Detective Reardon if the courtroom would ever
empty out and the media would go away. There were always fewer
people and news media around later in the day, the detectives told
Hodgkins, who then asked to postpone his arraignment.

After Hodgkins waived his right to an immediate arraignment, the
detectives conferred with Gribouski, who had an idea that would potentially lock up the case. The prosecutor's office had a new piece of
technology—a video camera—maybe Hodgkins would be willing to reenact the crime on tape. Hodgkins agreed and signed an additional Miranda waiver and a statement consenting to describe the crime scene
and to have the interview recorded.

When state policeman Brian O'Hara finally showed up with the
video equipment, it didn't work. The battery needed to be charged, but
O'Hara had failed to bring the charger. The detectives' secretary tracked

down an electronic equipment distributor who agreed to lend the officers a battery. Gribouski, Reardon, Ryan, O'Hara, and Rockport police officer Clifford Brooks took Hodgkins into the woods, carrying two video cameras: one belonging to the DA's office and for backup, Officer Brooks's personal camera, which he used for recording his favorite TV shows.

A handcuffed Hodgkins led the men, who didn't know their way around this far extreme of Dogtown. Along the way, Hodgkins told them the names of the small abandoned quarry pits they passed and something about their history. He then explained the area's myriad paths and where they each led. Peter Hodgkins had just confessed to a heinous crime, but he told Gribouski and the officers about "his castle," as if he were merely conducting a gentlemanly tour of the woods on a pleasant summer afternoon. "Murder in the murderer is no such ruinous thought as poets and romancers will have it;" as Ralph Waldo Emerson once wrote, "it does not unsettle him or fright him from his ordinary notice of trifles." Likewise, killing an innocent woman in cold blood in Dogtown produced no change in Peter Hodgkins's love for this place. It would affect an entire community's feelings about this land, but not the strange man at the center of this drama.

After walking for about twenty minutes they passed the Whale's Jaw and continued through a maze of trails to the bottom of a hill and onto yet another path. Hodgkins then walked up to a pine tree and said, "There's where I left the bike."

The officers turned on the cameras. Reardon read Hodgkins his rights once again. O'Hara's equipment malfunctioned, but Officer Brooks's camera was rolling tape over a previously recorded episode of *Star Trek* as Gribouski asked Hodgkins to show them where and how he executed the crime.

Here came the dog. There went the person in the yellow rain gear who he didn't think knew he was there. Hodgkins walked ahead. The camera followed.

"This is where I hit her," he said without any emotion or significance, as if he were merely talking about where a pinecone had dropped. "That's it there." Hodgkins pointed to the ground. "That's the rock."

"What rock?" Reardon asked.

"The one I hit her with."

Reardon thought the forty pounds of granite "looked like something out of a fieldstone wall." An old highland Commons Settlement build-ing block turned deadly weapon.

That probably set the old Commons Settlement ghosts on their ears. All their hard work, trying to take the devil out of this place, to build a New Canaan, and one of their own descendants turns it into a Land of Nod.

There wasn't a single, visible speck of blood on the rock. Detective Ryan wrapped it inside his police jacket to carry it back to the lab.

It had turned into a perfectly picturesque day. Gribouski, who lived seventy-five miles away in Worcester and had never been to these woods, couldn't help but admire their seemingly primeval splendor. But the contrast between their beauty and the incredible brutality that Peter Hodgkins described without any emotion whatsoever was "ut-terly chilling." The woods were so peaceful. Isolated. It was almost hard to imagine that such a cruel and atrocious crime could be committed there. To Gribouski, who did not have the small-town familiarity with Hodgkins that Reardon and other members of the Gloucester Police Department had, Hodgkins was a killer, plain and simple, and an espe-cially cruel, cold-blooded one at that—a sociopath. Gribouski had tried only two cases at this point in his career, both of which he had lost. But there was no way he was going to let "this monster" walk with a second-degree-murder conviction; nothing short of first-degree would do.

By the time they returned to the police station, it was after 5:30 P.M. Chemist Robert Pino took some swabs from Hodgkins's soiled hands for analysis. Upstairs, the courtroom was nearly empty—the majority of the onlookers and reporters had moved to the other end of Main Street, where the Fiesta opening processional was about to begin—but Erik Natti was still there, waiting.

Peter Hodgkins was arraigned on the charges of murdering Anne Phinney Natti in the first degree and assault with attempt to rob. Ed-ward O'Reilly, Hodgkins's court-appointed attorney, entered a not-guily plea to both charges.

Judge Lawrence Jodrey ordered that Hodgkins be escorted to the hospital for a full body check and treatment of the foot injuries he had complained about. Hodgkins would then be transported to the Law-rence Jail, where he would be held without bail. The arraignment would continue after a court psychiatrist examined Hodgkins to determine if he was criminally responsible and capable of aiding in his own defense.

Chapter Sixteen

In Gypsy Ways

A S AN OXCART was about to cross the Alewife Brook Bridge, the driver steadied his team and looked apprehensively to Thomazine "Tammy" Younger's house, which marked the entrance to Dogtown. Throughout the early 1800s, whenever a hoof landed on the wooden planks of the bridge, Tammy would fling open a window covered with a little wooden door and begin to yell. It was unseemly for a woman of any class to raise her voice, but propriety was not Tammy Younger's concern. Hunger was. And as people recalled, the rag-clad woman had a "very choice vocabulary, especially in the line of invective." Her "torrents of vocal pyrotechnics" could be heard half a mile away.

Tammy Younger had inherited her dilapidated little house from her aunt, Luce George, a notorious witch. Though some had questioned whether Tammy was also a witch, Luce George had managed to pass her reputation on to Tammy along with the house, which was enough to make people more than a little wary. And while Tammy was short and roly-poly and looked nothing like her aunt, who was all angles and lines, few paid attention to the women's physical differences: both were reputedly hard on the eyes. Passersby hurried past the little abode, but the oxcart drivers, who worried that Tammy could vex their carts and beasts, always stopped long enough to leave whatever she desired—mackerel, wood, pumpkins, apples, corn—before speeding away.

Tammy Younger's house stood at the intersection of Poplar Street and a route informally called the Back Road, a rough shortcut to the village of Annisquam that passed through Dogtown. If anyone had turned onto the Back Road, he would have passed other derelict homes, occupied by a predominantly destitute, tatterdemalion population of forty individuals. But people rarely went that way. As Salem's Rev. Bentley observed when he visited Cape Ann in 1799, the highland routes were "in a neglected State & by far the worst of any we found upon the Island." Washington Street, a new road that followed the shoreline, made for an easier journey, unless one needed to get to Annisquam in a hurry. Even so, in the words of Rev. Bentley, most Cape Anners would "never think of stretching 3 miles over the worst roads, when they can sail pleasantly only one"—travel via water was preferable to either route. And as bad as the roads through Dogtown were, the good people of Gloucester had another reason for avoiding the area: its residents.

By the early 1800s, the Commons Settlement had changed from a village of hardworking families to a tumbledown hamlet of desperately poor individuals. With them, the area's reputation transformed almost entirely, as if someone had rolled up the Commons Settlement's roads and let the place go to seed. The highland village became known as Dogtown at about this time.

There is something about the way curiosity sniffs out a name such as Dogtown, then scurries away, looking back over its shoulder, only to circle in again. In the 1890s, the area and its name piqued the interest of *Gloucester Daily Times* editor Charles E. Mann, who documented its history and interviewed "sweet-faced old ladies" and "men with whitened locks" to produce a slender little volume titled *In the Heart of Cape Ann or the Story of Dogtown*. "The name 'Dogtown,'" Mann wrote, " . . . came from the canines kept by the so-called 'widows' of the place, when the evil days came that saw their natural protectors either in their graves or buried beneath the ocean." But other than this explanation there are no stories about dogs in this place. What changed the Commons Settlement to Dogtown was the people: women who dressed like men, men who did housework, alleged witches, and former slaves, who lived according to what Roger W. Babson called "gypsy ways," as if these people were wanderers, when in fact Dogtown's population was so deeply tied to this place that its name and reputation would forever be associated with them above all others.

During the 1800s and early 1900s there were at least sixty different places called Dogtown in nearly thirty different states: Alabama, Arizona, Arkansas, California, Colorado, Florida, Idaho, Illinois, Kansas, Kentucky, Louisiana, Maine, Maryland, Mississippi, Missouri, Nebraska, Nevada, New Jersey, New Mexico, New York, Ohio, Oregon, Pennsylvania, Tennessee, Texas, West Virginia, Wisconsin, Wyoming, and, of course, Massachusetts.

As in Gloucester, other places named Dogtown tended to have local explanations for how the pejorative evolved, but from Maine to California, people shared the idea that these places and their inhabitants, human or animal, were feral. Sometimes the name Dogtown was employed to refer to a spot that was little more than a trail and a hitching post or some miners' camps, but in most instances the name referred to towns that were populated by an underclass or that had been abandoned. In the latter meaning, the moniker typically evoked a fiercer, more sinister state of desertion than the term "ghost town." Whether occupied or not, a Dogtown was a place that was considered to have reverted back to nature, red in tooth and claw.

A few Dogtowns were literally overrun with dogs. When more than 150 dogs overtook Jonesborough, Tennessee, in 1841, the editor of the local paper reported, "This is emphatically Dog-Town." Residents fired at the dogs with pistols and double-barreled shotguns. "Hitherto in the dog killing line, we have been operating upon a small scale," but, the article concludes, "we shall make them squat." Others ranked townspeople with the animal namesake. In the 1850s a California town became known as Dogtown because, people said, the Chinese miners' huts were "good enough for dogs to live in." The term also was applied to other minority communities, including a Wisconsin Chippewa village and a St. Louis neighborhood where members of the Igarots, a Filipino tribe on exhibit at the 1904 Universal Exposition of St. Louis, allegedly captured neighborhood dogs and ate them.

Without a doubt, it was an insult to call someone a "Dogtowner." This may account for why places that were once known by the pejorative were quick to change their names, but not in Gloucester.

What set Gloucester's Dogtowners apart, and added to the strangeness of their reputations, was their choice to live outside of society. Having a place in society was a literal, not a metaphorical, construct in early America and was reflected in laws such as the 1662 Settlement Law, which gave local jurisdictions the power to "warn out" or send their nonnative charity-dependent residents back to their town of origin and thus be "put in their place," as the practice was called. Destitute native residents were sent to live with town-approved families who received a local government stipend to cover their charges' costs. Though some children ended up in the poorhouse, many often were sent away as indentured servants. By 1796, Gloucester constructed a poorhouse to better manage its destitute native inhabitants, while those originating elsewhere continued to be "warned out."

Life in the poorhouse was filled with mandatory and lengthy sermons meant to rehabilitate its inhabitants (or inmates, as they were sometimes called) from their spiritual and moral failings. These lessons were reinforced with destitution's worldly remedy: work, which kept poorhouse expenses, paid for by the town, to a minimum.

Opting out of this system to take up residence in abandoned highland homes, early-nineteenth-century denizens of Dogtown lived off the land, made butter, wet-nursed for women in town, brewed "dire drink" (which alluded to both herbal remedies and home brew), rented pastureland, told fortunes, traded in vice, or earned income as laborers, slaughterers, and healers. All had colorful reputations inadvertently (or purposefully) cultivated by themselves or, most likely, others, including their fellow Dogtowners.

Three of Gloucester's Dogtown residents reputedly had unusually long incisors: the former slave Cornelius Finson, a woman named Judy Rhines, and Tammy Younger. It seems highly unlikely that all three individuals in fact had noticeably long incisors—this characterization was possibly just another way of portraying them as bestial—but the story goes that Tammy's bothered her so much she decided to have them pulled. John Morgan Stanwood, a ship's captain who had worked in the town's foreign trade and had stayed on in Dogtown in his family's old home after the Revolution, was up to the job.

Like his neighbors, Captain Stanwood was eccentric, if not crazy. He was crippled and eventually "became convinced that his legs were made of glass and refused to use them." But before that happened, he sat Tammy in a chair and, wielding a pair of pincers, pulled one tooth partway so it stuck out over her lip, making her snaggle-toothed. He decided to let that tooth rest a minute and began working on the other, drawing it to a matching length. The old captain leaned back, admired his handiwork, and claimed that the teeth would not move any farther.

With half-extracted teeth, Tammy went about her life, which allegedly included hosting "buccaneers and lawless men" in her little house on Fox Hill, holding card games, reading fortunes, and drinking rum that she had cadged. During the day she went to the harbor to beg for fish and to sell butter. Eventually someone took pity on Tammy and informed her that she needed to tell the old captain that his joke was over. She did, and Stanwood removed the teeth.

The Dogtown stories that Mann collected reveal townspeople's perceptions of the area's populace as much as they capture the reality of the Dogtowners' lives. While most of Dogtown's women were reputed to be witches, Mann also claims that townspeople said, "If a person sawed a barrel in two and made two tubs, they called him a witch." Indeed, there were two types of women (primarily) who were referred to as witches in eighteenth- and early nineteenth-century America: the midwife/folk healer and the social outcast, who was often destitute, accused of licentiousness and of possessing unusual, if not supernatural, power. Historian Christine Heyrman notes that the six Gloucester women who were accused of witchcraft in 1692 as part of the Salem witch trials were poor or "shrewish" and "prone to violent or unseemly behavior, and usually reputed for practicing malefic arts against their neighbors." And while most of Dogtown's women were outcasts, some also were legitimate healers.

Though the minister sometimes was called upon to tend to parishioners' "bodily diseases," in Gloucester's earliest days, as elsewhere, women were the town's primary healers. Serious medical cases that could not be treated under this informal system were sent to nearby towns where university-educated doctors lived. Yet even after Gloucester got its first doctor in 1712, town records list women healers and payments received for their services. As the formally trained (and male-dominated) medical profession grew, such healers often were scorned, but that did not keep people from calling for their services when physicians could not cure their ailments. Nor did it prevent them from purchasing the women's tonics, herbs, and other reputed health-boosting concoctions. Dogtown resident Rachel Smith hawked a beverage she made from foxberry leaves, spruce tops, and other botanicals by going door to door in town and saying, "Now, ducky, I've come down to bring a dire drink, for I know you feel springish." Fortunately for these healers, Dogtown abounded in useful wild plants, making for a natural pharmacy growing right outside their doors. White thoroughwort made good medicine for gout. Witch hazel bark was used for lotions and astringents. Catnip quieted crying babies. Burdock soothed tender gums sore from teething. Boiled bayberry mixed with mutton tallow relieved chapped skin.

Then there were women such as Luce George, Molly Jacobs, Judy Rhines, and Molly Stevens, whom people believed deserved their evil, witchlike reputations. Later generations of Cape Anners claimed that these Dogtown women were prostitutes, but perhaps out of deference to contemporary mores, Mann, author of the aforementioned 1896 Dogtown history, makes no such claim. He merely states that these women "seem to have done a great deal to give to Dogtown a reputation which also was undeservedly conferred on Gloucester as a whole." (In 1840, residents living to the east of Dogtown wanted no truck with the heathen folk in Gloucester and separated to form the town of Rockport.)

Irrespective of whether the Dogtown women were truly deserving of their bad reputations, most were feared and held in contempt for no reason other than the fact that they were destitute and lived outside of societal norms. Years after Judy Rhines's death, people actually acquainted with her tried to set the record straight. They maintained that she was merely courageous and outspoken, two distinctly unfeminine traits for the time. In one incident, two boys who claimed that any witch's livestock was public property tried to abscond with her geese. Rhines chased after them with a hoe yelling, "Now, ye hell birds, I've got ye!" One boy swung a goose at Judy, hitting her in the face and knocking her to the ground. The boys ran off with her birds.

Though Dogtown was characterized as a rural slum, its population was not limited to the underclass. Dorcas Foster had remained there since the Revolution, when her father relocated the family from the harbor village out of fear of attack. Isaac Dade, who was crippled while fighting in the war's decisive battle at Yorktown, resided there with his wife, Fanny Brundle, a Virginian whose family were close associates of George and Martha Washington. William Pearce, brother of David Pearce, owner of the ill-fated privateer *Gloucester*, had a farm in the area that the British raided for its sheep during the War of 1812. Yet even some of these "good people" of Dogtown succumbed to vice. Mann claims that the aristocratic nurse Easter Carter also "entertained" young lovers and a "staid old citizen" who arrived with "a parcel of girls," delicately suggesting that Carter's house was a nineteenth-century version of the no-tell motel.

Though Mann reports that only six of the forty-one houses that filled the Commons Settlement in 1741 during the First Parish dispute were left standing by 1814, more than half a dozen residents remained in the moribund highland village. After Captain Stanwood and his family moved away, he invited three Dogtown women to live in his old home: Molly Jacobs; Sarah Phipps; and a Mrs. Stanley, whose grandson Sammy Stanley, a nurse who had been raised as a girl and wore a kerchief on his head, took care of them. Though the house was slowly falling down around them, Cornelius Finson or "Black Neil," one of Dogtown's two former slaves, moved into the cellar. Finson, who earned his living as a hog slaughterer and did some menial clerking for fishing boats in Annisquam, allegedly dug for buried treasure under the captain's old house. During the winters, Captain Stanwood's grandchildren brought them all food. One day they found the three women huddled in bed underneath a "coverlet white with snow where the wind had sifted through the night." The overseers of the poor soon came and carted the women away, but not Sammy Stanley, who moved to Rockport and worked as a launderer, or Cornelius Finson. Finson might have already moved on to live with Judy Rhines, who had invited him to live in the unoccupied portion of her house.

STARTING IN THE 1740S Gloucester participated in the rum, sugar, and slave trade like other New England ports. The town's earliest slaveholders were farmers, but by the 1770s many merchants and ship captains owned slaves, too. At least three hundred slaves had lived in Gloucester, according to historian James Pringle. They were put to work as oarsmen, livery drivers, field hands, clerks, dockhands, domestics, and laborers. A small percentage were granted their freedom prior to Massachusetts' 1783 emancipation.

Some former slaves, such as Gloucester's Robert Freeman, lived in town and prospered. Freeman owned a house, a barn, a garden, oxen, horses, livestock, and various rights to common lands. But it was more typical for black men and women to leave the communities where they had lived a life of bondage; cities such as Boston were a popular destination. Yet many former slaves simply disappeared from official records across the region. Some may have lived on the outskirts of towns in small communities that were not unlike Gloucester's Dogtown. In nearby Beverly, a former slave named Cloe Larcom resided just beyond town in her former owner Mary Larcom's "tumble down old house innocent of paint, and black with age." Larcom opened her home to other manumitted slaves from the area until the 1840s, when the house was torn down to make way for the railroad.

In 1790, Gloucester's census accounted for thirty-nine black residents. The 1801 federal census—the nation's first accounting of all its residents—listed a mere twelve. The two former slaves who lived in Dogtown, Cornelius Finson and a woman named Old Ruth, who also went by the names "Tie" and "John Woodman," do not appear on either of these lists.

Cornelius Finson may have been a Gloucester native born to a slave named Dill, who belonged to Ambrose Finson, an Annisquam resident, or he may have moved to Gloucester from elsewhere; Gloucester's Vital Records account only for his death. Old Ruth does not appear in Gloucester records under any of her various names. There were no Woodmans in Gloucester, but a slave owner named John Woodman lived up the coast in Newburyport. Old Ruth may have relocated to Gloucester from Newburyport or elsewhere—she does not appear in any of the records of nearby towns. Mann reports that when Old Ruth was a slave, she was forced to dress in men's clothes and work outside. After her emancipation, she claimed to simply prefer pants to skirts; they were more suitable for the fence-building and other "heavy toil" she did to earn a living. Eventually, after the house she shared with Easter Carter collapsed, she was taken to the poorhouse, where she was forced to conform to the norm and start wearing skirts.

The poorhouse overseers planned to come for Cornelius Finson, too. Judy Rhines's house had deteriorated to such a degree that she had moved out of Dogtown altogether, but Finson stayed on.

Folklore holds that the Commons Settlement lived a more colorful afterlife as Dogtown, but life there in beggary only got harder as people left or were taken away and the houses continued to collapse. One woman recalled that the Dogtowners "never had white flour but once a year, at Thanksgiving, when they brought their pans down to a merchant in the Parish, and had them filled." Ladies from an organization called the Reading Society provided "much-needed clothes" and commented on the Dogtowners' "unfortunate moral and physical condition." Abraham Wharf, a descendant of a Commons Settler, was so distraught over his destitute state that he crawled under one of Dogtown's large boulders and slit his throat. Jack Bishop Smith, son of the healer Rachel Smith who brewed the "dire drink," also killed himself.

It is impossible to say how many people were left in the winter of 1829 when Tammy Younger died at age seventy-six. Tammy's nephew wanted to give his aunt a proper burial and ordered a coffin from cabinetmaker John Hodgkins. One stormy, candlelit evening, Hodgkins had finished rubbing beeswax into the wood and left the coffin in his kitchen to dry. His children were accustomed to having coffins in their home, but on this particular night, little John Jr. was on his way to the bedroom, which was through the kitchen, when his candle cast an eerie glow over Tammy's coffin, terrifying the young boy. John Jr. began "to whimper" and ran out of the room. Next, Hodgkins's daughter peeked through the door and became "panicky." The children refused to go to bed with Tammy's coffin in the house. Ready to put a stop to all of the nonsense, Mrs. Hodgkins, who was never afraid of anything, went into the kitchen and caught the same horrified chill her children had. All three determined that Tammy was indeed a witch and that her ghost was in the house. They insisted that the coffin be removed to the shop at once. Hodgkins resisted; the rain would spoil the wood. But this point did nothing to stop his family's protests. Hodgkins wrapped the coffin in a blanket and carried it out in the storm.

Dogtown had long been a dying village, but the time finally came when only a single resident remained: Cornelius Finson. On a bitter February 1839 day when Judy Rhines's old house "was full of ice," the constable arrived to take him away. Finson was "cold, dirty, half-starved, and shaking with the combined infirmity of old age and fright." Severe frostbite on his toes prevented him from walking. En route to the poorhouse, Finson was so badly chilled the constable had to stop inside a store for half an hour to warm him up. He died seven days later.

With Cornelius Finson went Dogtown, never to be officially populated again. All that was left were the ruins, this lore, and a haunted reputation that settled in among the village's remnants.

"They say that on stormy nights you can still hear the beat of the drums that marched the fated patriots out of Dogtown," The *Boston Sunday Herald* reported in 1897. "They say this sound gradually dies away and the wailing of women is heard, and that finally this also becomes an echo and only the barking and howling of dogs break the silence of the deserted village."

Chapter Seventeen

"Viva San Petro!"

S INCE THE LATE 1920S, Gloucester, ever tradition bound, has given the last Friday in June over to St. Peter, its protector. And despite the rain, June 29, 1984, was no exception. While Peter Hodgkins's arraignment was under way just a few blocks up Main Street, a crowd, drawn by the sounds of a band warming up, began to gather in front of the St. Peter's Club on Main Street's west end to watch the statue of St. Peter come to life as it had every year for nearly sixty years. If any Fort Square residents had given it much thought—in such a provincial city as Gloucester, the downtown waterfront neighborhood could not have been farther from Dogtown—having Peter Hodgkins, that "crazy lumper," out of the woods and off the streets would have given them all the more reason to celebrate.

A few years before the statue of St. Peter came into Gloucester people's lives in 1926 (maybe it was 1927—no one remembers exactly), Peter Favazza, a Gloucester fisherman, built a small shrine to the saint in his Fort Square backyard. The Favazzas invited family, friends, and neighbors, most of whom also were of Sicilian descent and grew up with similar traditions, to come and pray for protection and good fortune from St. Peter for nine days. On June 29, the day of St. Peter's feast, these prayers ended with a large party. One year around this time, Favazza's sister-in-law Maria became seriously ill. The family begged St. Peter for help. Somewhere in those prayers, Salvatore Favazza, Maria's husband and Peter Favazza's brother, made a deal: if St. Peter intervened to spare his wife—and mother to his ten children—he would do something special in thanks. Something big.

Salvatore's wife survived, and that big promise he'd made weighed in at six hundred pounds: a life-size painted plaster statue of St. Peter commissioned from a sculptor in Charlestown. Once the statue arrived, the backyard celebration upgraded to a block party that grew into a street festival, which evolved into a celebration involving the entire Fort Square neighborhood until Fiesta, though predominantly an Italian-American celebration, became the city of Gloucester's largest annual party.

When St. Peter was not busy being feted back in the early days—he looked so young with a head of black hair, ruddy-cheeked, and handsome, too, like the man who had commissioned him—he stood in the front window of Peter Favazza's Fort Square commercial fishing supply shop. By 1984, St. Peter had moved up in the world to the Main Street storefront window of the Italian social club named in his honor, a prominent locale befitting the first leader of the Christian Church.

From his storefront niche, St. Peter spent days and nights watching the town go by, witnessing each year bring small changes that would amount to noticeable differences over the decades: suit lapels widening, then shrinking; women's hair growing long, falling loose, then cut short; hemlines rising and falling. While the world transformed around St. Peter, his eyes maintained the same tender expression, but his eyebrows, beard, and the thick hair framing his face had begun to gray thanks to the quiet intercession of a clever individual wielding a paintbrush with a gentle touch.

To the rough-and-tumble drunks who couldn't give a hoot about some sandal-clad, halo-topped, toga-sporting statue, he faded into the backdrop of Main Street's west end storefront windows along with Vergilio's crusty loaves of bread, Palazola's Gloucester High School Fishermen T-shirts, and the charred remains of Mark Adrian Farber's shoe store. But St. Peter, whose right hand is forever raised in benediction, blesses everyone silently, surreptitiously, while his left hand holds the keys to the heavenly kingdom. Of course, not everyone who dies makes it to heaven, nor does everyone who wishes to die, as Peter Hodgkins did that weekend, actually succeed.

Detectives Reardon and Ryan took Hodgkins to Addison Gilbert Hospital for a body check and X-rays before officials would transport him to the Lawrence Jail. While Hodgkins waited to be examined, he talked as if thoughts of being pumped full of lead by the fifty armed men who had searched for him in the woods continued to haunt him.

"Viva San Petro!" The crowd shouted down on Main Street.

The women, many of whom wore their Sunday best, held white tapered candles. Passing the flame from candle to candle, they greeted family and friends, as well as any strangers who had walked over from the midway to see what all the excitement was about.

Two men entered the St. Peter's Club's storefront window niche and began to tip the statue of the saint backward into the arms of a third. The men, members of the St. Peter's Club, received all six hundred pounds of the saint's earthly weight. They carried the statue to a wooden litter adorned with gold cherubs and hoisted him on top. Little boys crawled underneath to tighten a set of bolts securing St. Peter in place. Women straightened satin bows adorning his chest, affixed dollar bills to them, and draped gold chains across his palm. Eight men lined up—four to the front, four to the rear—alongside poles that extended horizontally from under the litter tabletop. A man fell to one knee, raised his arms overhead, and called toward the sky, *"Me chi samiou, dute mute? Viva San Petro!"* (Shout it louder, are we all mute? Long live St. Peter!) The crowd called back, *"Viva San Petro! Me chi samiou, dute mute?"* The kneeling man responded *appassionata, con fortissimo.* Louder, stronger, they shouted, too. *"Viva!"* he called out. *"Viva!"* they answered at the top of their lungs. *"Vi-i-i-va-a-a!"* he bellowed, arms quivering overhead, back arched as he pressed the melismatic cry from his chest. *"Vi-i-i-va-a-a!"* they yelled, wild with excitement. Children jumped up and down. Applause went up. A whistle blew. Together the eight men knelt, as their fathers and grandfathers had done, slid their shoulders under pads secured to the poles, and stood. The statue of St. Peter was lifted onto the men's shoulders, high above the cheering crowd, and began to move.

BEFORE THE LAST SUPPER, Jesus washed his twelve disciples' feet. But when Peter's turn came, he refused to allow Jesus to bathe him. Though Jesus had changed the fisherman's name from Simon to Peter, in recognition of his rocklike faith, Peter could also be dense like a rock. "If I wash thee not, thou hast no part with me," Jesus said. Finally grasping the significance of Jesus' gesture, Peter replied, "Lord, not my feet only, but also my hands and my head." Jesus bathed him and said, "You are clean, but not all," referring to what he knew in his heart: that Peter would later deny having any involvement with him.

PETER HODGKINS'S X-RAYS revealed no breaks, no briar nor thorn lodged in his feet. Nurses swabbed and soaked his feet and treated the blisters they found, but no one could wash Peter Hodgkins of his crime.

ONE YEAR, AFTER a Fiesta novena Mass, the statue of St. Peter was carried to the home of Simone Sanfillipo, an octogenarian who had recently died from cancer. Little girls holding flower arrangements led the way. St. Peter followed through the beams of the headlights from cars that were waiting for the procession to pass. The children turned onto Beach Court, a small street backlit by the sun's descent from a wilting light blue sky. St. Peter passed under the street's filigreed lights done up in red, white, and green—the colors of the Italian flag. A cloth-covered medallion suspended amid lights and colored foil hung over the entrance to Pavilion Beach next to Sanfillipo's house, the last on the street, or first, if you were coming in from the shore. Sanfillipo's widow, dressed in black, emerged from the house onto its front deck. Her children and grandchildren pressed in at her side. She made the sign of the cross and held out her arms, as if St. Peter had walked across the water and the men's shoulders to comfort her and her family, to give her strength to carry on. Mrs. Sanfillipo began to wail, *"Caro San Petro, aiuta mi! Che dio mi salvi!"* (Dear St. Peter, help me! God save me!) The processional girls held out their flowers for the family. A boy riding on his father's shoulders reached up and pulled a string attached to the cloth, revealing a medallion-shaped image of St. Peter and a dedication of that year's Fiesta to Simone Sanfillipo. Older boys let off poppers. The crowd cheered, *"Viva San Petro! Viva! Viva!"* and began to sing in Italian about how the saint guides one safely through the darkest storms. They sang to the Madonnina del Mare (Madonna of the Sea), voices nearly falling into time with the waves washing over the beach. Two Sanfillipo girls held little white dogs and stroked their fur. Tears streamed down their grandmother's face. *"Viva San Petro!"* she cried one last time as St. Peter ambled away, and the street grew quiet but for the nearby shouts of carnival barkers and the shrieking cries of roller-coaster riders.

ANNE NATTI'S DEATH was significantly more public than Simone San-fillipo's, but Erik Natti's grief, like his Finnish heritage, was private, reliant on a different force of the spirit, *sisu*. His elders had handed down stories of centuries of Finns calling up spirits from the woods, and while Erik was not the sort of guy to go in for talking to trees, the forest always had profoundly consoled him—that is, until finding his wife's body led him into an unmappable internal wilderness. More than anything, Erik wanted to function even in this dark place, to keep moving forward. He submerged himself in the numerous mundane tasks that must be completed when someone dies a violent death: talking to the police, letting them clip Woofer's fur for evidence, breaking the news to Anne's parents, arranging for cremation, and planning a memorial.

The Natti family regularly gathered on Saturdays to take a sauna, and on Saturday of Fiesta weekend they also went to church.

For Erik, the memorial service was a blur: the names and faces of the three hundred people who came; what the minister, who had married Erik and Anne ten months before under a big oak tree in the woods, had said; the eulogy that Dr. Charles Drake, founder of the Landmark School, read; and the comment his sister Isabel made that some remembered years later: "Don't anyone go in the woods." What Erik retained from the event was a change in his awareness of Anne's death: it became more real to him; the ritual gave his most amorphous feelings a vessel in which to take shape.

After the service, people traveled to Erik's uncle Bob's house for a reception, which included a sauna. Erik stayed behind, sitting alone in the church and weeping. He stopped crying half an hour later and left to join his family, but his grieving had just started.

In the *Kalevala* the evil witch Louhi sends a warship after the Kaleva people who have taken back their *sampo*, an elaborate mill with magical properties that Louhi had stolen from them. The Kaleva manage to escape, but Louhi sends a scourge of diseases to their land in revenge. In need of healing and comfort, the Kaleva take to the sauna, where the shaman Väinämöinen sings an incantation to the sauna rocks to release their curative properties: "send away evil vapor / so that it will not burn your sons, / harm your offspring." But this song soon turns into a curse on anyone who would do the Kaleva people harm: "Whoever may destroy us without cause, may his own magic words go into his mount, / his evil designs into his head, his intentions redound upon himself."

PETER HODGKINS'S INTENTIONS were doing just that, turning in on him. He arrived at the Lawrence Jail, where he was processed and sent to the showers. He then cracked open a standard inmate-issue plastic razor and removed the blade.

ST. PETER WAS incarcerated twice in his life. The first incident occurred in Jerusalem, when Herod began imprisoning members of the early Christian Church, of which Peter was the leader. Herod planned to execute St. Peter, but an angel miraculously intervened and set Peter free. When St. Peter was imprisoned a second time, in Rome's Mamertine Prison, he demonstrated his miraculous powers by conjuring up a spring from the prison floor to baptize his fellow inmates. But no angel came to his aid. St. Peter was crucified upside down, as he requested, so as not to be confused with Christ.

ON SUNDAY MORNING Bishop Charles P. Greco led his twenty-third Fiesta pontifical Mass under a gray sky that made the carnival colors seem even brighter in contrast. So many people came for the service—about two thousand, some say more—that many had to sit in the motionless carnival rides to hear the eighty-four-year-old bishop's sermon. Policemen helped usher the crowd to communion. "A year ago I hovered between life and death and prayed to God to be able to stay a little bit longer," the Louisiana-based bishop said, "and I was able to return to this wonderful celebration today." The crowd listened, solemn, exuberant, inspired.

PETER HODGKINS SLICED into himself with the razor blade, attempting suicide, but he did not hover between life and death for long. Guards quickly intervened.

LIGHTS WENT UP on the carnival rides. Bumper cars whirred and crashed. Sugar was twisted and spun into pink bouffants. Bells rang out from the midway games. Hundreds of red, white, and green balloons filled the sky, as if buoyed by the smells of fried onions and peppers, grilling sausage, and cinnamon-sugar-coated fried dough. Fishermen dressed in crisp whites shouldered St. Peter for a larger, longer procession through Gloucester's downtown. This time his entourage included a statue of the Portuguese saint Our Lady of Fatima, a variety of floats on which children acted out scenes from St. Peter's life, local dignitaries, ten marching bands, and a police escort. Accompanying the saints on the two-mile walk was the sweetest devotion. Some of Gloucester's most devout followed in bare feet.

THERE WAS ANOTHER tradition of walking on Cape Ann that people affiliated with a different sort of spiritual practice: traversing Dogtown. Many had wandered in this place in search of some form of inner peace. Now, weekend hikes, picnics at ancestors' cellars, orchid-hunting walks, and berry-picking trips were cancelled. This time the devil in the wilderness had been real. Peter Hodgkins had voluntarily removed himself from Dogtown, but he continued to cast a shadow over it that blended with those from years past.

In 1873, Thomas Wentworth Higginson—the renowned transcendentalist minister, abolitionist, soldier, writer, and literary mentor to Emily Dickinson—had a bone to pick with Nathaniel Hawthorne over his critique of John Bunyan's Christian allegory *Pilgrim's Progress,* in which two characters named Christian and Hopeful get lost and end up in a dark land that belongs to a monster called Giant Despair: "What can Hawthorne mean by saying in his English diary that 'an American would never understand the passage in Bunyan about Christian and Hopeful going astray along a by-path into the grounds of Giant Despair, from there being no stiles and by-paths in our country'?" Though Giant

Despair captures Christian and Hopeful, locks them away, and tortures them, nearly convincing them to commit suicide, the pair escape when Christian realizes he has a key called Promise. As allegories go, *Pilgrim's Progress* is especially heavy-handed, but to Higginson, Dogtown was the key that unlocked Hawthorne's polemic: "So much of the charm of American pedestrianism lies in the by-paths! For instance, the whole interior of Cape Ann . . ." Higginson went on to describe Dogtown's "couchant monsters," "wild foot-path[s]," and "devious tracks" that he had wandered summer after summer. And while Higginson certainly did not encounter Giant Despair in Dogtown, somewhere along the way it had snatched Peter Hodgkins in its meaty grip.

AS THE PARADE returned to St. Peter's Square, the saint's statue was placed back in its altar niche in front of a painted seascape so it appeared that St. Peter stood firmly, solidly on the surface of the sea. Participants in the weekend's most anticipated event, the greasy pole–walking championship, hoped to do as well as their patron.

St. Peter took his siesta as a procession filed down to the waterfront to watch the bishop cruise by in the bow of a yacht to bless the Gloucester fleet. Meanwhile, the greasy pole walkers peeled off to have their feet blessed by a man surnamed Foote. They then invoked an earthly order of spirits: bottled ones, in copious quantities; however much it took to inspire some of Gloucester's brawniest men to don outlandish costumes and dresses and take turns stepping out onto an axle-grease-coated forty-five-foot-long telephone pole that extended ten to twenty-five feet above the water, depending on the tide. The challenge was to be the first to remove a flag nailed to the pole's end. Risking broken bones, concussions, and other dangerous injuries, participants walked out onto the pole one after the next. Most slipped and went flying off, hitting the water with great force. Others, less fortunate, smacked the pole on the way down or, worse yet, managed to slip and fall to straddle the pole with an excruciatingly painful whack to the groin. A huge crowd, watching from the beach and in boats, egged them on. The greasy pole is a brutal, masochistic competition that called on its own kind of inner fortitude: bravado and tolerance for alcohol.

Though it was officially reported that the greasy pole champion won fifty dollars and a case of beer, the contestants most lusted for the glory of victory, a year's worth of free drinks in all the town bars, and the women. "You win the greasy pole, you're gonna get laid every night for a year!" a pole walker boasted, as if winning was the key to an earthly heaven. It was a good thing old St. Peter napped while such talk was going on. As much as Fiesta was a sacred event, "happy people," as the *Gloucester Daily Times* described all the inebriants, reveled in its profane moments.

After the greasy pole walk and the final competition of the seine boat races (Gloucester fishermen formerly used seine boats to haul fish that they caught in their floating nets), the statue of St. Peter was taken out for a final nighttime spin through Fort Square. Overwhelmed with memories of family and friends now departed, St. Peter's attendants accompanied him with tears in their eyes and "put him to bed" for another year just before Gloucester's clocks struck midnight.

Chapter Eighteen

Life's Book

I'M BEGINNING TO feel things!" a woman merely identified as "the Wife" told her friend Sarah Comstock as they walked across Dogtown one dusky 1919 evening. Hoping to have a variety of spooky, hair-raising encounters, Comstock and company had been searching for traces of New England witchcraft in Salem and on Cape Ann along what they called the "Broomstick Trail." Each site they had visited seemed drab and ordinary until they reached their final destination: Dogtown.

In the seventy years between the area's abandonment and Comstock's peregrinations, Dogtown's barrenness intensified its desolation. Grazing cattle ate the shoots of everything that tried to take root except the blueberries and the occasional juniper tree. The old village's stone ruins, the colossal glacial erratics, and the numerous boulders of the terminal moraine now stood out in stark relief against an otherwise empty landscape. To Comstock and company, the area was a "New World Salisbury Plain"—an American version of the English plateau where Stonehenge is located. In Dogtown, according to this *Harper's Monthly* magazine writer, the "spellbound victims" of the area's witches had been turned to stone along with "the monstrous shapes of prehistoric beasts and birds and reptiles" that the glacier had carved out of its boulders. Of all the haunts they had discovered, Comstock concluded with authority, Dogtown was the one and only "true home of the witches." And those witches—"a few of whom so blackened the reputation of the settlement that early historians pursed their lips and dwelt

148

as briefly as possible upon its records"—had turned this land into "the very dwelling-place of all the powers of darkness."

While this sounded perfectly, mysteriously entertaining to Comstock and friends and others who came in search of this "wonderworld," it made Comstock's contemporary, the Prohibitionist Roger W. Babson, purse his lips, too. Babson, an eccentric Gloucester-born millionaire, wanted people to understand that Dogtown's "real history was not that from 1750 to 1927 . . . but rather from 1650 to 1750 when it was a thriving community settled by fine people"—that is, Babson's ancestors. And to give his idea of Dogtown the monumental permanence he believed it deserved, Babson planned to turn the area's eerie boulders into principled counterforces against society's ills.

Something of a household name from 1910 until his death in 1967, Roger W. Babson was a financial guru and nationally syndicated investment advice columnist whose articles ran in the *Saturday Evening Post*, *Collier's Weekly*, and the *New York Times*; the author of forty-three books about business and sundry topics; the founder of a gravity research institute as well as Babson, Weber, and Utopia Colleges; an investment statistician; and a real estate developer. He served as assistant secretary of labor in Woodrow Wilson's administration and is recognized for predicting the October 1929 stock market crash and subsequent economic collapse. (Economists refer to his prediction and its effect on the market as the "Babson Break.") A few months before his 1929 economic prediction, the public relations–savvy Babson, who had his sights set on a bid for the White House, began fashioning an Abraham Lincoln meets Horatio Alger–style autobiography set in Dogtown.

"Boston Millionaire Deserts Civilization to Live With Birds in Wilderness of Witches and Pirates," a July 28, 1929, *Boston Sunday Post* headline stated in reference to the 500-square-foot cabin that Babson had built in the style of an original Commons Settlement home and filled with colonial furnishings and curiosities. Babson built the house after purchasing 1,150 acres of Dogtown land with his cousin Gustavus Babson in 1927. They also purchased the stone cooperage that their ancestor James Babson, the vision-seeing Ebenezer Babson's father, built in 1658 along Dogtown's eastern periphery, as well as its adjacent land. That same year Roger W. Babson published an address to the Gloucester Rotary Club in which he extracted and embellished Charles E. Mann's accounts of the area's venerable colonials. To Babson, this village's demise was "more tragic than the history of almost any other American community," but it offered "many great lessons" for "those who visit and catch its spirit," a spirit that was decidedly different from the one that Comstock felt.

Roger Ward Babson's interest in Dogtown was not steady throughout his lifetime, but its influence, he claimed, was enduring. Born in Gloucester in 1875 "by the light of a kerosene lamp," as he described the event in his autobiography, *Actions and Reactions*, Babson claimed that childhood summers spent tending to his grandfather's Dogtown cattle had a profound impact on his upbringing and moral outlook, though it did not keep him from getting into trouble as a boy. Dragged by his ear to Sunday school classes, Babson amused himself by sticking gum in other boys' hair, "twisting up pins for the teacher to sit on," and hiding the collection plate. He then started running with a gang of Irish immigrant kids who lived in a nearby tenement. According to Babson, in these late-nineteenth-century days, Gloucester had grown into a small city where "liquor actually flowed in the streets." A row of saloons and a whorehouse called the Busy Bee were a mere three hundred feet from his respectable, middle-class home. (In 1856, less than fifty years earlier, Hannah Jumper and two hundred hatchet-wielding women went on a temperance raid and destroyed rum shops in the adjacent town of Rockport.) But in 1890, at age fifteen, Babson was visited by "the greatest event of my life": an "old-fashioned" revival meeting that lifted him out of the mire and into the trusting hands of the Lord. His act cleaned up, Babson graduated from the Massachusetts Institute of Technology, married a preacher's daughter, triumphed over a bout of tuberculosis, and went on to amass a fortune selling financial forecasts.

In making these financial predictions, Babson applied lessons gleaned from Newton's laws of motion, principles of mass psychology, and Dogtown. "Some phase of every industry, and some branch of every family is experiencing the same four period [*sic*] of improvement, prosperity, decline and depression, as has occurred in this village of Dogtown," Babson stated in his 1927 pamphlet *Dogtown: Gloucester's Deserted Village*. "Thus connected with the story of Dogtown is a great economic lesson as well as a story of romance." Babson's conviction that the story of Dogtown offered financial and moral instruction was so strong he planned to carve its lessons in stone. "I believe that reading should be used by physicians perhaps more than pills," he once wrote.

If people were not going to sit down and read books, they could walk through Dogtown and read his huge rocks for a little lesson in self-improvement.

But first, Babson set out to improve Dogtown, his would-be classroom. Grazing cattle had knocked down the numbered posts he had erected next to the colonial cellars that corresponded to a map listing the owners' names. To replace the posts, Babson hired out-of-work masons to carve these numbers in stone. He then turned his attention to writing his *Life's Book*. For inspiration, Babson pondered the lives of his colonial ancestors—Babson believed that ancestry had an especially strong effect on character—and searched his "Good Cheer Library," a collection of self-help and inspirational books that included the following titles: *Blessed Be Drudgery, Tune in for Your Birthright*, and *Guide to Literature for Character Training*. From these and others, he compiled a list of mottoes for twenty-four of Dogtown's largest boulders: SAVE, USE YOUR HEAD, IDEAS, BE CLEAN, TRUTH, STUDY, GET A JOB, INDUSTRY, INTEGRITY, HELP MOTHER, SPIRITUAL POWER, NEVER TRY NEVER WIN, BE ON TIME, PROSPERITY FOLLOWS SERVICE, KEEP OUT OF DEBT, BE TRUE, IF WORK STOPS VALUES DECAY, IDEALS, INITIATIVE, KINDNESS, COURAGE, INTELLIGENCE, WORK, and LOYALTY.

These were good years for large-scale rock carving projects. Gutzon Borglum's carving of larger-than-life-size profiles of Confederate generals on Georgia's Stone Mountain had been stalled, but Borglum was off in South Dakota chiseling Mount Rushmore into George Washington's likeness. (In 1963 Gloucester sculptor Walker Hancock, Erik Natti's uncle by marriage, completed Borglum's Stone Mountain carvings.) But Babson claimed it was the billboard, America's new advertising medium, with its "debauching outdoor poster talk," that inspired his messages and chosen medium. Moreover, he thought his *Life's Book* was so fetching that "many other cities which happen to be blessed with boulders will likewise adopt [the practice] and make it a part of their educational system." But Babson's most important gift to the people of Gloucester lay underneath the land.

ON JUNE 5, 1930, a year before Hartley set foot in Dogtown, a "picturesque geyser" shot up from the ground along Gloucester's harborfront.

While initially it might not have looked serious, just an undersea seismic belch, the ground around it soon started to cave in. An electric pole fell. Then part of the sidewalk disappeared. The hole became a puddle, which became a pond that swallowed twenty square feet of land. A cascade teeming with fish gushed over the seawall, as though something of biblical importance were at work. All over town, as housewives prepared to make breakfast and wash up their children before school, faucets went dry and pipes produced a hollow, sucking sound. A pipe carrying water from the mainland to the island had broken. Island Gloucester had run dry.

It was the second year in a row that something happened to cause Gloucester to run out of water. Scarcity of potable water had long been a problem on island Gloucester. When Thoreau visited Cape Ann on September 23, 1858, he noted in his *Journal*, "There is a scarcity of fresh water on the Cape, so that you must carry your water a good way in a dipper." And Babson once remarked, "Our main fire protection was that it sometimes rained!"

The day after the water main break, service was temporarily restored with water from various sources in West Gloucester. Town business leaders and city councillors held an emergency meeting. State Department of Health officials urged the city to dam Dogtown's Alewife Brook, but an extremely vocal group of concerned citizens rose up in opposition to the idea.

After city water commissioners seized 130 acres of Roger W. Babson's Dogtown land under eminent domain, the voice of this opposition, former mayor Henry Parsons, fired off a letter to the editor of the *Gloucester Daily Times* in objection. Colonists had abandoned an Alewife Brook mill because the brook's flow was insufficient, Parsons asserted, but the water's dubious quality was his greatest worry. Though officials stated that Briar Swamp's iron ore, which produced the Alewife Brook's reddish color, could be filtered, Parsons was more concerned about the land the water flowed through. A hog cholera epidemic had recently killed a thousand pigs that were then buried in the Alewife Brook watershed. An animal-rendering factory also occupied other parts of this land, as well as the city's night-soil dump. Then there was the issue of how to deal with the railroad that ran through the area. Parsons did some math and figured that one hundred toilets passed through the watershed each day, dropping "several other things too numerous to mention," plus oil and pollutants from the trains' engines. "Of course we never thought that we would be compelled to drink the drainage from that diseased place," the former mayor pleaded. Spurred on by Parsons's claims, on July 19, a hundred people gathered in Dogtown at the Alewife Brook and staged a protest.

Engineers and state health officials contended that the Alewife Brook's supply and quality were more than adequate. Fed by sixteen underground springs created by a subterranean stream, the water was said to be of "unusual purity." Night soil and any animal carcasses would be removed. Trains would be regulated to close their toilets when passing through the region, and the reservoir would undergo a mandatory chlorination period.

Parsons was mildly appeased, but now opposed the reservoir's projected expense. The newspapers alluded to whispers, especially among the old-timers, that the old witch Tammy Younger was still at work vexing the ancient highland.

Into this argument stepped Roger W. Babson and his cousin Gustavus, who offered to sell the city the 500 acres of watershed land that it needed for just $1 as long as it also purchased an additional 650 acres, including their ancestor James Babson's stone cooperage. For these combined acres, the Babsons charged the city $14,201, a fraction of the estimated value of $50,000 for the watershed acreage alone. Their proposal carried two important stipulations: that the land would remain "a natural park and bird sanctuary" to be accessed "on foot only" and that Babson's masons be allowed to continue carving his inscriptions on the area's boulders.

Construction on the dam began almost immediately. Nearly two hundred crewmen were brought in, including twenty-year-old poet Charles Olson, who was home for summer vacation from Wesleyan University. At the end of his first day, Olson and others were fired in a labor scandal that he would include in his epic *Maximus Poems* some twenty years later. By December 8, 1930, the reservoir construction was complete.

Not everyone was pleased with Babson's arrangement. Hartley referred to the carvings as "an intervention of the worst sort," but Leila Webster Adams was nearly apoplectic. When Babson's masons carved a cellar hole rock on her land without seeking her permission, Mrs. Adams launched a public invective against Babson's "defacing of the landscape."

"Just look at that horrible thing; just look at it!" Mrs. Adams exclaimed to reporters. "Why the idea of a man like Roger Babson, so well-known and popular, going about carving such things as 'Prosperity Follows Service,' 'Keep Out of Debt,' and 'If Work Stops, Values Decay.' Whoever heard of such foolish notions?" Blue-blooded Mrs. Adams was convinced that her ancestors, whom she made a point of letting people know had been in the country as long as Babson's and included the pirate-slayer Captain Andrew Haraden, were rolling in their graves over his "propaganda."

In 1932, when the reservoir finally opened, Roger W. Babson addressed the city: "As a warning to future generations, I have carved . . . these words: 'When Work Stops Values Decay,' . . . a situation is developing in the United States today which is similar to that which developed here on this watershed two hundred years ago." Thus began a Dogtown history lesson embedded within Babson's plans for pulling the country out of the Great Depression.

By 1940, Babson was at last on his way to taking his message to the White House. He ran for president on the Prohibition Ticket against Franklin Delano Roosevelt in a values-based campaign that pledged to outlaw alcohol, drugs, gambling, and indecent movies and publications, and to foster spiritual awakening. He finished in fourth place with 0.12 percent of the popular vote. Babson has long since faded from public memory, but his boulders endure.

Like Moses, Roger W. Babson handed down a set of stone commandments and made water flow from rock. But over time, his *Life's Book* would add to the strangeness that he had hoped to expunge from this place. Likewise, his attempt to establish an orthodox Dogtown history would merely serve to perpetuate the area's myths rather than set the historic record straight. After watching Dogtown's wildflowers bloom Babson once wrote, "Dogtown teaches me clearly that progress comes only slowly," but he had no idea how slowly future efforts to ensure his legacy would progress. The greatest good Babson found in Dogtown was the one that had been there all along: the land itself. Babson's bequest would ensure the area's continued existence as a natural landscape, but not its care or its reputation.

Chapter Nineteen

Island Heart of Darkness

I LOST MY WOODS," Annie Melancon, a ceramic artist who worked out of a studio nestled in the forest on Bob and Lee Natti's land, said after Anne Natti's murder, as if Dogtown was her own private sanctuary. Anne and Erik Natti had felt that the woods were their personal haven, too. So did Peter Hodgkins and others, including people who had not set foot in the area for years.

At first, Melancon thought about getting a gun. She eventually settled on getting "a very large, scary dog," but for now—July 1984—Annie had simply put the place off-limits. Many others, women in particular, did the same. The murder was not only tragic, it also was infuriating. Not only did people lose "a wonderful spirit" in Anne Natti, they had lost their woods, and they wanted them back.

These were no ordinary woods to these Cape Anners. That Dogtown's forest had recovered from the despoliation colonists and quarry companies had wrought made it all the more compelling to those who saw wilderness as a means back to a purer, more natural, Edenic state, as well as a place of solace. It reassured people that all things eventually heal; maybe even they would, too.

There is something especially disturbing about a murder in a natural setting. It shatters our illusion that nature is our protector, a force that inspires goodness. But people had failed to see the human wildness that had been quietly, slowly evolving in Dogtown. Boys who had once run through these woods aiming slingshots at squirrels had grown into men whose woodland escapades became increasingly deviant. Peter

Hodgkins was merely part of it. Joe Orange, one of Gloucester's more outspoken residents on the subject of Dogtown, described "numerous 'close calls' with various subhuman, lowlife types" there, including "gangs of trail bikers with German helmets, German crosses, guns, and knives." Peter Anastas, a social worker and Gloucester writer, stated in his *Gloucester Daily Times* column, "In essence, a 2,300-acre area in the middle of this city is being held hostage by punks and law-breakers." Though a handful of concerned citizens, Anastas among them, had been pleading for people to do something about Dogtown's worsening state of neglect, most did not respond to these impassioned appeals until an innocent woman was brutally murdered in cold blood.

"TAKE BACK THE WOODS," proclaimed signs leading to Dogtown's Babson Reservoir a month after the murder. This vigil for Anne Natti was a twist on the Take Back the Night rallies protesting violence against women. Organizers of and participants in these events frequently get a lot of mileage out of the metaphorical implications of nighttime; Take Back the Woods's planners were no exception. "The gate to Cape Ann's 'heart of darkness,'" the *Gloucester Daily Times* reported, "was lit by candlelight, memories of Anne Natti and plans for a safer Dogtown."

"In order for there to be wilderness," as mailman Jack Chase once remarked, "you have to will some sort of spirit into a place." In the 1600s, the Puritans willed a dark, evil spirit into this land. After colonists cleared the original primeval forest and eradicated the scourge of wilderness, they built fences and houses, ushering in a new spirit, one called home. But home did not take to such a hardscrabble, isolated habitat; loss did. It settled among the ruins and the boulders, "that multitude of couchant monsters" that Thomas Wentworth Higginson described in 1882, where "there seems a sense of suspended life; you feel as if they must speak and answer to each other in the silent nights, but by day only the wandering sea-birds seek them, on their way across the Cape, and the sweet-bay and green fern imbed them in a softer and deeper setting as the years go by." By the second half of the twentieth century, this setting indeed softened until it eventually yielded trees. Moreover, people's attitudes about wild things had also grown increasingly tender. Dogtown was reverting to something resembling its original, primeval state. But the human world that surrounded it had changed, too. Dogtown did not change after Anne Natti died; people did. And on this night in the woods, two hundred people holding candles came together to illuminate the area's previously unexamined shadows.

Cape Ann's "Heart of Darkness" was a phrase that echoed in speeches shifting this tragedy away from the story of the "quiet, gentle, and compassionate" woman most had turned out to honor and whose loss they mourned. As in the way of sudden, violent trauma everywhere, Anne Natti's murder became something else altogether: an opportunity for people to impose their own fears, desires, and agendas upon the event. Political candidates and incumbents took to their soapboxes and pumped their fists, promising tougher courts, more jails, and safer woods; it was an election year, after all. The police issued a hero's commendation to Lawrence Davis, the man who brought Peter Hodgkins into the station to surrender. Staff members from Gloucester's social service agencies stumped for better mental health care. People condemned violence against women. Women took to the microphone and spoke about how very angry and frightened the murder had made them feel.

"You will not find violence only in the woods, that heart of darkness," Gail Seavey, one of the vigil's organizers, said. "As long as we leave these woods to people we refuse to take responsibility for, there will be special problems in the woods." But a few years after the murder, even Erik Natti conceded, "There had always been trouble in there—there's always been strange people of one sort or another walking around—but [we] were among them. We were some of the strange people."

For decades, there had been governmental and community indifference toward Dogtown. The City of Gloucester owned 1,150 acres of Dogtown land thanks to Roger W. Babson, but it had allowed much of it to fall into neglect. The rest of the land, an area that covered at least an additional 2,000 acres, was of mostly unknown ownership, which meant that no one took on the responsibility of caring for it. Dogtown did not need to be manicured like a garden or a park, but a publicly accessed natural landscape in a densely populated setting requires at least some regular hands-on management. The area's unique archaeological and natural features ought to have been a point of pride for the community—a place to provide spiritual and maybe even moral uplift, as Babson had envisioned. Yet, after Professor Norton and a group called the Dogtown Foundation spent twenty years clearing a series of bureaucratic hurdles to buy tracts of Dogtown land for conservation and to develop a management plan that would cover the entire area's use, they were met with utter disinterest from the majority of Gloucester's residents. Thus, Dogtown became a physical and a metaphorical dump for trash as well as human beings.

When Dogtown faced imminent critical threats, though, people could always be counted on to come out in protest. Over the years, proposals to use parts of the land for a U.S. Army defense site, a small-craft municipal airfield, an antiballistic missile site, a wind farm, a drive-in movie theater, and a colonial theme park had all been stopped thanks to the efforts of various Cape Ann activists. So it was after the murder, too. When former mayor Bob French announced at Anne Natti's vigil that a new volunteer task force on Dogtown was in need of volunteers, many were suddenly eager to take up the cause.

With passions flowing and a newfound resolve for change, these Cape Anners headed home for the night. Only time would tell if people could find their way back to the land they professed to love but had allowed to fall into neglect, the place where poet Charles Olson went to write among "the blossoming apple trees / in the Paradise of Dogtown."

PART TWO

Chapter Twenty

Maximus, to Dogtown

POET CHARLES OLSON'S JOURNEY to the "paradise" that was Dogtown was not that different from Marsden Hartley's. In 1957, Olson moved to Gloucester to devote himself to writing full-time. He had just left his post as the rector of North Carolina's Black Mountain College, the center of America's avant-garde, where choreographer Merce Cunningham; architect, author, and inventor Buckminster Fuller; composer John Cage; painter Willem de Kooning; poet William Carlos Williams; and other late-modernist luminaries also had taught. But within a year after moving to Gloucester the forty-seven-year-old poet was feeling increasingly anxious about his career. After attending a Beat poetry event where Allen Ginsberg and Gregory Corso were the stars, Olson, who dabbled in the occult—at least insomuch as it served his poetic purposes—went home and started a poem titled "A Maximus Written to Throw Back a Hex on Allen Ginsberg and/or Gregory Corso." Olson, who frequently left his second wife, Bet, and his young son Charles Peter at home without telling them where he was going or when he'd be back, once left them a note that said, "Don't mind anything—I just feel such a load of bullshit I'd like to hide out somewhere until I can believe in some part of me again." Dogtown was one of the places he hid. By the end of 1959, Olson was starting on the second volume of *Maximus Poems*, which he claimed was "all really essentially Dogtown."

In the *Christian Science Monitor*, Steven Ratiner wrote, "It is impossible to describe in this small space the immensity of Charles Olson's achievement—as poet, theoretician, and explorer of the 'human universe.' Just as Ezra Pound's writing energized Western poetry in the first half of this century, Olson in the 1950s redefined its direction and inspired the next generation of writers." The pinnacle of this achievement was Olson's epic *Maximus Poems*, which were hailed by the *Los Angeles Times* as "probably the most ambitious poems ever written by an American." Taken at their simplest, most personal level, the Maximus Poems are Olson's poetic love letter to his muse, Gloucester. Olson was so passionate about the old port city that when his former student Charles Boer was visiting, he took him to a rock in Gloucester's village of Magnolia. "Sit on it and feel the energy," Olson said. Boer later recollected, "I felt nothing but a cold pointed stone sticking me in the ass." But Olson felt the force of the universe pulsing through that stone and nearly every animate and inanimate thing in the town. It was all intensely, enthrallingly alive to him.

CHARLES OLSON'S ARDENT love for Gloucester dropped anchor in 1915, when he was five years old and his family started spending their summers in a modest cottage near Stage Fort Park. The Olsons, who lived west of Boston in the industrial city of Worcester, where Charles was born on December 28, 1910, were not from the class of rarefied summer people who flocked to Gloucester each summer. Olson's father, Karl, was a letter carrier who spent summer weekends in Gloucester with his wife and only child, but had to return to Worcester for work during the week. Olson continued the family summer tradition and returned to Cape Ann while on break from his undergraduate and graduate studies at Wesleyan University. When Olson's father died in 1935, his mother moved to Gloucester permanently, making Cape Ann Olson's official home.

After dropping out of a Ph.D. program in American studies at Harvard in 1939, and spending a year on a Guggenheim Fellowship writing *Call Me Ishmael*, a book-length experimental meditation on Herman Melville's *Moby Dick*, Olson moved to New York City, got involved in politics, and eventually landed a position in Washington, D.C., with the Democratic National Committee. Olson abandoned politics in 1945 after Franklin D. Roosevelt died, and dedicated himself to writing poetry. He began visiting Ezra Pound, then confined to St. Elizabeth's Federal Hospital for the Insane in D.C., and eventually became Pound's literary secretary. With support from Pound, *Call Me Ishmael* was published in 1947. Around this time, Olson started envisioning a response to Pound's *Cantos*, which literary scholars consider to be one of the seminal works of twentieth-century modernist poetry. Olson's idea would eventually take shape as his Gloucester-based *Maximus Poems*.

His career now off the ground at age thirty-seven, Olson went on to publish, among other works, "The Kingfishers," a mosaic-like poem that literary critic Paul Christensen claims "ushered in postmodernism" (a term that Olson has been widely credited with coining). Soon thereafter, Olson started teaching at North Carolina's Black Mountain College. In 1950, Olson published *Projective Verse*, his influential poetic manifesto that rejected writing according to closed or "academic" principles—meter, line, form, and meaning—in favor of writing "open" verse according to the poet's breath, the sound of language, the openness of the page or "field," and letting content dictate form. In other words, poems were not meant to be contained structures; they were meant to project and transfer their subject's energy to the reader. As Olson once said, "A Foot Is to Kick With," referring to both the appendage and the poetic foot of classical meter. A movement was launched. The Black Mountain Poets, who followed Olson's projectivist principles, included Robert Creeley, Denise Levertov, Joel Oppenheimer, and Ed Dorn. They were closely affiliated with the New York School and became a major influence on the Beats.

By 1951, Olson was appointed Black Mountain College's rector and president ex officio. Around that time his correspondence with Gloucester poet Vincent Ferrini formed the beginning of his *Maximus Poems*. Though Olson was then primarily living in North Carolina, he regularly visited Cape Ann, which was undergoing a dramatic change.

Since the colonial era, the small drawbridge crossing the Cut had been the only overland way to Cape Ann. But in 1948, Massachusetts State Route 128 was extended over the newly built A. Piatt Andrew Bridge. As Cape Ann became better connected to the outside world, Olson and many others began to feel that the island was becoming less like Cape Ann—a relatively isolated community that had kept its distinct character in a world that was rapidly homogenizing.

Written over a twenty-year period, the *Maximus Poems* is a sprawl-
ing, six-hundred-page epic-cum-manifesto against Cape Ann's modern-
ization in which the poet exhorts readers to see Gloucester as he did: a
timeless, mythical setting. The poems' narrator, who is a combination of
Olson and the second-century A.D. philosopher Maximus of Tyre (the
Phoenician city to which Rev. John Wise had compared Gloucester in
1721), urges Gloucester's "polis" to "let them not make you / as the nation is." To argue his point, Olson filled the *Maximus Poems* with details
of what distinguished Gloucester from other places—its geological history; stories of contemporary and historic residents; colonial records,
including ship manifests, logbooks, nautical charts, store accounts, and
legal disputes; Josiah Batchelder's 1741 First Parish survey—and fused
these with references to Greek, Norse, Algonquian, Mayan, and Sume-
rian mythologies; tarot cards; zodiac signs; and Olson's personal history.
The poems read kaleidoscopically, creating a dazzling array of associations. Underneath their intricate allusions there is a man, at turns vulnerable and bold, passionately pleading with his reader to embrace the
physical setting of his beloved historic port, its history, and the mythic
significance with which he imbues it. And in these poems Dogtown
inspires Olson's most far-reaching spiritual and mythological associations. Marsden Hartley, who filled his Dogtown paintings with so much
lifelike energy, was another important influence on the poet.

One cold spring day in 1953, Olson was visiting from Black Mountain and drove into Dogtown to find the Whale's Jaw, which he had
recalled from Hartley's paintings and a photograph of his father posing
inside the monolith as if he were pushing its jaws apart. Olson had once
met Hartley quite by accident in the early 1940s, when the painter
dropped in unannounced at novelist Edward Dahlberg's Greenwich
Village apartment, where Olson was staying. Olson, flustered by the
surprise of such an esteemed guest, offered Hartley some tea but mistakenly served him a cup of plain hot water instead. Without noticing
his gaffe, Olson went on to talk incessantly about poet Hart Crane, having no idea that Crane's 1932 suicide had plunged Hartley into a deep
depression. Hartley took offense and left without saying a word. Olson
was chagrined, but never lost his admiration for Hartley or his work.

In "Letter 7," which comes toward the beginning of the *Maximus
Poems*, Hartley is a creative father figure the poet struggles to follow:

But what he did with that bald jaw of stone,

> *(my father differently usurped it,*
> *took it as he took nature, took himself*
> *until all bosses struck him down)*

such cloth he turned all things to,
made palms of hands of gulls,
Maine monoliths apostles,
a meal of fish a final supper
—made Crane a Marseilles matelot

Such transubstantiations

> *as I am not permitted,*
> *nor my father,*
> *who'd never have turned the Whale Jaw back*
> *to such humanness. . . .*

Olson eventually found Dogtown's animated "humanness" in the second volume of the *Maximus Poems*, which he began working on in late 1959.

That November, Olson's friends—editor Don Allen and writers LeRoi Jones (now Amiri Baraka) and Michael McClure—came to Gloucester for a visit. Olson took them to a Dogtown field that once belonged to a legendary Gloucester sailor named James Merry and told them his story. In the late 1800s, Merry had sailed to Spain and charmed his way into a bullfighting competition, which he won. After returning to Gloucester, Merry pastured a two-month-old bull calf in Dogtown and began to wrestle it regularly. The bull grew larger and stronger, as did Merry's boasts about his ability to subdue the beast. When townspeople reacted skeptically, Merry invited them to watch him fight the bull. Arriving in Dogtown on the appointed day, people discovered a bull peacefully grazing in a pasture strewn with blood and gore. The bull had smashed Merry upon the rocks. Olson showed his friends the rock inscriptions commemorating James Merry's death: "1st Attacked" and "Jas Merry died Sept 18, 1892." While telling them this story, Olson, who stood six-foot-eight and had a powerful, commanding presence, moved across the pasture as if being in the very place where the drama had taken place enabled him to channel all the hubris and violence that were bound up in the tale and to actively bring them to life in his narration. But being in Dogtown meant this was no ordinary New England pasture. The spirit of the place was there, too, and Olson was gathering up its energy for the poem he planned to write as soon as his guests departed.

In *MAXIMUS, FROM DOGTOWN—I,* Olson captured the vigorous spirit of this telling in situ. He also drew allusions between Merry and Melville's Billy Budd and populated Dogtown with various ancient gods and spirits. In Olson's version of events, when James Merry dies next to Dogtown's "Soft soft rock," he is not alone.

> *The four hundred gods*
> *of drink alone*
> *sat with him*
> *as he died*
> *in pieces*
>
> *In 400 pieces*
> *his brain shot*
> *the last time the bull*
> *hit him pegged him*
> *to the rock*
>
>> *before he tore him*
> *to pieces*
>
>> *the night sky*
> *looked down*

The sky watches, as if it knows something. To Olson, eternal, living spirits are everywhere and in everything, including the rocks inside Dogtown, "this / park of eternal / events."

Olson soon began expanding his Dogtown research with title deeds and other historic records, which he used to amplify his larger, poetic aim: to project through the poem *all* of the energies or spirits bound up in its actual, physical setting, what Olson called "an actual earth of value." This was not just some poetic conceit. Olson believed that places have a spirit, if not a consciousness of their own—what Hartley referred to as "livingness"—that also shapes human consciousness. Olson once wrote, "Anybody that's ever lived on this earth knows that the earth is the geography of our being."

To capture his philosophy on the page, Olson covered his apartment walls with Dogtown maps marked with settlers' names and set out to "map" Gloucester's past and various energies along Dogtown's two principal roads, which became the structural bases for the second volume of the *Maximus Poems*. Sometimes he composed his poems at a tree-stump-cum-writing-stand in a Dogtown orchard to better infuse his work with the spirit of the place.

Throughout the span of Olson's opus, he continued to push the boundaries of poetic form and content. The poems become visually dynamic. Words cascade and tumble across the page as in a waterfall, or take the form of arcs and rays in imitation of landscapes and maps. They run to the page's far corners, shooting outward, expanding on his idea that the page is a field, a map of experience and energy. These field compositions come across as extended thought gestures, the poetic parallel to action painting. (Olson, in fact, wondered why poems were not commissioned like paintings.)

When "the Mighty O," as he was sometimes called, read his work aloud, he exuded a cool yet enigmatic reserve as if the verses themselves were living, breathing extensions of his being. At his tiny Stage Fort apartment, he sometimes performed his poems as a modern dance, twisting and shaping words into ephemeral, physical forms. He once challenged Vincent Ferrini to a poetic sparring/dance match during a crowded party. The two men, both of whom stood well over six feet tall, jousted with off-the-cuff lines and wild, expansive gestures—Olson's poetic transfer of energy was no passive thing.

In 1964, Olson's wife died in a car accident that some think may have been a suicide. Olson worried that his singular focus on his career and lack of attention to his wife had brought on her death. He also became increasingly aware of his own mortality. Meanwhile, urban renewal, or "renewal by destruction," as Olson liked to call it, had arrived in Gloucester, and the rate at which the three-hundred-year-old cityscape was changing began to accelerate. Olson turned his interest away from Dogtown to the city's harborfront downtown—parts of which were being razed and replaced with modern buildings—and its wetlands, which were being filled in to accommodate additional construction. He began writing letters to the editor of the *Gloucester Daily Times* in protest. In one such letter titled "A Scream to the Editor," he protested the razing of a historic building. In another he urged the city to restore its original seventeenth-century selectmen and colonial commons system. Olson had previously found a poetic wellspring of timelessness in the city's landscape; in its changes he saw premonitions of his own death, as captured in the first stanza of his beautiful, haunting poem "COLES ISLAND":

> *I met Death—he was a sportsman—on Cole's*
> *Island. He was a property-owner. Or Maybe*
> *Cole's Island was his. I don't know. The*
> *point was I was there, walking, and—as it*
> *often is, in the woods—a stranger, suddenly*
> *showing up, makes the very thing you were do-*
> *ing no longer the same. That is suddenly*
> *when you thought, when you were alone, and*
> *doing what you were doing, changes because someone else*
> *shows up. He didn't bother me, or say anything. Which is*
> *not surprising, a person might not, in the circumstances;*
> *or at most a nod or something. Or they would. But they wouldn't,*
> *or you wouldn't think to either, if it was Death. And*
> *He certainly was, the moment I saw him. There wasn't any question*
> *about that even though he may have looked like a sort of country*
> *gentleman, going about his own land. Not quite. Not it being He.*

Olson once wrote that Gloucester's geography "forever . . . leans in / on me." Now, each time a part of his mythic landscape was destroyed, it took a piece of him with it.

A few years later, while he was in England researching Gloucester's first settlers, Olson learned of the city's plans to tear down a condemned 1713 house to straighten a bend in the road. This sharp turn, which dated to the 1620s, was a remnant of Gloucester's colonial past, something no modern road planner would allow. To Olson, the house and bend were important relics that, though mundane, gave him "a sense of auspice of life and being." Hoping to save both, Olson immediately sent a cable to city hall, asking if he could have the house. The city agreed, but only if he would move it off the land in the next six months and pay the relocation expenses; they would still straighten the bend. Olson came back to town and put $2,500 in escrow, part of which came from a National Academy of Arts and Sciences award he had recently received. But in the end, Olson could not pull the money together in time. The house was razed, and the city later abandoned its plan to straighten the bend.

Olson's career had long been thriving. By the mid-1960s he was internationally famous and had become something of a literary cult figure. In 1965 alone, he was invited to read at the Festival of Two Worlds in Spoleto, Italy; the PEN International Congress in Bled, Yugoslavia; and the Berkeley Poetry Conference, where he was chosen over Ed Dorn, Allen Ginsberg, and Robert Creeley for the event's most honored slot as its final reader. In addition to the National Academy of Sciences award, he received other literary prizes, including two Guggenheim Foundation grants. He had also published the first two volumes of the *Maximus Poems* and other works. The "Big Fire Source," as novelist Robert Duncan called him, was burning bright. But when yet another part of Gloucester's landscape faced destruction, this time the filling in of a historic wetland to build a car dealership, Olson wrote, "The soul of man is worth more than the sale of automobiles." Gloucester's changing landscape continued to have a devastating effect upon him.

Like many midcentury avant-garde artists, Olson did not attain his consciousness-expanding states unaided. He experimented with psychoactive drugs and was one of Timothy Leary's guinea pigs at the Center for Personality Research. In 1966, Olson's friend and fellow poet Ed Dorn claimed that "all the drinking and the pills" were catching up to him. (Robert Creeley once got the impression that Olson was "working his way through the whole history of drugs in America in about two weeks.") Olson had been hospitalized at various times over the years with heart problems and emphysema, but by 1968 friends began to wonder if he was more seriously ill than he wanted them to know. A young poet about Gloucester named Linda Crane began helping him take care of himself—the two also became romantically involved—but others observed that Olson was truly not well. In 1969, an audio engineer from the Beatles' record label, Apple Records, came to his Stage Fort home to record Olson reading his poems for possible release. During the session, Olson pointed out something on one of the many maps that covered his walls but seemed not to notice that the maps were so badly faded they were nearly blank. He later wrote in one of his notebooks, "I drink to live to go further," but like the landscape that was disappearing around him, Olson was already too far gone. As if he knew death was near, he began drawing the *Maximus Poems* to a close. Toward their end, this place that had so passionately inspired Olson for so long becomes a void:

> *the fake*
> *which covers the emptiness*
> *is the loss . . .*
>
> *Gloucester too*
> *is out of her mind and*
> *is now indistinguishable from*
> *the USA.*

Dogtown was the Gloucester that became lost in the 1800s, while Gloucester, Olson's muse, was now lost to him. "I despise Gloucester," Olson told his former student Charles Boer after moving in the summer of 1969 to Connecticut to take an academic appointment that Boer, now a professor, had arranged for him. Four months after leaving Gloucester, Charles Olson died from cancer of the liver.

Charles Olson had revolutionized American poetry, but his impassioned poems, though they celebrated much of what made Gloucester so unique, could not change the direction the city was taking. Today Olson is virtually unknown outside literary circles, but his passion for Gloucester would influence a generation of Cape Ann individuals. After Anne Natti's death, some of these people would work to save Dogtown. But like the effects of Gloucester's changes upon Olson, Anne Natti's death would eventually bring on a dispiriting change of heart for many.

Chapter Twenty-one

The Masked Man in Yellow

P ETER HODGKINS SURVIVED his suicide attempt and was put on special watch. On Tuesday, July 3, he waited in a Gloucester police department holding cell before Dr. David Swenson, director of the Salem Court Clinic, presented the findings of his psychiatric evaluation to the Gloucester district court. Outside of Hodgkins's cell, Officer John Brosnan pulled two chairs together, propped his feet up on one, and opened the *Gloucester Daily Times*. Brosnan, who knew Hodgkins and his father, looked back over his shoulder and asked Hodgkins if he wanted anything.

"No," he replied.

Brosnan's paper crinkled loudly as he turned a page. Silence settled back in around them.

"Did you read about my case in the *Times?*" Hodgkins asked.

"No." Brosnan kept scanning the paper. Even if he had read about Hodgkins's case, there would be no discussing it.

It was quiet again. Disturbingly so, at least for Hodgkins.

"I'm pissed off about the stories in the *Times*," Hodgkins volunteered. "Most of what was said in the *Times* was wrong."

Brosnan turned another page.

"I was in the woods," Hodgkins said. Brosnan and everyone else already knew that. What of it?

"I was running out of food and cigarettes."

Brosnan held the paper up, as if making a tent to shelter his thoughts from the criminal his former neighbor had turned out to be. Hodgkins continued talking about how he had lost his job. His girlfriend was pregnant. He was desperate.

"I only meant to rob her," he claimed. "I didn't hit her hard. I hit her with a rock. It was a small rock." Hodgkins shed these words as if he were trying to molt, the shape of his story changing form. Brosnan buried himself deeper inside the rustling sheaves of newsprint.

Hodgkins kept talking, this time about army helicopter school. He may have mentioned his service as a warrant officer and helicopter pilot in Vietnam—experiences he would certainly tell other authorities about—describing the 157 chopper missions he had flown in Quang Tri and Soc Tran. Hodgkins claimed that he had crashed twice and suffered head injuries, a broken arm, and a leg injury that required extensive treatment and physical therapy, but he said he did not understand why when he applied for helicopter piloting jobs "halfway around New England," no one hired him. Hodgkins was now worried that he would never fly again.

It was a seemingly random comment, but an outfit called Trauma and Stress Consultants, Inc., would later claim that Hodgkins's actions that 1984 summer might have been caused by combat-induced post-traumatic stress disorder from his time in Vietnam. PTSD is an anxiety disorder that can occur after a traumatic event. It can make one feel either numb or agitated and experience traumatic flashbacks. And in some instances, PTSD has been found to provoke criminal behavior. But Hodgkins did not linger over his helicopter talk for long. He simply changed the subject to the time he "got into a lot of trouble with a woman when he was home on furlough" from the army. "I had to do a lot of fast talking to get out of that one," he said.

Hodgkins's words fell into the silence and evaporated. Brosnan didn't say a word.

Hodgkins reached through the quiet one more time: "When I left that girl she was alive," he insisted. "There was someone else nearby. He was on a dirt bike." But before Hodgkins could get any further with this new story, the bailiff arrived to escort him to the courtroom.

DR. SWENSON TOOK the stand to give his assessment of whether Hodgkins was criminally insane and/or mentally competent to stand trial.

The basic definition of a criminal is someone who consciously engages in wrongdoing or harmful activities, whereas someone who is criminally insane has a mental defect that makes it difficult, if not impossible, for him to understand the wrongfulness of his actions. While many defendants have psychological problems, few are actually found to be criminally insane. It is more common for a defendant to be insane *and* also have a criminal mind-set, meaning that he knows he is engaging in wrongdoing and is therefore criminally responsible. Competency to stand trial is a related but separate matter that gauges a defendant's understanding of the charges against him and his ability to actively assist in his own defense. A defendant can be found incompetent to stand trial because he does not understand the wrongfulness of his act or is incapable of assisting in his defense due to a mental defect or, in some cases, a severe physical condition.

Dr. Swenson stated that Hodgkins understood the charges against him and seemed capable of assisting in his own defense. But he recommended that Hodgkins undergo further evaluation at Bridgewater State Hospital for the Criminally Insane to determine if he were indeed criminally responsible. The judge ruled in favor of this recommendation; he most likely factored Hodgkins's weekend suicide attempt into his decision. Bridgewater not only had the appropriate psychiatry staff to conduct a more thorough evaluation, it was also better staffed to deal with potential suicides than other facilities in the state. But Bridgewater was not without its own problems.

In 1967, Bridgewater, which operates as both a mental hospital and a prison, achieved national notoriety for its inhumane conditions and abusive inmate treatment as captured in the documentary *The Titticut Follies*, a film that was banned for thirty years after its release out of concern that its graphic footage violated patient/inmate privacy laws. By 1975, Bridgewater had cleaned house. The state opened a new facility with a new medical staff that many judges believed was the best place in Massachusetts to send defendants such as Hodgkins, who were mentally ill and/or a potential risk to themselves and others. Hodgkins had actually been evaluated at Bridgewater in 1980, after his attack on Linda Crane, but by the time he returned there in July 1984, Bridgewater had become seriously overcrowded and was again the subject of ongoing allegations of inmate abuse. In fact, a federal lawsuit had just been settled earlier that year. As part of the settlement, the Department of Corrections agreed to curb the use of solitary confinement and physical restraints at the facility.

Because of a caseload backlog, Peter Hodgkins's 1984 stay at Bridgewater was extended from twenty to forty days. Bridgewater's deputy medical director, Dr. Robert A. Fein, eventually determined that Peter Hodgkins was criminally responsible *and* mentally fit to stand trial. He was released back to Essex County authorities. (Two weeks later, a Bridgewater inmate hanged himself in his cell.)

Immediately upon his release from Bridgewater, Hodgkins was scheduled to be transferred to the Salem Jail but was mistakenly sent to Gloucester. Because of the seriousness of his crime and prior suicide attempt, an officer was once again stationed to watch over him.

"Joe, I fucked up," Peter Hodgkins said to patrolman Joseph Aiello, who sat outside his cell. Aiello was yet another policeman Hodgkins knew from growing up in Riverdale; they had once lived on the same street. "I really fucked up this time. I have to tell you something. I have to tell somebody. I didn't do it. I witnessed this thing, but I didn't do it."

Aiello told Hodgkins he should not say anything else without his lawyer present and offered to call his attorney.

Instead of taking up his offer, Hodgkins asked, "Is Ed Hardy here?"

Sergeant Ed Hardy was an old neighbor of Hodgkins's who had known Peter "since he was a youngster." He also knew his father; Hodgkins considered him a friend.

Aiello got Hardy. "Sit down," Hodgkins said, "this is going to take some time. I want to tell you I was not alone." Hardy read Hodgkins his rights, and asked about Hodgkins's attorney, but Hodgkins said, "I don't care for my lawyer."

Hodgkins seemed not to care for lawyers in general. As soon as Edward O'Reilly was appointed his counsel at his arraignment, Hodgkins began talking about finding a different attorney. Four days later, when Hodgkins was back in court for his competency hearing, a lawyer named Lawrence Maguire was appointed to be his counsel. Things didn't work out with Maguire, either.

In 1984, the Essex County Superior Court had a list of five lawyers who took pro bono capital cases. Robert Kalis, a Salem-based criminal defense attorney with no Gloucester connections, was one of them.

Kalis had been appointed to the case in late July, but Hodgkins started talking to Sergeant Hardy as if he were the only person who could advocate for him.

Hodgkins later told the same story he recounted to Hardy to Gloucester reporter Wendy Quiñones, who covered his case for *Boston* magazine:

"I pulled off the trail, under some pines, and sat for ten or fifteen minutes. . . . A dog went by. . . . A minute later somebody walked by in yellow rain gear. . . . In less than a minute I started hearing another bike. On the hill where I was, the main trail is washed out. It's a steep upgrade. [The] other bike went by and then stopped. . . . Even I've fallen there, and I figured the guy might have fallen.

"I started to walk up the hill. I saw the bike laid down at the top of the hill, and about twenty feet further I saw another person. He had a rock and I saw him drop it on the back of the other person, headwise. The person went down and the guy picked her up and half carried her. She was still groggy. They started heading into the pines, off the trail.

"I went back to my bike and started walking in through the tree farm, figuring I'd come out somewhere close to where they were. . . .

"When I got to where I could see, he was sitting on her knees. I could see it was a girl; she was nude. I couldn't see what he was doing. He got up [and left]. I walked over to her. She was lying on her back, moving; her eyes were open and she was speaking but I couldn't understand what she was saying. I couldn't see her clothes.

"I tried to pick her up. I put an arm under her knees and tried to pick her up . . . [I] got hit from behind. I dropped her and fell over her.

"The other person had a yellow Yamaha riding suit, a yellow helmet, no gloves, and a face mask. . . . He came at me, and he had a hunting knife. I grabbed him, and we pushed each other down. I had him by the throat and ripped his face mask off. I saw who it was. . . .

"He threatened to kill me in such a way that if I said anything to anybody he'd go after my girlfriend. . . . I got up and started running through the pines. . . .

"At the police station the state trooper asked questions. Dave Reardon asked questions. I couldn't understand what they were saying. When I walked in, I was worried, scared. At one point I even cried. They started asking questions back and forth, back and forth. They asked me to describe the area where this happened, so I did. They asked,

'Would you go back there? Just to give us a rough idea where it was?' . . . During the questions, half the time I wasn't sure what I was saying. I can't even remember what I was saying. . . . There were no other witnesses. Nobody saw me that day. . . . Nobody else was in the woods the day it happened. If I'd told them I wasn't there, I wouldn't be here. That police statement, half of it isn't what I said. . . . All the *I's* I'm going to deny."

It is not unusual for a defendant awaiting trial to backpedal and re- vise a statement, but Peter Hodgkins's new story was a literal revision- ing of the murder with a vanishing point in the center—the identity of the killer.

Either Hodgkins was now merely lying in an attempt to wheedle his way out of the charge or he was innocent and had confessed to the murder to avoid retribution from the real killer. Then again, he might also have been suffering from some form of PTSD, which influenced either his killing of Anne Natti or a false confession. It was also plausi- ble that he had in fact killed Anne Natti but genuinely believed he was innocent—in other words, he could have been delusional. With Peter Hodgkins, it seemed that any of these scenarios was possible.

Hodgkins's suicide attempt did not shed much light on the situa- tion. He had either acted out of remorse or out of desperation about his situation. But the white heat of his attempt on his own life had cooled by the time he got to Bridgewater. Dr. Fein's report explicitly stated that Hodgkins did not show any signs of depression, strain, or duress stemming from the charges against him.

MEANWHILE, AFTER Anne Natti's vigil, various local natural history ex- perts, city officials, and Dogtown aficionados signed on to join the Dog- town Steering Committee. They met with Mayor Richard Silva and gave their assessment of the problems that confronted the area. The committee also organized a volunteer cleanup day to haul away the trash, including the skeletons of cars that had been burned for insur- ance money, abandoned appliances, and other junk that had been dumped there over the years. Before making any decisions about how to proceed with Dogtown's management, the Steering Committee began conducting a study of the area's history, geology, and flora and fauna. By late August, local botanists, ornithologists, historians, geologists, land-use consultants, and the like were turning binoculars, magnifying glasses, and cameras on Dogtown to begin figuring out what—and who—was truly there.

Soon thereafter, Robert Kalis, Hodgkins's lawyer, successfully advanced a motion with the court to hire a private investigator to also search the area for the masked man in yellow.

IN THE MONTHS leading up to Hodgkins's trial, which was scheduled to open in March 1985, Hodgkins was confined to the Salem Jail, then the oldest continually operating jail in the country. The Old Salem Jail, as it is called today, is located in the heart of the city's downtown and overlooks a cemetery where colonist Giles Corey, a farmer accused of witchcraft at age eighty in 1692, was pressed to death with stones for refusing to stand trial. This being Salem, people say Corey's ghost haunts the facility, even though the jail that stood in Corey's time was replaced in 1813. This newer building, known as the "Stone Gaol," was constructed with granite from Cape Ann's quarries. The same type of stone that Hodgkins had used to kill Anne Natti now walled him in.

Kalis had an office in downtown Salem just a few blocks down the street from the jail and regularly walked there to meet with Hodgkins. They would sit at a corner table in the jail's library, where other inmates would be reading up on law for a deeper understanding of the charges against them and trying to find any angle their attorneys could use to help their cases.

In his thirty-two years as a criminal defense attorney, Robert Kalis had never met anyone like Peter Hodgkins. Kalis, who was in his midfifties, had previously taken five court-appointed murder cases that carried mandatory life sentences. Out of these clients, Peter Hodgkins was the only one who repeatedly insisted he was innocent. Kalis took Hodgkins at his word.

As Kalis reviewed evidence in the case, it began to seem wholly plausible that Hodgkins, who, after forty-eight hours of running and fearing for his life, with dogs and helicopters and men coming after him with loaded guns, had come into the police station in a completely deranged state. Hodgkins told Kalis that he had not eaten or slept in two days and was pressured and coaxed with promises of food and sleep as rewards for his confession. In spite of Peter Hodgkins's size, Kalis found him to be "pretty docile" and eager to please. Hodgkins then told Kalis that his confession "was what I thought they wanted me to say," as if it was simply something he made up out of fear and a willingness to get out of a pressured situation. Add to this that Hodgkins was the outsider, the kid who had always been scorned. And here were his old neighbors, the same people with whom he had probably always wanted to fit in, even some of the ones who might have bullied him, who were able to coax the story out of him without any struggle. Kalis strongly believed that Hodgkins had been manipulated into making the confession that was tantamount to giving his life away. Hodgkins was inscrutable and strange, to be sure, but being strange did not make him guilty.

Though there was blood on the bike and under Hodgkins's fingernails, by September an FBI lab determined that the blood samples were too limited for conclusive grouping and could not be typed to Peter Hodgkins, Anne Natti, or anyone else for that matter. (DNA testing was not put into forensic practice in the United States until 1987.) It was a much-needed break that bolstered Hodgkins's case, but the odds were still stacked against him. Kalis needed to overcome the most damning pieces of evidence: Hodgkins's two confessions. Doing that required convincing the jury that Peter Hodgkins was the type of person who, might easily be coerced into falsely confessing under extreme duress. Kalis simply had to get more information from him.

Hodgkins, ever courteous, would listen attentively to Kalis, but as soon as Kalis finished explaining what he needed for the sake of his defense, Hodgkins would say, "Can you give me three bucks for candy?"

It was nearly always the same response.

"You mean you were sitting here pretending to listen and this whole time you were waiting to ask me for money to buy candy?" Kalis would ask.

Yes. Candy or cigarettes.

To Kalis, Hodgkins's response was mind-boggling, but he always made sure there was a little something in Hodgkins's commissary account for cigarettes or sweets.

Hodgkins's disinterest in his own case became a mounting concern for Kalis. After the private investigator reported that he never found anyone or any clues leading to the mysterious man in yellow, another FBI lab report came back with a positive match between hair and fibers found on Brian Langley's motorbike and Anne Natti. The hairs in particular were now the strongest link between Hodgkins and Anne Natti's murder. Taken together with the confessions, they pretty much confirmed his guilt. Yet Hodgkins continued to insist that he was innocent.

At some point that same autumn, Hodgkins attempted suicide again, this time by lacerating his throat at the Salem Jail. He survived this second effort to kill himself, but his seeming disregard for his own life alarmed Kalis, who began to wonder if Hodgkins was truly competent to stand trial. He successfully advanced a motion persuading the court to hire a private psychiatrist to give Hodgkins another criminal responsibility and competency evaluation.

In mid-October, Dr. Stevan Gressitt, a clinical psychiatrist who worked in the Lynn, Massachusetts, courthouse, spent three hours interviewing Peter Hodgkins. Hodgkins did not want to go back to Bridgewater, not even for one day's worth of tests, but Dr. Gressitt sent him back to the facility on November 26, 1984, for an in-depth neurological examination. And in mid-December, Dr. Gressitt sent Hodgkins to a private laboratory in Brookline for an additional battery of tests to discern if Hodgkins suffered from either a neurological impairment or a medical condition that could have made him criminally irresponsible.

While waiting for these results, Dr. Gressitt began interviewing Peter Hodgkins's family, former teachers, and coworkers, and also examining Hodgkins's criminal, military, and school records. One of the things Dr. Gressitt pieced together from these records and that Hodgkins's family confirmed was that Peter Hodgkins never attended flight school. And he never went to Vietnam.

Chapter Twenty-two

The Geography of Being

URING THE SUMMER of 2002, New York was still pulsing with a sense of loss from the events of September 11 and anxiety over the potential for another terrorist attack. And although the intensity of these feelings had waned, their persistence overwhelmed me. Hoping to find a way to restore some sense of normalcy, I made a plan to divide my graduate school summer break between Cape Ann and Maine with a trip home to see family in Georgia.

One reason I preferred going north, especially to Cape Ann, was that each time I went home to Marietta, Georgia, I would get lost. One patch of kudzu-covered woods that had been a landmark for much of my life would disappear, then another. Strip malls, subdivisions, and new roads that went places I did not know soon followed. The woods and farms that once seemed to expand for miles in all directions had been boxed into vanity strips framing these developments, creating the illusion of depth where none existed. Nathaniel Hawthorne wrote, "Nothing gives a sadder sense of decay than this loss or suspension of the power to deal with unaccustomed things, and to keep up with the swiftness of the passing moment. It can merely be a suspended animation; for, were the power actually to perish, there would be little use of immortality. We are less than ghosts, for the time being, whenever this calamity befalls us." My hometown may have been thriving, but what made it home to me—the landscape I knew as a child—was disappearing. Going home made me feel as if I had become a ghost of myself in search of some place, some thing, someone gone.

Kennesaw Mountain is the one place that has remained relatively unchanged. Marking the southern end of the Appalachian foothills, this 1,808-foot-tall granite mound was the site of an important Civil War battle. Growing up, I took my dog to the mountain nearly every day after school. We ran along trails that flex and twist for 18 miles over Kennesaw Mountain National Battlefield Park's 3,000 rolling acres. The park, which is roughly the same size as Dogtown, encompasses two mountains, two prominent hills, a forest, expansive fields, and a restored 1836 farmhouse. And while, like in Dogtown, I only occasionally saw other people there, the experience of being at Kennesaw was nearly the opposite of visiting Cape Ann's interior.

Though 5,350 soldiers died in the Battle of Kennesaw Mountain (whose name is derived from the Cherokee word *gah-nee-saw*, meaning cemetery or burial ground), the park has never felt funereal or haunted to me, which is not to say that it is at a loss for spirit. Perhaps because the mountain belongs to a dominant narrative, the Civil War, its ghosts don't seem to be searching for an ending, a resting place. No matter what side of the conflict the soldiers who died on Kennesaw Mountain were on, or the hardships they endured, I like to think they died with a sense of purpose. Or maybe it is because "the mountain"—as we locals call the park in its entirety—which is neither wild nor wholly tame, is so well kept that it seems to take care of itself, though I know this is not the case. The National Park Service owns and tends to the land and enforces state and federal laws, as well as a few of its own, such as a curfew and the prohibition of mountain bikes, camping, and use of metal detectors. I rarely saw a park ranger there, but every so often one would ride through on horseback, wearing a wide-brimmed hat and shiny steel-toed boots. More often, an employee could be seen off in the distance riding a giant mower across a large field. These fields partly account for the extreme difference between Dogtown and the mountain. Most of Dogtown's open space has filled in with trees, whereas Kennesaw goes from trees to wide, rolling fields. The woods are open enough that fingers of light stream through them with a liquid clarity that washes away all eeriness. And while one can go to the northern side of Kennesaw Mountain to a Park Service welcome center, as more than a million visitors do annually, and watch a video about the battles and tour an exhibit, the rest of the park is significantly less trafficked. But the previously underexplored parts of the park have changed in recent years, along with the view from the mountaintop.

When I was younger, I could look out from Kennesaw's summit and see Atlanta, which is twenty-five miles away, a little less than Boston is from Dogtown. Now, a curtain of smog hides this view. Looking out from Kennesaw makes me feel anxious, trapped. I begin to worry about the air, the trees, the birds, the people, the strip malls, the roads, the cars, the huge crush of something I wanted to stop but could not: growing up in the suburbs made me part of it.

That Dogtown, a jumble of property of known and unknown ownership and lackadaisical management, continues to exist as close to Boston as Kennesaw Mountain is to Atlanta, amazed me. And though by this particular summer I understood more about Dogtown's mysterious origins and decline, I still could not stop marveling over how this forgotten American landscape had remained undeveloped with its wild, abandoned atmosphere intact, particularly given its proximity to Boston. I did not yet know the complications that were involved in bringing this land back from its recent nadir after Anne Natti's murder, but I was interested in more than just facts. Being at Kennesaw had brought me back in touch with how very different Dogtown *feels* from most places. While it was clear that the distinct aura Dogtown emanates could not be pulled up to expose its roots and held to the light—whatever lends the place its unique presence is too elusive for that—this mysterious quality had inspired such rich lore, eccentric carving projects, poems, and paintings, including that object of my obsession, Hartley's *Mountains in Stone*. In this painting, a lone stone works its way above a surrounding jumble of rocks. I hoped that finding the site of the painting's creation and experiencing its "actual earth of value," to use Olson's turn of phrase, would similarly help me rise up out of the sense of loss and anxiety that had weighed me down in New York and that Kennesaw Mountain could no longer assuage. I had not yet exhausted every nook and cranny of Cape Ann's secret woods in search of *Mountains in Stone*, but made it my goal to do so right away.

LUCKILY, THAT SAME SUMMER I was invited to stay with one of Dogtown's tending spirits, Carolyn O'Connor, a former Gloucester city
councillor who had overseen the town's Watershed Advisory Committee for seven years. Because the Babson Reservoir and Goose Cove Reservoir, two of Gloucester's main water sources, were in Dogtown,
Carolyn had been heavily involved in protecting the place.

Decorative lobster buoys painted in bright stripes hung from trees
in front of Carolyn's august nineteenth-century sea captain's home. As
I waited for her to come to the door, I admired her widow's walk and
multiple balconies that looked out onto Wonson's Cove and Gloucester's outer harbor. The scene reminded me of a Winslow Homer painting in which a woman in a long, white Victorian dress stands in front of
a similar house and looks out to the sea. Carolyn, who was in her early
sixties and sported highlighted short brown hair and glasses, opened the
door, leaned out, introduced herself, and said, "It's beautiful out. Let me
show you around."

Wearing a short-sleeved shirt patterned in varying shades of blue
and aquamarine that looked like a watercolor impression of the sea,
Carolyn seemed to be the essence of water. She gingerly made her way
to the garage and located a wooden oar that she leaned on as if it were
a cane. We walked across her lawn to a deck that overlooked the cove.
Carolyn then began telling me about the scarcity of fresh water on "island" Gloucester and the years she spent trying to protect its primary
source, an aquifer "just loaded with water" underneath Dogtown, the
same one that fed the Babson Reservoir.

As we were talking, Carolyn suddenly swept her arm in a broad arc,
gesturing to the other side of the cove. She pointed out all the land-
marks in sight: the houses where Marsden Hartley had lived in 1920
and 1931, Niles Beach, the mansions along Eastern Point, the Dog Bar
breakwater and lighthouse, and the outer harbor. The sun was setting
behind us, casting a warm, pink glow over the scene. A perfectly formed
half moon was on the rise. "Would you look at that?" Carolyn asked,
oozing contentment. "Just gorgeous."

Carolyn returned to her story and explained that though Roger W.
Babson's 1,150 Dogtown acres are protected under state and federal
wetlands legislation, some developers on Cape Ann, whom she referred
to as "a bunch of cowboys," have a way of ignoring the laws. "If we get

one toxic spill up there," Carolyn explained, "and cook the water supply, we're gonzo."

"Did you monitor the boundaries when you were on the committee?" I asked.

"Sometimes, but the main man on the ground was Joe Orange.
You've heard of him?"

Had I ever. At this stage I had been visiting Cape Ann for almost a
year and a half and had spoken to a fair number of people. Nearly all of
them mentioned Joe Orange and volunteered their opinions on Dogtown's septuagenarian constable who wears shorts year-round and
crashes through the woods, commando-style, to issue citations to people for what were, in their opinion, innocuous activities such as drinking alcohol or smoking pot. No one ever called him "Joe" or "Mr.
Orange," just "Joe Orange," or sometimes a string of expletives that they
tossed off like a handful of tiny firecrackers; the man clearly incited ire.
And though most of these people said the name Joe Orange as soon as
I said the word "Dogtown," few had ever seen him there or elsewhere.
Yet they all claimed to know he was in the woods. To the people of
Gloucester, Joe Orange and Dogtown seemed to have a lot in common:
ever present, but rarely directly experienced; the subject of various bits
of lore; thorny and rough around the edges, but maybe not so bad at
heart.

Numerous rumors concerning Joe Orange had been floated past me,
all of them rife with contradictions. Joe Orange has breakfast every
Friday morning at Sailor Stan's, each day he goes to the YMCA and
works out for hours, he then "runs across Dogtown with a backpack full
of chains" as part of his workout regimen. He had "saved Dogtown," he
was "single-handedly destroying Dogtown," he "knew what was best for
Dogtown," he "controlled City Hall," he "spent winter nights atop
Mount Washington in blinding snowstorms," he "spends every evening
at Wheeler's Point to watch the sunset," he lied about his age to enlist
in World War II, he "slit enemy throats behind the lines at the Battle of
the Bulge," he was in his eighties, he was in his sixties, he was "a teenager at heart," he was violent, he "runs around the Common goosing
butterflies"—in other words, wasting his efforts. I could find him "out
chasing after a car, biting at the tires" or "setting dogs off their leashes."
He walked up to a friend of mine who was very involved with Gloucester's only synagogue, asked him if he was Jewish, and then confided that

he, Joe Orange, was "actually a Jew," too. That was funny, my friend said.
Everyone in town always thought Joe was "more of a Nazi." Others alleged he was "a misanthrope," or "a misogynist," or simply "inconsistent
in his attitudes toward women." I heard that Joe was "a fucking idiot,"
an anarchist, a right-winger, a jackass, a bastard; that his father had dis-
owned him, that he had been raised in Dogtown by a pair of sea captains. No, Indians! No, wolves! One day the phone rang and he was
offered a substantial inheritance because his estranged father, who lived
in North Carolina, had died, but Joe Orange slammed down the receiver, refusing the money; he hasn't answered his telephone since.

At least the answering the telephone part of the story was true. Joe
Orange's number was unlisted, but according to Carolyn, he still
changed it every few months. I had knocked on his door once, but no
one answered. I also had been to Wheeler's Point, Sailor Stan's, and the
YMCA, hoping to bump into him. Out of all of these attempts to track
down Joe Orange, I only spotted him once, outside the Y. "Have a good
swim, Mr. Orange," the door attendant said before buzzing him through.
"Joe Orange!" I called out from behind a line of navy sailors in dress
whites, as if seeing the hyperfit, perfectly tanned elderly figure in shorts
and a baseball cap was like catching a fleeting glimpse of a celebrity. Joe
Orange looked over his shoulder, winked at me with a devilish grin on
his rugged face, and disappeared.

In 1984, after Anne Natti died and the Dogtown Steering Committee was planning to close the area to motorized vehicles, Joe Orange
wrote a guest column in the *Gloucester Daily Times:* "As for the Steering
Committee, a well meaning but totally unqualified body, the words of
the late Oliver Cromwell would seem to be in order. Speaking to the
long, do-nothing Parliament, the Lord Protector said, 'In the name of
God, go.'" Such was the essence of Joe Orange, people assured me: in-
corrigibly hard-assed and ornery, but passionate about protecting Dogtown.

"You *have to* talk to Joe Orange," Carolyn insisted as she pivoted
around her oar and led me past one of her summer rental properties,
the former summer residence of American Impressionist painter John
Twachtman, to the Wonson House, a smaller but no less handsome
Victorian home, where I was going to stay for a few weeks. "But finding
him is always a challenge."

After showing me the house's inner workings, Carolyn got down to business, giving me explicit instructions in the art of communicating with Joe Orange: letter-writing. "Just give him the facts," she explained. "Tell him Judy Peterson [the town archivist] gave you his name and that you are staying with me. Leave the address and number of the Wonson House and ask him to meet you at Sailor Stan's," which was just up the road. As if to entice me further, she added, "He has stories about Dogtown that will curl your nails."

"Write it tonight so it can go out in the six A.M. mail, then come on over. I have envelopes and stamps and will take you to the post office." And just like that, though it was past ten P.M. on a Sunday night and I had just driven five hours without stopping, I wrote a quick letter and walked across the street to Carolyn's house. As promised, she had an envelope and stamp waiting for me.

Soon after we got into Carolyn's old Mercedes, it was apparent that we were heading out for a moonlight drive with a little post office mailbox stop along the way. "When you live on the ocean," Carolyn advised, "you always have to take the scenic route."

As we explored the waterfront, Carolyn told me about city councillor Gaspar "Gap" LaFata, who had proposed building a historic theme park in Dogtown with costumed actors spinning wool and firing muskets just like at Virginia's Colonial Williamsburg and Massachusetts' Old Sturbridge Village. LaFata's proposal angered many people, most of whom found the idea ridiculous, but Carolyn was particularly averse to the plan because LaFata wanted to build in the watershed.

LaFata's "Pewter Pot and Muffin Shoppe," as people referred to his faux colonial village, sparked Carolyn's political awakening. Once her three children were old enough, she went to work as a congressional aide. After someone tipped her off that John "Cackle" Morse, a developer whom others had referred to as a "dirt merchant," was building an industrial park uncomfortably close to the watershed line, she made the move into local politics and ran for City Council.

I dropped my letter in a mailbox in front of the main post office, and Carolyn pointed the car not home toward Rocky Neck, as I had expected, but in the direction of Portugee Hill, so we could pass by Joe Orange's house. Carolyn just wanted to see if he was in town, or away in the White Mountains, as often was the case. We crept by an old Cape in need of serious upkeep and surrounded by a weather-beaten picket fence. A gray station wagon sat in the driveway. "You should hear from him by Tuesday," she proclaimed authoritatively, and continued up the steep hill.

Atop Portugee Hill, densely packed houses lined a ridge and suddenly ended at a small park and a jumble of barbed vines. Before Route 128 came through, one could walk from this hilltop to Dogtown's abandoned colonial village without encountering a paved road as Joe Orange used to do when he was a boy. I had never been up this way before, but Carolyn explained that this was also Dogtown and pointed to a few large granite boulders guarding a dense growth of wild rugosa roses that gleamed menacingly in the headlights.

Carolyn then told me about the time she was walking with Joe Orange near the Cackle Morse industrial park when they came across a page torn from a book that was floating on the surface of a puddle. They reached into the water and removed the paper. "Of all the places in the world and of all the poems ever committed to print, we had happened upon a copy of Edgar Allan Poe's 'The Raven.'" Carolyn spoke as though coming across a poem about death and madness in Dogtown was not just a random act; to her, Dogtown had conjured it. "It was a terrible omen of things that were going to come," she said, lowering her gaze at me.

Suddenly Carolyn turned to me and asked, "Are you comfortable in the woods by yourself?" I nodded and felt Carolyn fix me with a piercing stare that suggested she was not so sure about me. "The place just gives me the heebies," she said. "My son used to have these terrible dreams in which someone in Dogtown would be screaming and calling out to him. You know a young woman was murdered there?"

There she was again: Anne Natti. Why could people not just let her be? One woman dies in some woods *twenty years ago*—many people around this town did not even know her—but people still talk about it. Why is that? It would have been a fair enough question to ask, but I was at a complete loss for words.

I had originally hoped that finding the original site of *Mountains in Stone*, exploring this alternate, unsung America, and unearthing its myriad tales would complete some part of me. The surge of hope that rises up in *Mountains in Stone* is made all the more powerful because it comes out of such a melancholic, lonesome place, the same kind of place that I had felt inside ever since I had turned to those family ancestral portraits for comfort as a child. I kept coming back to Dogtown because Hartley's painting and story had opened up something in me that had long been shut down: the hope that I could better endure that anxious, lonely feeling that I had carried around with me for most of my life and that had recently engulfed me yet again. This was exactly what Dogtown had done for Hartley, and I hungered after its possibility to do the same for me. It was an altogether naive yearning, but it was mine. Now, each time someone so much as suggested that I should not go to Dogtown alone because of this murder, I felt angry.

Carolyn turned the car around to a lookout where we could see the city of Gloucester slope dramatically to the sea. We sat in silence for a while, watching the indigo night sky and the platinum-hued harbor glitter in the moonlight. I was stewing, feeling completely agitated, but the peaceful scene was slowly, quietly getting through to me.

That was how I slowly came to realize that the story of Anne Natti's murder and its impact upon the community was the *zuihitsu*, the Japanese calligraphic principle that following the brush would lead to its own story. It was not as though people had been carrying around Anne Natti's memory with them. My coming along asking about this place sent people back through that leafy, dark forest of memory to the shadowy place where they had hoped to leave this event behind. But a cold-blooded and brutal murder is not something that can be quietly forgotten. This type of random, unexpected violence can affect a community for decades to come. Yet the impact of Anne Natti's killing also served to sear even deeper into the collective conscience the already prevalent perception that Dogtown was a dark and dangerous place. As a result, Anne Natti's murder became all the more poignant and haunting. I had followed the brush not to a place that was of Hartley's making, but to one that called up the community's turning point, loss of innocence, and darkening perspective about this land.

IN BETWEEN MY EFFORTS to locate the site of *Mountains in Stone*, I continued to meet other people who had been involved with Dogtown in some way, including Peter Anastas, one of the volunteers who had vowed to help "take back the woods" after Anne Natti's death. Anastas, a Gloucester native, worked for a social services agency that helped destitute individuals who sometimes lived in Dogtown during the summer. He also possessed an intimacy with the area through childhood trips berry-picking with his grandmother and his teenage explorations there with a gentlemanly amateur naturalist group called the General James A. Cunningham Marching and Chowder Society, whose members had created the Dogtown Foundation along with Professor Norton.

After college and the completion of a Fulbright fellowship in Italy, Anastas was about to leave Gloucester again to enter a Ph.D. program when Charles Olson said, "Why are you going to Berkeley? There's graduate school right here at my kitchen table." Anastas stayed and began "studying" Gloucester along with others who had congregated in the elder poet's Fort Square apartment. Anastas's study yielded an oral history about Gloucester and other writings, mostly about the city. Prompted by Olson's ideas and an activist streak, Anastas also began fighting various proposals to develop Dogtown.

Nine years after Olson died—Anastas was a pallbearer at the poet's funeral along with Allen Ginsberg and six other literary and counterculture luminaries—Anastas, Gloucester writer Jonathan Bayliss (then conceiving an idea for an epic novel about Dogtown), and a science professor named Steve Heim set up a free four-year college that was roughly modeled on Black Mountain College, and invited any local with specialized knowledge to come teach. They named their program Dogtown College in honor of the collective ideal of the area's colonial commons and appointed Anastas as rector. Using the Cape Ann landscape as their classroom, Dogtown College's instructors held sessions around kitchen tables or outside and aspired to teach their fellow Cape Anners what they had learned from Olson: that "all the meanings of life" could be gleaned "through their place, because the destruction of place is like the destruction of life itself." After a few successful years in the early 1980s, the enthusiasm for Dogtown College waned, but not Anastas's enthusiasm for Olson's ideas, which drove him to take up the helm of the Dogtown Steering Committee in 1986 after its initial chairman, former Gloucester mayor Bob French, stepped down. Anastas ran the organization for ten years, but after retiring from this post he eventually stopped going to Dogtown altogether. And he claims he has not wanted to go back ever since.

"Everybody who goes to Dogtown says there's something magnetic about the place," Anastas told me one day as we were sitting at Carolyn's Wonson House, "there is something magical about it. People would go up to Dogtown to get away, but the darkness, the darkness is—I mean, don't people really need to be in touch with the subconscious? I think that's what Dogtown is for people: the subconscious." Anastas's big green eyes lit up underneath his dark, orbicular brow. He was an extremely animated talker whose short white hair and deep tan made him resemble Picasso. "It's sort of like everybody has to have a place to go, not just to escape, but to get to the other side of yourself." This was certainly one of my reasons for going there, as it was for many others. "People went to Dogtown with great delight, particularly in the summertime," Anastas said—he splayed his hands on the table between us and stretched his fingers wide in a gesture that reminded me of photographer Robert Doisneau's famous portrait of Picasso in which loaves of bread are substituted for the artist's hands—"but that still doesn't mean they weren't aware of the darkness. You see this in Gloucester. People accept the darkness." From my limited exposure to Gloucester thus far, it seemed that this acceptance of tragedy had long been part of life in this seafaring town. From its earliest seventeenth-century days to the present, thousands of Gloucester's lives had been lost at sea. Plus, the town's most emblematic stories—such as Henry Wadsworth Longfellow's poem "Wreck of the Hesperus," which was based on a true story about a shipwreck off Gloucester—had a sense of tragic inevitability. In the poem, an aged sea captain lashes his daughter to the ship's mast in a hurricane, hoping to save her from being swept overboard, but the vessel crashes upon an ominously named reef called Norman's Woe. The next day, a fisherman is horrified when he sees the dead girl's body, still tied to the mast, drift past the Gloucester shore. There are contemporary stories, too, such as the one about a man who, upon learning that his wife had died, walked straight into Gloucester Harbor and drowned himself. As much as people seemed to accept tragedy—if not despair— in this seaport community, it still struck me as odd that both Anastas and Carolyn O'Connor had worked to protect Dogtown but then put the place off-limits to themselves. "Is the darkness why you stopped going there, then?" I asked.

"For most of my life, Dogtown was in my bloodstream," Anastas replied, as if the area had been a life-sustaining part of him, "but then something changed." It was not because of Anne Natti's murder alone, but because of a dark foreboding sense he began to feel there. When he was in high school in the 1950s, a classmate's brother had shot his own best friend and allegedly buried the body in Dogtown. (This was the murder that Shep Abbott had been referring to when I first met him.) In 1982, the homeless man Donald Pinkham was found beaten to death up near the Babson Reservoir; then there was Anne. Three murders over a fifty-year period did not make a particularly dangerous or menacing place, but Anastas knew all the victims. There were other goings-on, too, which, over time, started to bother him. After Anastas had returned from Italy to Gloucester and sat at Olson's table, the elder poet talked about people who went to Dogtown, got lost, and were never found again. (I had heard similar stories myself. That they could not be verified did little to keep people from thinking that they might, in fact, be true.) Anastas was also friends with Olson's lover Linda Crane, the shaman who had instructed Shep Abbott about the rocks and whom Peter Hodgkins had attacked. ("It took her years to work through that," Anastas remarked, adding that Linda Crane took over the Dogtown Committee after he retired.) Then two people whom Anastas knew committed suicide there. Though Anastas had dedicated much of his life to protecting this land and helping its denizens, he wondered, "Why did all of these terrible things happen in this one place?"

When I met Anastas again a few days later at the Sunny Day Café to continue our conversation, it was obvious that he had been thinking about Olson's idea that place shapes consciousness with regard to Anne Natti's murder. "Dogtown is the wild part of Gloucester, the *uninhibited* part," he said, "and I think that, in a Jungian sense, Dogtown gave Peter Hodgkins permission to kill Anne Natti." Though I had considered Dogtown to be a powerful place, at least insomuch as the effect it had had on Marsden Hartley, Charles Olson, and other creative people was concerned, Anastas's statement had much stronger implications than notions of artistic inspiration. Dogtown was remote and isolated, a fact of geography that was only reinforced by its dark reputation. This reputation was primarily an artifact of folklore and rumor, at least until the years leading up to the early 1980s when it became increasingly neglected, a dump for trash and humans alike. When a place declines to such a state, it can start to seem as if bad things always happen there, as if the place itself is deeply troubled. But people make the place, and the place, in turn, makes the people. Did Dogtown's desolation inspire the mentally disturbed Hodgkins to escape from society to a place where he believed humanity's laws did not apply?

CURIOUS TO SEE if Peter Hodgkins's trial revealed any clues about what happened to make him pick up that rock on that ill-fated June 1984 Monday and kill an innocent woman in cold blood, I returned to the library and spooled up some microfilm. As the reel spun and the light flickered, it landed on a picture of Robert Kalis, Hodgkins's attorney, and prosecutor James Gribouski, surrounded by jurors standing in Dogtown and staring at the ground on a damp, early spring day.

Chapter Twenty-three

Into the Deep Woods

WEDNESDAY, MARCH 13, 1985, was a dreary, wet day, which to prosecutor James Gribouski, seemed perfectly fitting for starting the process of sending Peter C. Hodgkins Jr. away for life. Hodgkins's trial opened in Newburyport, an old seaport town along the Merrimack River, twenty-five miles north of Gloucester. Newburyport's Essex Superior Courthouse sits in the northeastern corner of the town's original 1645 commons, Bartlet Mall. In the late 1880s, Frederick Law Olmsted's partner Charles Eliot redesigned a pre-existing park to include a tree-lined promenade and a skating pond from the remnant of a geologic formation known as a kettle hole that was created by a chunk of ice from the same Pleistocene Epoch glacier that had filled Dogtown with boulders.

Both John Quincy Adams and Daniel Webster had tried cases in the redbrick courthouse, which was designed by Charles Bulfinch (architect of Boston's Faneuil Hall) and constructed in 1805. On July 1, 1976, three days before the Bicentennial, the radical group the Fred Hampton Unit of the People's Forces (named in honor of a slain Black Panther leader) attempted to blow up the courthouse in conjunction with bombings at Boston's Logan International Airport, the Dorchester National Guard Armory, and the Seabrook, New Hampshire, post office. The building survived the blast and remains the oldest continually operating courthouse in the country.

Before the trial began, Hodgkins's attorney, Robert Kalis, advanced a series of motions in an attempt to get the prosecution's most damning pieces of evidence—Hodgkins's confessions—thrown out of court. In the end, Kalis succeeded only with the statement Hodgkins had made to Officer John Brosnan when he was sitting in the Gloucester holding cell before being sent to Bridgewater—Brosnan never read Hodgkins his Miranda rights. Kalis also tried to get the court to toss out the inconclusive blood evidence, but to no avail. Meanwhile, the report that Kalis had commissioned from Dr. Gressitt concerning Hodgkins's criminal responsibility and competency to stand trial was scheduled to arrive that afternoon. Rather than wait for it, the elderly, soft-spoken Judge Paul Rutledge, Gribouski, and Kalis agreed to accept Bridgewater doctor Robert Fein's earlier assessment so the proceedings could commence as scheduled.

Once Hodgkins's trial began, the man on whom Anne Natti's death weighed most heavily, Erik Natti, felt a roomful of eyes on him and his family, who sat straight-backed and stern-faced in a corner of the second-story courtroom. All eyes were on Peter Hodgkins, too, whose face wore a blank, inscrutable expression. Hodgkins sat behind Kalis rather than at his side, as was customary at the Newburyport courthouse. Their table, like the old courtroom, was small by modern standards, especially for two big men such as Kalis, who stood around six feet, and the six-eight Hodgkins.

Good trial lawyers are like writers with heavily plotted stories and sharply defined characters. They lay out each detail precisely to create an illusion of seamless inevitability, leaving no room for doubt, no possibility for an alternate ending. Gribouski approached his statement to the twelve jurors in this timeworn fashion. "Now . . . you will hear the story of a tragedy," he began, and immediately expounded upon recently married Anne Natti's love of teaching and nature, her desire to be a good wife and stepmother, and the couple's plans to start a family of their own. What could be purer, more wholesome?

Gribouski completed his long opening statement, telling the jury that he was going to present thirty-four witnesses who would detail the manhunt and the conditions around Hodgkins's written statement and videotaped confession. Now it was the defense's turn, but surprisingly, Robert Kalis made no opening statement at all. Gribouski worried that the older, more experienced Kalis had a special trick up his sleeve.

As the prosecution brought up Linda Ryan, its first witness, Kalis kept looking over his shoulder, past an unmanacled Hodgkins, to Erik's children from his first marriage, Matthew and Diana, who sat with their father. It is well established that placing visible restraints on a defendant in the courtroom can prejudice the jury and impair the defendant's right to a fair trial. However, the defendant's right to attend his trial unrestrained is not absolute. If a defendant is considered a potential threat in the courtroom or a potential escapee, the judge can decide to place him in restraints. Kalis believed that Hodgkins was not one to act out violently, but he couldn't help but be a little bit concerned that something might potentially go awry. Matthew and Diana's presence continually reminded him of this.

Erik had fretted over his decision to bring his children to the trial. They had already lost their stepmother and their sense of safety, but now he was also concerned about the trial's potential impact on them. Ultimately, Erik decided that the best way for Matthew and Diana to gain closure was to see justice served. To protect them, though, he only allowed them to attend on days with less gruesome testimony. Yet, before there could be closure there had to be a reopening of the murder in all its heartrending detail. And though a victim's services advocate had helped Erik prepare for the trial, he did not realize how hard it would be until he, too, was summoned to the stand.

As a teacher, Erik was accustomed to being in front of a crowded room, but he also is an excruciatingly private, mild-mannered individual who can easily be mistaken for being meek. With an anxious look on his bearded face, Erik described how the ground had turned soft because of the rain and revealed footprints. All of the emotions and sensations of Monday, June 25, 1984, vividly came back to him. How Woofer came bounding out of the darkness with ripe, damp fur, tucked his tail at the sound of a bike, and led Erik into the thickening, deep woods, where Anne's rain pants glowed yellow.

When Erik spoke, benches creaked as people shifted forward in their seats, rapt with attention. Hodgkins sat motionless, his shadow looming over the proceedings.

"I touched her back," Erik said. "It was cold. She was dead."

Across the courtroom muffled, damp sounds rose. Husky, shallow breaths held back tears. Bags unzipped. Tissue wrappers crinkled.

Years later, Erik recalled that testifying had been so intense, he felt as though he were reliving that June 1984 day all over again, this time with a greater awareness of what he had actually experienced beneath the original moment's numbing shock. Erik was relieved that he had somehow managed to describe the scream he let out the moment he realized his wife was dead, rather than actually screaming on the witness stand. It was a small thing, but a major accomplishment.

Gribouski asked Erik to reach into a bag and remove the items inside, which were sealed in evidence bags. As Erik extracted the bloody raincoat, the courtroom stiffened. With each item, Gribouski asked, "Did this belong to your wife, Anne Natti?" Yes, Erik answered, and to each question that followed. One by one, he removed her pants, shirt, boots, turtleneck, and sweater. When Erik held up a green chamois shirt, a sound as though birds were being flushed from tall grass went up from the Phinney and Natti families; the shirt had been Anne's favorite. Erik continued with a blue shirt, her jeans, socks, belt, Erik's bandanna, Woofer's "in-town leash," and Anne's underpants, until he felt around in that bag, as if some final, forgotten trace of his wife could possibly have been hiding somewhere inside, but it was empty.

After Erik's testimony, the jury was instructed to dress for a hike for the following day's trip to Dogtown and then dismissed. It was just after lunchtime, but it had already felt like a long day.

DR. GRESSITT'S REPORT arrived at the courthouse that afternoon. In it, the doctor stated that the preponderance of Hodgkins's results on his medical and neurological tests fell well within normal ranges. Hodgkins had no condition that could have made him criminally irresponsible. A CT scan of his brain did reveal a prominent right temporal horn, common among schizophrenics, and suggested a potential loss of brain tissue in his medial temporal lobe, the region of the brain that processes memory. This, however, was not supported by any history of Hodgkins having memory problems. Through an examination of Hodgkins's prior criminal history, interviews with his family and acquaintances, and a review of his confessions, Gressitt concluded that he was fully capable of distinguishing between right and wrong. In his estimation, Hodgkins was not criminally insane.

As for his competency to stand trial, Hodgkins seemed to have no problem understanding the charges against him or the roles of the various members of the court. Yet, even though Dr. Gressitt had repeatedly reminded Hodgkins that the defense had hired him to help his case,

Hodgkins was uncooperative, and went from seeming to fear the doctor to showing open hostility toward him. Moreover, Hodgkins's multiple confessions and various statements after the fact were rife with inconsistencies. Placed in context with his history of lying, the doctor believed it was simply impossible to depend on anything Hodgkins might say. Thus, Dr. Gressitt seriously questioned Hodgkins's competency to stand trial.

Dr. Gressitt also thought that Hodgkins might be the type of person who would confess to a crime that he did not commit. Hodgkins's history of exposing himself, plus his boasts and outright lies—such as his invented stories about Vietnam—suggested that he had a serious need for attention, which could have led him to falsely confess for the sake of gaining notoriety.

Kalis was disappointed by the report. While it confirmed his suspicions about Hodgkins's incompetency to stand trial, he was hoping for a more definitive conclusion showing that his client was the type of person who could be easily manipulated by others. Kalis could then have made a stronger case to the jury that Hodgkins was likely to have falsely confessed under duress. Instead, most of Gressitt's report focused on Hodgkins's propensity to lie, which painted him in an unfavorable light and did nothing to advance the defense of his case.

That afternoon, Kalis gave Hodgkins a copy of the report in a courthouse side room where they had some privacy. Hodgkins read it over several times without saying a word. The air was tense, the room quiet. Suddenly, Hodgkins turned and slammed a windowsill with his handcuffed fists. There was nothing wrong with him, he declared. The commotion alarmed the tough and tetchy court officer Earl McCurdy, who came bounding into the room asking if everything was okay. Kalis assured McCurdy that Hodgkins was just a little upset over the report, and sent the officer away, but McCurdy was now on alert. McCurdy, an old salt who brooked no trouble in his courthouse, made a point to keep a close eye on the defendant, who towered over everyone in the building.

Kalis explained Hodgkins's options. He could be sent back to Bridgewater, where he would stay until he was deemed capable of standing trial. Alternatively, he could have a third competency evaluation right away. Hodgkins requested the latter.

Kalis then took Hodgkins's request to Judge Rutledge, who put the matter to Gribouski. Any suggestion that Hodgkins could walk because of a competency claim disturbed Gribouski. He had seen Hodgkins confess. He was convinced that Hodgkins was fully competent and therefore agreed to the third evaluation. Because Hodgkins had requested not to be present at the viewing of the crime site the following day, Judge Rutledge ruled that Dr. David Swenson, who had recommended Hodgkins's transfer to Bridgewater the preceding summer, use that time to evaluate him at the Salem Jail.

THAT THURSDAY MORNING, the jurors, Kalis, Gribouski, Judge Rutledge, and the court stenographer traveled via bus to the Rockport train station, where various members of the court gallery and a police escort met them. It was another bleak day, but they were loaded into Jeeps and the open backs of four-wheel-drive pickups belonging to the National Guard and a volunteer citizen group, and started toward the woods.

As houses gave way to trees, the sky began to darken. The court piled out of the vehicles at the end of a private dirt road. Before starting on their twenty-minute walk into the heart of the woods, Gribouski instructed the jurors to notice how far they had traveled from town. See how remote and dense this stretch of woods happens to be—it will only thicken. Take in the silence. The quiet. Just "stop, look, and listen." Gribouski let Dogtown do most of the talking, let it whisper and moan, creak and whine. The jurors took to the chilly path in silence. Every so often, the sky spit an icy drop of rain. Judge Rutledge, who was sixty-nine at the time and only months away from retiring, ambled along slowly, bringing up the rear.

"Pay attention to the seclusion, the isolation of the paths," Gribouski said once they reached a cluster of pine trees on a small path next to the main trail. "Look at that area . . . [as] if someone was walking on that path as you are standing . . . here." Gribouski did not tell the jury that this was where Woofer first came to sniff Hodgkins's motorbike tire like some fabled wolf in this ancient forest, taking in the high and low notes of the wild's musky perfumes. This is the place where Peter Hodgkins looked through the visor of his blue helmet in the mineral-like haze of the rain and first noticed Anne Natti, appearing small and delicate in the company of her piney friends.

Gribouski led them a hundred yards down the path and pointed out an X and a number that had been marked on a tree in red spray paint. It was not meant to show that the tree "bear[ed] ackhorns," as trees chosen to remain standing were marked in Ebenezer Babson's day when most of this land was being cleared, but to identify where Hodgkins claimed he had first struck Anne Natti. Gribouski let the jurors' imaginations do the work of envisioning being all alone in this desolate place and having an unsettling feeling, as if they knew they were being watched through the pouring rain and suddenly, unknowingly, followed.

Next, Gribouski took them off the path into some underbrush surrounded by small trees. Professor Norton had walked out to this place in his bare feet to check on his woods after Anne Natti was found underneath their low, sheltering boughs. So many people had told the professor that growing a forest on Dogtown's granite ledge simply could not be done. He did not listen, nor did his neighbors, Bob and "Jimo" Natti, Erik's uncle and father, who endeavored their own reforestation projects. Over the years, the professor placed more than a hundred thousand seeds in trays full of rich soil, and gently covered them in more of this velvety earth as if he were tucking children into bed. He gave them enough water and sunlight to coax the life secreted away inside those hardened pods to take root, to rise and grow. Once they were planted, the professor surrounded his trees with more than forty different species of ferns, cut firebreaks, and lined paths with rocks he split by hand. Years later, his daughter-in-law, Marcia Norton, said that of all the professor's accomplishments, "these woods were probably the most important thing to him in the world." That his forest became a place where the life had been beaten out of an innocent woman simply "did a job on him." The trees kept growing in the same place, and in the same way as before, but Marcia Norton claims the professor was never the same. Neither was his little corner of the earth.

Here at the edge of Professor Norton's land, Gribouski told the jurors to touch a depression in the ground. One by one, they pressed their fingers to this cool, damp, hollow spot with no knowledge of its significance. More than eight months had passed since Anne Natti had been killed but the imprint from where her face had been shoved into the ground was still there, "like a cast of the face," as Kalis and others recalled. The details had been softened by rain, snow, and ice, but the depression remained clear enough to be recognized for what it was: a suffocating death mask made of Dogtown clay.

Chapter Twenty-four

City Bred Tenderfoots

D OGTOWN HAD IN FACT been on its own trial after Anne Natti's death, and the ensuing debate over how to manage the area became a defining moment not just for Dogtown but for Gloucester, too.

In December 1984 the issue of whether to save or develop Dogtown headlined a City Hall referendum. New houses were going up along Dogtown's periphery in the early 1980s. And though people such as Gloucester resident Joe Kaknes believed that "to develop the Dogtown Common area of Cape Ann is in many ways tantamount to building a Safeway Supermarket on the site of the Acropolis," developers saw the events of 1984 as a chance to lobby for more construction there. But these developers and the newly minted Dogtown Steering Committee faced a major complication: with the exception of the 1,150 acres Roger W. Babson sold to the city no one knew who owned the land's remaining 2,000 acres.

That same fall, while trying to assemble a large tract of land for conservation, the Dogtown Committee and the city were offered 130 Dogtown acres for purchase. This acreage made a better, more manageable parcel if 20 additional, adjacent acres could be included in the acquisition. But these 20 acres had "clouded titles," meaning that their ownership, like that of much of Dogtown's land, was unknown. Determining who these parcels belonged to was where things got thorny.

Eminent domain laws enabled the City of Gloucester to seize the land, but first the City Council had to agree to the plan. Next the city needed to figure out where individual parcels lay and to identify their owners, which was a Byzantine process. There were few records for settlers who arrived before 1722; some had been issued grants; others had simply staked a claim. Many records dated after 1722 were incomplete or had been lost. Determining ownership required searching through centuries of deeds and probate records that read like this: "I Benjamin Ellery . . . do hereby grant sell and convey unto the said George Girdler Smith—a certain piece of land . . . beginning at the corner of William Centers land near the house that formerly belonged to John Brewer, then running eastward as the brook runs to a corner wall joining to a pasture formerly Mr. Pulsifers . . . thence northerly as the wall runs 'till it comes to the corner joining Millets pasture, thence westerly and southerly as the highway runs, thence southerly until it comes to the first mentioned bounds containing twenty acres be it more or less." Reviewing more than three hundred years of such records was going to be complicated, slow, and costly. And that was just the beginning; years if not centuries of back taxes on individual parcels then needed to be assessed.

Starting in the late 1950s, Professor Norton and the Dogtown Foundation had attempted to purchase 375 Dogtown acres, but it took them fifteen years to jump through all the necessary bureaucratic hoops, identify the owners, and have their targeted parcels assessed. In 1978, when these legal notices were published in the *Gloucester Daily Times*, many of these Dogtown properties were still registered to their original eighteenth- and nineteenth-century owners, such as Granny Day, who had run a Commons Settlement school in the 1700s, and Abraham Wharf, the man who had committed suicide there in the early 1800s. Though they had been dead for two hundred years, Granny Day and Abraham Wharf's names were listed in the paper for owing $149.20 and $116.20, respectively, in property taxes for 1978 alone. One of the lots that appeared on this 1978 list was believed to have approximately fifty thousand owners, an astounding, if not wholly improbable, figure. Members of the extended Hodgkins family owned six different parcels of this land. Foreclosing on abandoned Dogtown lots, even though in some instances taxes had not been paid on them for centuries, remained far easier said than done.

Once these notices had been published, the eminent domain claims needed to be filed with the Massachusetts state real estate court. A claimant could show up in court and fight the case, but this would have been unlikely for most of Dogtown's land: the back taxes owed could be more than what the land was worth. Moreover, the real estate court only accepted a mere five claims for review at a time. At this rate it would take years to clear the titles on Dogtown's two thousand unclaimed acres. The alternative was to push a foreclosure bill through the state house and senate, which would amount to more bureaucratic and political wrangling. Dogtown's land was largely undesired, but nearly impossible to obtain.

To purchase their 150 acres in the aftermath of Anne Natti's murder, the Steering Committee received a $266,000 state grant that required them to raise an additional $85,000 in private, matching funds. To raise this sum and to pass a new management plan through the City Council, the Steering Committee needed the support of Cape Ann's hunters and Norval Barkhouse, owner of the Cape Ann Sportsmen's Club.

Like elsewhere, Cape Ann's hunters and conservationists butted heads on how nature ought to be experienced. At a heated 1968 Rockport City Council meeting to discuss stocking Rockport's side of Dogtown with snowshoe hares, a woman who opposed the plan asked, "All I want to know is what do the rabbits think?" "They like to be chased by dogs," a hunter replied. "It's fun for them." Rockport never passed the measure, but the Sportsmen's Club had long stocked snowshoe hares and pheasants on Dogtown's Gloucester side. Its members also tagged some of Cape Ann's deer population, which had been multiplying in the years since the forest had grown back. The members of the Sportsmen's Club (which included Peter Hodgkins's father) were concerned that the liberal-minded Steering Committee would ban hunting.

Here was another hurdle to developing a unified management plan for Dogtown: many conservationists were morally opposed to hunting, while the hunters, who had used Dogtown as much if not more than the conservationists during the area's worst years of neglect, believed that Dogtown belonged to them as much as to anyone else. Beginning in the 1950s, though, hunting and the random shooting of firearms in Dogtown were among people's reasons for staying away from the area, a fact that contributed to Dogtown's further decline.

The other problem was the trees. Many old-timers claim that once the woods grew back, Dogtown changed completely. It was no longer an inviting, sun-filled place that abounded in wild blueberries and majestic boulders that commanded an otherwise empty landscape. Instead, it had become a dark, thick forest, the same kind of place the settlers had feared. But despite what then-president Ronald Reagan claimed while campaigning in 1980—that "trees cause more pollution than automobiles do"—no one was going to debate the merits of the woods. Yet, access was an altogether different matter.

Though Roger W. Babson had stipulated that his 1,150 acres were to be used "as a natural park and bird sanctuary, but on foot only," the area had never been officially managed for either purpose; people, including Charles Olson, had driven across its dirt roads for years.

And so it was on the Friday of the first week of Peter Hodgkins's trial when a group of teenagers drove up the Dogtown Road with radios blasting. Rocks spun under their wheels and ricocheted off trees. Eight four-wheel-drive trucks, Jeeps, and ATVs turned across a pasture and dipped back into the woods, piping exhaust into the cool, piney air. Wherever trees and low branches blocked the way, the kids stopped and gathered around. A starter rope was pulled. A chain saw began to whine. Gasoline vaporized in the late spring afternoon. Resin flowed, and sawdust flew like tiny little fairies coming to join the party. Grabbing branches and limbs, the revelers tossed the freshly cut wood into the back of their vehicles and sawed a new path through the forest toward a place where there are no consequences, parents, teachers, or cops for miles, just freedom and whatever feels right.

They corralled the vehicles inside a stand of red pine, threw the wood into a pile, anointed it with gasoline, and tossed in a light. Gusts of woodsmoke deadheaded the sun's fading bloom and seasoned the oncoming dusk. Giddy hands pumped a keg, pressed the tap, and steadied cups. Beer flowed. The woods glowed in the firelight. What these Gloucester teens would eventually come to remember was how exhilarating it felt going to that place where freedom tastes like Budweiser, smells of campfire and cigarettes, and sounds like a sizzling match and a crackling fire, all set to the tune of a radio playing into the night.

The kids had cleared out early Monday morning before Dogtown Steering Committee chairman Bob French walked up the Dogtown

Road following their tire treads to the freshly cut trees, discarded Styrofoam cups, and a giant fire scar. The treads branched off toward a gate blocking Dogtown's Gee Avenue entrance, which was now broken, and to the Goose Cove Reservoir dam. The sight left as deep an imprint in French's mind as the tracks had left upon the earth. Peter Hodgkins was gone and hopefully not coming back, but in spite of any hunter's or emergency planner's claim that motorized vehicle access to the woods was necessary, French was resolute in his belief that such access had to be cut off. Motorized transport brought a "savagery" to this place that he resolved to eradicate.

The Massachusetts Department of Environmental Management (DEM) offered to help. Noting that Dogtown was the only place targeted under its Olmsted Historic Landscape Preservation Program that was not in state hands, the DEM proposed to take care of Dogtown for an annual fee. Their plan actually resembled a proposal that Professor Norton's Dogtown Foundation had drafted in the 1950s: regulate hunting, ban cars, create new maps for hikers, and hire a hands-on manager to enforce these rules and maintain the landscape. (The City Council agreed to the Dogtown Foundation's 1959 plan, even after vociferous opposition from the hunters, but support for the proposal fizzled after it took so long to clear titles on the land.) In response to the DEM proposal, Joe Orange, who had not yet been appointed Dogtown's constable, but already was its ever-vigilant watchman, fired off a letter to the *Gloucester Daily Times* calling the Steering Committee "a group of city bred tenderfoots." He urged people not to let "the mayor and his elitist team of greater Boston carpetbaggers destroy Dogtown forever," and insisted that people simply let "Nature work her magic unmolested," meaning this quite literally. Though Joe Orange's opinion carried a lot of weight with officials in City Hall, Bob French disagreed. French, a retired industrial psychologist (and avid collector of Hartley's Dogtown paintings), believed that Joe Orange's wish to "lock the place up and throw away the key" would spell disaster for Dogtown. People had to go there and be able to use the place to appreciate it.

Dogtown had long been part of Cape Ann's identity, a holdout from the Gloucester that had been lost to bulldozers and wrecking balls. Many people were concerned that under the DEM plan, Dogtown would lose something of its unique tumbledown character. This special, pleasurably forlorn setting would be turned into someplace ordinary.

Eventually, it was decided that no outsider could be trusted to manage Dogtown. Thus, when the time came to vote on the proposal, Gloucester city councillors rejected the plan. There was simply too much at stake: Dogtown's character and, by extension, Cape Ann's.

Chapter Twenty-five

"No Intention of Leaving This Courtroom Alive"

EFORE PETER HODGKINS'S TRIAL resumed, on Friday, March 15, court officer Earl McCurdy, who had witnessed Hodgkins's violent outburst after he read Dr. Gressitt's report, broached the topic of manacling Hodgkins in the courtroom with Judge Rutledge. The judge put the matter to Kalis, who admitted to being wary of Hodgkins's size, but remained resolute in his belief that manacling his client would prejudice the jury. "Okay," McCurdy told Kalis, "if you're the person that is attacked in court, you are on your own." But the court's concerns about Hodgkins would not end there.

Next, Judge Rutledge called in Gribouski and Dr. Swenson to confer about his competency assessment. Dr. Swenson stated his belief that Hodgkins was indeed mentally competent and fit to stand trial. With two out of three doctors finding Hodgkins competent and Judge Rutledge's own observations of Hodgkins's cooperative behavior, the trial resumed immediately. And though by all accounts, Hodgkins seemed mentally present, his mind was elsewhere.

The trial's sequence approximated that of the murder investigation. Police officers and detectives testified about the state of Anne Natti's body, which had been covered in leaves and pine needles as if the murderer had tried to hide it, and how hard it was to remove. They also revealed to the jury the significance of that cold depression in the ground where they had been asked to press their hands.

During the trial's second week, pathologist John Guillemont detailed the injuries Anne Natti had suffered. From his description of the blood that had filled the victim's mouth and ears to the pie-shaped piece of bone that had been completely dislodged from her skull and the multiple ripple-like fractures that radiated into her forehead, Guillemont's testimony was so graphic, Judge Rutledge had to call a recess because a juror became ill.

Robert Pino, assistant chemist of the Massachusetts Department of Public Safety crime lab, testified about the blood evidence. In his cross-examination of Pino, Kalis stressed that the blood found on the bike and under Hodgkins's nails was diluted beyond typology and could not be matched to Anne Natti, Peter Hodgkins, or anyone else, for that matter. There had to be a lot of blood on whoever killed Anne Natti, Kalis concluded, but there were only meager traces on the bike and under Hodgkins's nails, which could have come from Hodgkins's scratching an insect bite.

Testimony followed about the stronger pieces of physical evidence: the hair and fiber samples found on the bike. FBI special agent Warren Oakes stated that when viewed under a microscope, these hairs were "consistent with having originated" from Anne Natti. After agent Oakes stated there was a one-in-a-thousand chance that these hairs could belong to someone else, Kalis questioned whether this could indeed be that one chance.

If Erik Natti ever had had any doubts that Peter Hodgkins killed his wife, they were being dispelled by those tiny traces of hair and fibers, but FBI special agent Maureen Higgins's testimony brought him the greatest relief thus far: lab tests definitively showed that Anne Natti had not been raped.

THAT TUESDAY NIGHT Kalis stopped in at his office in Salem, where his partner John Tierney asked to see him right away. Tierney had learned through sources at the Salem Jail that Hodgkins was planning to escape if he was found guilty. As Kalis was walking to his car, he ran into a Salem police officer and former guard at the jail who repeated the rumor. It was as though everyone at the Salem Jail was privy to what was really on Hodgkins's mind, thoughts that he did not share with his lawyer.

Kalis spent a sleepless night mulling over the situation. Was the rumor just a typical inmate boast, or did Hodgkins in fact have something up his sleeve? Hodgkins may have seemed docile, but he demonstrated an inscrutability that made it difficult to gauge whether he was truly dangerous or not. At the very least, his suicide attempts suggested that he was desperate. Who knew what he was going to try to do in that small, crowded courtroom.

AS SOON AS Kalis arrived at the courthouse the next day, he planned to ask Hodgkins point-blank whether the rumors he had heard the night before were true, but Hodgkins had his own issue to take up with his lawyer and Judge Rutledge.

Massachusetts Supreme Judicial Court rules allowed one television news camera at a time in a courtroom while a trial was in session, but when the sheriff's cruiser carrying Hodgkins pulled up to the Newburyport courthouse the following morning and Hodgkins saw a Channel 7 news camera set up in front of the building, he refused to get out of the car. After the camera was shut off and officers coaxed him into the building, an agitated Hodgkins told Kalis that if he were found guilty, he had "no intention of leaving this courtroom alive."

Fearing that Hodgkins might grab a hostage in an effort to escape, Kalis informed Gribouski, Judge Rutledge, and Officer McCurdy about the rumor and Hodgkins's remark, including his insistence that "he will never spend the rest of his life in jail."

McCurdy believed that of all the people whom Hodgkins would potentially attempt to harm, it would most likely be Kalis, who sat closest to him. "I told you," McCurdy admonished Kalis, "that if he harmed you, you were on your own." McCurdy had had enough problems in his courthouse in recent months. Defendants in two separate cases had attempted suicide in the building, but he didn't bother to mention these embarrassments. The other person whom Hodgkins might attempt to harm, McCurdy believed, would be the judge, who would deliver his sentence. And while Kalis did not waver in his opinion that restraining Hodgkins in the courtroom would jeopardize his right to a fair trial, he asked to have Hodgkins placed in leg irons and handcuffs if he wished to see Kalis alone. "The way he hit that windowsill with the handcuffs the other day . . ." Kalis said, making his trepidation clear. Kalis, Mc-

Curdy, Gribouski, and Judge Rutledge all agreed to increase the security around Hodgkins and in the court at all times. The judge then called Hodgkins in to address his concerns about the camera.

Hodgkins told Judge Rutledge, "I could finish my trial with no problem, but I wish not to be on the film. I wish not to be here during the trial when the cameras are here." Judge Rutledge reminded Hodgkins of his right to be present at his own trial and to confront any witness against him, including the videotape of his confession, but Hodgkins waived all these rights. Because Massachusetts Supreme Judicial Court rules also allowed a defendant to sit freely at his own trial, Judge Rutledge honored Hodgkins's request to sit in a room just off to the side of the courtroom while the cameras, which the judge had restricted to recording the taped confession alone, were operating.

Once the trial resumed, Hodgkins would remain unshackled, be escorted by two guards instead of one, and be seated next to Kalis in order to be slightly removed from the public. The court also decided that once testimony was complete and the jury returned from deliberations, court officers would place Hodgkins in leg irons before the jury delivered its verdict.

THE TRIAL RETURNED to session with Detective David Reardon and state policeman Carl Sjoberg, who each testified about Hodgkins's cooperative behavior during, before, and after giving his initial confession, as well as during the videotaping. Hodgkins had signed every single waiver placed before him and had willingly agreed to go into the woods and reenact the crime, they claimed. Reardon also testified about how Hodgkins even gave them a little history lesson about the area's granite-quarrying industry and helped the detectives find their way back to the patrol cars when they almost got lost. There was no coercion whatsoever, Reardon and Sjoberg had separately contended under cross-examination.

Kalis could tell from the jury's reaction to these testimonies that his coercion defense alone was not working. His only hope for an acquittal was in Dr. Gressitt's expert testimony, which was scheduled for the next day.

Later that afternoon, Hodgkins was escorted to the court side room, where he could listen to the proceedings but not be seen. A television was wheeled into the courtroom and placed in front of the jurors who were about to become the first in the history of Massachusetts' Criminal Court to hear a defendant confess on videotape. Erik Natti and his family got up from their seats and moved closer for a better view. The Channel 7 news camera started to roll.

The videotape, which originally belonged to Officer Brooks, had been cued to where an episode of *Star Trek* was suddenly interrupted by wobbly shots of trees (dark pines and bright, newly leafed oaks), a rocky path (so blurry it appears to be flowing like a stream), and the sounds of leather-soled shoes creaking, the earth crunching underfoot, and someone breathing heavily. A bird chirps loudly, repeatedly. Figures appear around a bend. The camera catches a gaunt Hodgkins from behind, looking over his shoulder with a drawn look in his hooded eyes. Horizontal lines of distortion cut through each scene. The words "Gloucester Police" appear in large white letters on the back of a detective's navy blue windbreaker and disappear into thick, green woods that look as if they could swallow this whole scene, which comes off as an exercise in cinematic abstraction with some official police business thrown in for grit.

The camera zooms in and out on Hodgkins, whose hair is as black as the shaded tree trunks. Red spray paint on some of these trees marks where Anne Natti's body was found. "Well, I had that rock," Hodgkins said, referring to the murder weapon. "How do you know that's the rock?" Reardon asked. "The two-handed one," Hodgkins answered impatiently. Towering over Reardon and Gribouski, Hodgkins stared at the ground then over his shoulder like a bored teenager. When Reardon asked what he did with the rock, Hodgkins rolled his eyes. "I hit the person from behind," he said, as if he had already spoken these words a thousand times that day. The camera then focused on the murder weapon, appearing no different from all the other rocks in this godforsaken place.

The breeze fluttered audibly. Sounds of people moving and clothing rustling overwhelmed much of the dialogue. (Jurors were provided with copies of a typed transcript.) Hodgkins's garbled answers to Gribouski's questions were enigmatic and marked by an archaic formality: "I had the intention to see what the person had and I checked her pockets." And "the clothing slipped off, *not* with the intention of raping anyone"—

Hodgkins emphasized this point—"just to look, I guess." Or they were so simple as to seem nonsensical. "The two-handed one" or "groggy," he replied when asked how Anne Natti seemed after he attacked her.

"I didn't know what I was thinking," Hodgkins said with complete detachment as if he were merely describing how the grass grows.

The jury took in Hodgkins's description of the brutal details of bludgeoning a woman to death, dragging her body, and leaving it for dead for no reason whatsoever as if it were merely an ordinary event, like something out of an old murder ballad telling the story of another time and place, not the summer of 1984 when Michael Jackson's *Thriller* topped the pop charts, Geraldine Ferraro was running for vice president, and the space shuttle had completed multiple successful missions.

Darkness was hiding behind every rock, tree, and shimmering blade of grass. It trailed Peter Hodgkins in shadows and met the distant, contemptible look in his eyes. Peter Hodgkins was part of the grainy, hazy illusion of these woods and their obscure aura. But before anyone could linger over the images of that beautiful summer Friday, it was all brought to a quick end just before Mr. Spock and Captain Kirk abruptly reappeared, worrying over the fate of the *Enterprise*.

For Kalis, the video was painful to watch. The quality was so poor everything appeared distorted, most notably his client. For Gribouski, this was nothing but a good thing. "Hodgkins knew exactly what he was doing when he killed her," Gribouski later said. "And it shows."

With the video confession, the prosecution rested.

EACH TIME ROBERT Kalis saw the video, the same thoughts came to his mind: when Peter Hodgkins walked into the police station that June Friday, waived all of his rights, and confessed not once, but twice, he might as well have committed suicide. Hodgkins had told Kalis that when he entered the police station that day he was tired and hungry, and most of all, he had feared for his life. But the two men who had met Peter Hodgkins in the woods that Friday morning, William Spinney and Lawrence Davis, and the various police detectives and officers who testified during pretrial motions and at the trial, painted the picture of a man whom they had tried to help and who, by all accounts, was essentially behaving as his usual odd self. With the case scheduled to go to the defense the next day, Kalis spent the evening preparing the last argument he could put forth in Peter Hodgkins's defense: that Hodgkins had falsely confessed.

That night, Kalis kept his eye on Channel 7, which ran at least three prime-time anchor breaks announcing that the defendant in a case being tried in Newburyport had confessed to his crime. Because the television station could only record the screening of the video, and was not given a copy of the actual tape, the excerpt it broadcast was even more distorted than the original. Peter Hodgkins came across as a madman who could barely be heard, much less understood. Kalis was livid.

THE NEXT DAY, Kalis motioned for a mistrial because of the media coverage. Judge Rutledge denied the motion. Kalis had not asked to sequester the jury. The judge had instructed them not to read the newspapers or consume any media during the trial. Judge Rutledge suggested sequestering the jury going forward, but to Kalis, it was already too late.

Chapter Twenty-six

Nature Working Her Magic Unmolested

T HE SOUND OF the ringing telephone shook me from my sleep
one morning at the Wonson House. Hoping that it would be
Joe Orange, I jumped out of bed, grabbed a pen and notebook,
and ran downstairs to answer it. Instead of Joe Orange, it was Carolyn,
who had called to invite me over for a little kaffeeklatsch.

Fifteen minutes later I padded across the road and updated Carolyn
on my progress. I had not had any luck with finding *Mountain in Stone*
just yet, but I had seen a man with shortly cropped white hair at the
wheel of a gray car decorated with American flags and rooftop speakers
blaring Sousa-style patriotic music. Though on approach the car looked
like it might be a station wagon—Joe Orange's station wagon, I hoped—
it turned out to be a sedan. Maybe Joe Orange was a zealous patriot and
had gotten a new car.

"Joe? No. Never."

I then told Carolyn that rather than wait around for Joe Orange to
call—there was no answering machine at the Wonson House—I was
going to go to Dogtown that day with Ted Tarr. Ted was a sixty-seven-
year-old, buttoned-down, dirt-under-the-nails kind of Cape Ann insider
who had devoted much of his life to Dogtown by building and main-
taining trails. He had also led weekly walks across the area for decades.
I had met Ted a couple of times before and had even joined one of his
guided walks. A former Rockport selectman and the town's sole repre-

sentative on the Dogtown Steering Committee after Anne Natti's death and for many years thereafter, Ted never talked about Dogtown being gloomy or dark. At Anne Natti's vigil he had referred to the land as a "church . . . a place for spiritual renewal," as if it were an inspiring, hopeful place, the Dogtown I had wanted to experience.

I presumed that Carolyn would approve of my going to Dogtown with Ted rather than alone, but she shot me that same concerned maternal look as before and said, "Be careful with that Rockport Republican." Many Gloucester people bristled at the mention of their wealthy neighbors, Rockporters (or Rockportericans, as Carolyn's sons called them, emphasizing the "rica," from *rico*, the Spanish word for rich, claiming they were snooty and condescending. Ted was the only native Rockporter I knew. A descendant of Richard Tarr, the first settler in a part of Cape Ann long known as Sandy Bay, now Rockport, Ted was the genuine article. But if I had to compare him to his Gloucester counterpart, Joe Orange, Ted would be Dogtown's fastidious Appolonian taming force, Joe the Dionysian advocate for letting "nature work her magic unmolested." And yet, somehow both men tended to get on people's nerves. Ted had a reputation for being bombastic, opinionated, offensive, and for having a way with spray paint in Dogtown, marking trail blazes on trees that upset people who wanted more of a wilderness experience. I had not experienced these sides of Ted myself and thought the blazes were necessary given how easy it is to get lost in Dogtown, but I knew many people who professed a strong dislike of the man simply because he was a Republican *and* an environmentalist *and* "drives that obnoxious machine"—a Hummer with red emergency roof lights (Tarr serves in the Rockport volunteer fire department), a safari-style roof rack, and an outsize bumper plastered with stickers that say such things as "Veterans for McCain" (Ted served in the Korean War), "Love Thy Wetlands," and "Open Space Our Common Wealth." I liked Ted for these very reasons; he keeps things interesting. He was a highly accomplished study in contradictions, not unlike Dogtown itself.

"Not to worry, Carolyn," I responded, "I'm a registered Democrat."

That did nothing to ease the worried look on her face. It seemed wise not to tell Carolyn that we were going to be searching for a rock called the Dream of Love.

Ted talked about nearly every Dogtown root, tree, toadstool, flower, leaf, and hole in the ground with the kind of familiarity that only someone with a life's worth of experience in a place could deliver, yet whenever I saw him he pumped me for what I was learning about the area. Each time I told Ted something I had learned, he would tell me a Dogtown story I didn't know, like the one about the guys who carved a hole in the roof of the old Babson cooperage and made off with its collection of antique tools, which later surfaced in California. Then he'd go on to another tale, such as how when Joseph Kennedy Sr. was smuggling rum off the Cape Ann coast, he would set fires in the woods to distract the authorities. Once he was done with his story, Ted would raise his eyebrows with a see-if-you-can-top-that-kiddo kind of look in his eyes. I had never discovered anything Ted did not already know about Dogtown until I asked if he knew who had carved the Dream of Love rock. Ted did not know the Dream of Love existed. I was astounded.

The Dream of Love was a rock in the style of the Babson Boulders, but instead of saying something a Victorian-era great-grandmother might have spouted, such as "Prosperity Follows Service," "Study," or "Be On Time," this rock was carved to say "Dream of Love." Shep had shown it to me on the same day that he told me about Anne Natti's murder. The incongruity between the tragedy and this rock was jarring, but it stayed with me as a touchstone of the good side of this place. And though I had done a fair amount of traipsing through Dogtown by this stage, I had not seen the Dream of Love since. Perhaps with Ted's expertise it would be easier to locate.

Ted seemed extremely eager to see the Dream of Love and suggested we try to find it as soon as possible. And in searching for the Dream of Love, I thought, we just might come across *Mountains in Stone*.

IT WAS TURNING out to be the kind of day when the air feels like flypaper. I had been waiting for Ted in front of the library for only about five minutes, but I was already feeling as though my clothes were sticking to my body. And it seemed to be getting hotter and muggier by the minute.

Ted pulled up in his black Saab convertible with the top down. He flipped down the driver's-side visor, ran a comb through his neatly trimmed brown hair, and adjusted his Ray·Ban–style sunglasses as I approached the car. I got into the passenger seat and Ted leaned over to give me a kiss on the cheek. Ted was not alone with the kisses. I had received similar pecks from more than one older Gloucester man.

"Where is Poppy?" I inquired, referring to Ted's sixteen-year-old springer spaniel who he said might be joining us for the day.

"The old girl is at home, resting," Ted replied with a heavy sigh, as if Poppy were getting her fur set with giant sponge rollers and taking her beauty sleep. Ted talked about Poppy as if they were a comfortable older couple deeply familiar with each other's moods and whims. Ted also happened to be very forthcoming about his lingering upset at Poppy for "nearly biting off John McCain's arm" when Ted was volunteering for the candidate during the 2000 New Hampshire primary. Ted assured me that he and Poppy were still working through this little issue, and then cheerfully asked if I wanted some lunch.

Lunch sounded great, I thought, especially if air-conditioning was going to be involved. In spite of the heat, Ted, who wore jeans, a double-weave nylon shirt circa 1980 with sporty white stripes on the sleeve, and ankle-high duck shoes with white tube socks, looked perfectly comfortable as he steered us away from the library and waved at passersby.

There was no air-conditioning inside the restaurant, and the slowly moving ceiling fan made a creaking sound, as if it were a mixer and the air were thick, glutinous dough. At least Ted's line of conversation was stirring.

I was about to ask Ted why Dogtown had such a continued hold on him, but somehow he got to talking about snakes.

Like most little boys growing up in the 1940s, Ted spent his childhood catching little animals, especially snakes: milks, greens, garters, ribbons, redbellies, and ringnecks. Ted and snakes "have a good history," as he put it. There was one black snake in particular that he never caught, but visited every summer near the Whale's Jaw. "The first two years, of course, she'd bite me. Then after that, she'd just go 'Oh,'" he said with a sigh, tilting his chin up as if putting on arrogant, effeminate airs, " 'there he is again.' So I'd show her my hiking boots and she'd give me this disdainful look and off she'd go. The same one." They had this rapport for ten years until the snake disappeared.

Ted's next love was Yasmin, a skunk he had captured. In what he described as his earliest business venture, little boy Ted bred Yasmin with the intention of selling her descented babies as pets. After Yasmin finally conceived, some kids attacked her. She would have pulled through, Ted claimed, but the vet unwittingly sliced into her womb, killing her.

"Miss her," he said, his brown eyes turning watery.

It seemed that Yasmin and this black snake had something to do with Ted's undying devotion to Dogtown. He rarely talked about friends or living family, just animals.

"Did you get another skunk?" I asked.

"No, I got an alligator."

Naturally.

Ted had previously told me about Alger Hiss, the six-foot-long female alligator he kept as a pet for forty years. I wondered how Alger Hiss managed the cold New England winters in her elder gator days. "She still had a good figure for an alligator," Ted volunteered, sounding more like a widower than a pet owner.

I began to feel as though Ted were telling me his romantic history; his pets were all female, and he had mentioned women only once, when he told me about a double date he went on with Salem's grand witch, Laurie Cabot. "She's a lot of fun," he had said. "Throws great parties." People like Ted were what had endeared me to Cape Ann: the blue-blooded elder Boy Scout rubs elbows with the witch and walks a pet alligator for half his life.

The little paper ramekin of coleslaw next to my fried haddock sandwich began to sweat. A group of kids came running in from outside, begging their father to take them to the beach. The beach sounded much better than Dogtown on such a hot and humid day, I thought. I could try to find *Mountains in Stone* any day, but I had promised to show Ted the Dream of Love rock, and he seemed so excited to see it. I also felt that I owed it to Ted. He had been extremely helpful to me with my research. Showing him something in this place he had known and loved for his entire life was small in comparison to how generous he had been with me.

But what if I could not find the Dream of Love rock? It was so well hidden, and seemingly so far away. And *Mountains in Stone*? I had identified nearly every possible Hartley Dogtown painting site except for the one I most wanted to see. It had to be in Dogtown. Although I was wary of the rising heat and humidity because of previous bouts of heatstroke, I convinced myself to buck up and deal. This was Massachusetts, not the tropics.

As we cruised toward Dogtown in the convertible, Ted asked me more pointed questions about the Dream of Love rock, but it was hard to talk because the hot wind was blowing my hair into my mouth and eyes and up my nose. We passed by a beach and I turned and stared as it slipped from view. Ted motored on diligently.

The moment we entered the woods, Ted whipped out a pair of pruning shears from a case that was attached to his belt as if he were holstering a gun, and started hacking away at the slightest trail obstruction with manly bravado. "Obsessive-compulsive," he muttered. "I take out my vengeance wherever I can." Today he was taking out his vengeance on the multiflora rose, an invader species that the Massachusetts Department of Transportation plants in the dividers on state highways. Ted said that the rose, which grows in thick, tangled, barbed vines, "eats cars and trash." I liked the idea of a car-eating plant.

I also liked the idea of having some nice, all-natural citronella bug spray. It seemed as if a heavy cloud of mosquitoes had descended on Dogtown and Dogtown alone. Ted's jeans were boldly insect-resistant. My high-tech hiking pants were not.

Cape Ann mosquitoes have actually headlined the *Gloucester Daily Times* in years past. In 1929, two years before Hartley had arrived in Gloucester, the paper reported a front-page story about the Chamber of Commerce's campaign against the insect. The author took the liberty to comment, "[T]his is another instance of life in which the 'female of the species is more deadly than the male.'" The Whale's Jaw had broken and Dogtown had changed in so many ways, but the mosquitoes had endured.

Ted showed me a cluster of red pines planted in the early twentieth century by Rayne Adams, the man whose tombstone I had stumbled upon on my first Dogtown trip, and whose wife, Leila Webster Adams, had protested Babson's stone carving projects. One tree had a split trunk, shaped like a trident, which was caused by an infestation of the pine weevil. The pine weevil problem could have been prevented, Ted explained, if Dogtown could be opened up again and the trees thinned out. Dogtown would then have a healthier, better-functioning ecosystem overall. And what stops Dogtown from being a healthier landscape, Ted happened to mention, was Joe Orange.

Of course.

"He'd arrest a grandmother if she was in the wrong place at the wrong time," he quipped. "He's just too strict and has managed to irritate a lot of people. I wanted controlled burning, especially right now, but he always fought against it."

Other people want controlled burning, too, such as a woman named Dina Enos, who grew up on the edge of Dogtown and recalls that before the trees grew back in, "the fog sets up there and it reminds me of *The Hound of the Baskervilles.* All the rocks and the colors. The grays and the dark cedars. You could see the derricks down in Rockport and in Lanesville in the quarries, sticking up in the air. It was eerie and wonderful and there was no place like it on Earth."

It's normal for the land to want to make trees, even in a place as rocky as Dogtown. Naturalist David Rains Wallace once wrote, "I could write an evolutionary history of the human species in which its main significance is not as an inventor of language or a builder of cities but as an ally of grasslands in their thirty-million-year struggle with forests." Ted and Dina were on the side of the open grasslands, but the trees had managed to keep Joe Orange on their team. I was somewhere between the two.

Dina now serves on the Dogtown Committee and has advocated for a controlled burn followed up with two hundred "eighteenth-century lawnmowers" (a.k.a. sheep). But sheep, Ted pointed out, would eat that sacred Dogtown fruit, the dark, dusky blueberry, and no one wants anything to endanger the blueberries. They had been in serious decline in recent years, but Ted believed that a good burn would bring them back.

I wondered what could bring back *Mountains in Stone.* Ted and I had been walking for a couple of hours and were not having any luck finding it or the Dream of Love. The day had become swelteringly hot. The air seemed to drip humidity and to press in with tiny, little-winged needles. I felt as if my entire body was beginning to inflate with histamines. Sweat dripped down my forehead and the backs of my knees. I felt woozy, disoriented. Even the trees appeared heavy and lethargic, as if their leaves were ready to drop right in the middle of the summer. The farther we went into Dogtown, the more overzealous flora of all sorts grew across the path. Milky sap dripped and oozed as Ted cut away at this growth, which seemed to start growing back as soon as he was done hacking away at it. It seemed as if all the plants in this place were closing in on us; the lazy-looking trees were going to start walking at any minute, too.

"Do you think the Dream of Love is around here?" Ted suddenly asked.

"No. I mean, sort of, but this looks familiar," I said. Not only did I feel completely turned around, suddenly the thought of showing Ted the rock just didn't seem right. It occurred to me only then that Shep might not have wanted me to share the Dream of Love, as if it were Shep's and Shep's alone. In fact, I began to wonder if Shep had carved the rock himself. A few years later I was having dinner with Shep and Sarah Dunlap, a friend from the Gloucester city archives staff, and asked Shep who carved the Dream of Love. "Oh, that was just a screen print I hung up in the trees," he replied with a poker face. For a moment I wondered if I had imagined the Dream of Love rock, but I knew I had definitely seen it. "That's right," I said, "it was a screen." Shep grinned widely, and gave me the same kind of look my eldest brother used to flash my way in the middle of the night when I helped him sneak back into the house via my ground-floor bedroom window. But on this day in the woods with Ted, I wondered if I had simply imagined the Dream of Love, even though I knew I had definitely seen the rock, not a screen.

Why were the Dream of Love and *Mountains in Stone* impossible to find? I could only provide a metaphorical explanation for the former, but it was wholly plausible that the painting was more the product of Hartley's imagination than Dogtown's reality. And while this possibility had occurred to me many times before, I had always brushed it off. I had discovered numerous sites that I was confident were the probable jumping-off point for Hartley's other Dogtown works, no matter how imagination-infused those final paintings might have been. Why did my beloved image continue to elude me?

Ted and I had arrived at the edge of Briar Swamp, where we both noticed that something appeared to be wrong with the trees across the water. A strange buzzing sound filled the air. Hundreds, if not thousands, of starlings perched their iridescent black bodies in the trees and were chattering away, making noises that sounded like so many socket wrenches whirring and spinning at different speeds. There were so many birds the trees looked as if they might collapse under their weight. It was as though Alfred Hitchcock's birds had broken free of his film and were living a separate life here in Dogtown.

Ted appeared shocked, almost stricken, by this sight. These birds didn't belong in Dogtown or anywhere in America. Like the multiflora rose, they are an invasive species. In the 1890s a man who believed that each bird mentioned in Shakespeare's plays needed to live in the United States brought a hundred starlings over from England and set them free in Central Park. Now they are everywhere across North America, flying around in massive flocks, aggressively evicting native birds from their nests.

Suddenly I understood why people thought Peter Hodgkins had a screw loose for spending so much time in this place. Dogtown seemed as if it belonged wholly to its own wild devices or to something else: Ebenezer Babson's hallucinations, Tammy Younger and her curses, the ghosts of the *Gloucester*, Thomas Wentworth Higginson's "couchant monsters," Roger W. Babson's maxims, Hartley's mystical rocks, the "four hundred gods of drink" from Olson's "MAXIMUS, FROM DOGTOWN—I" poem, the pine weevil, these weirdly cackling birds.

The huge flock of starlings appeared sluggish, but I worried that we might startle them and that they would come swarming after us. I wanted to leave. Immediately. I didn't care about the Dream of Love rock; I had only truly wanted *Mountains in Stone*, but I was running out of hope that such a place could ever be found.

"Perhaps today is not the day for the Dream of Love," I said. Ted nodded in agreement. We walked back to the car without saying much, and Ted continued snipping at every trail-obstructing branch and bramble along the way.

OF ALL THE things I had read, been told, or experienced in Dogtown, nothing was more upsetting to me than the sight of all those frightening birds. Because of some paintings and a story about their creation, I had believed that Dogtown could inspire me, change me, as it had changed Hartley, but the giant flock of starlings made me realize that I was doing nothing but spending my time being swept away by curious folklore and running around some peculiar woods turned all the more bizarre by a combination of man's manipulation and neglect. If this was nature working her magic unmolested, it was nothing but more of the dark and eerie kind. And though I had once wanted to lose myself here, Dogtown itself was lost in a way that was no longer inspiring to me; it was suddenly creepy.

I had gotten lost inside my imaginings and this stubborn, obsessive yearning, but now I felt I had gone too far. I no longer wanted to be in this forgotten place where every tree and flower seemed to be feasting on some deeper, wilder mystery. I thought of those stories Shep Abbott and Peter Anastas told me about people who had become lost here and were never found again. I had previously refused to believe them; now I was not sure I could dismiss them so easily. I began packing my bags immediately.

As I went outside to start loading my truck, I heard the phone ringing. I ran back into the house and managed to pick it up just in the nick of time. "This is Joe Orange," the voice of the man on the other end of the line said, sounding like a hard-nosed newscaster from World War II–era reels of Movietone news. "How can I help you?"

Worried that he might end the call at any pretext, I fumbled for pen and paper, my recorder, and asked Joe Orange if he would be willing to talk to me about Dogtown.

"I know nothing about Dogtown," he responded dismissively, enunciating each syllable as though he were biting into it. But clearly he had a thing or two he wanted to say, starting with "but Mother Teresa would be safe up there."

It was a funny thing for someone who had just claimed to know nothing about Dogtown to say. "Why is that?" I asked.

Joe Orange parried my question, saying, "What we have done is put the mechanisms in place to restore Dogtown and to keep it this way to *per-pe-tu-i-ty*." He struck each syllable in "perpetuity" as though the rest of us lazy people needed to make our consonants stand up straighter. "It cannot be violated. It cannot be encroached upon. It cannot ever be developed. It will stay as is. Nothing will change until the sun extinguishes itself and the Earth goes up in flames."

Joe Orange sounded like a drill sergeant crossed with a Pentecostalist prophet and Edward Abbey. "Hallelujah!" I wanted to cry out, but restrained myself.

"But that is what the modern era is all about," he continued, sermonizing rapidly and telling me about how Dogtown had been pasture for nearly three hundred years "until the internal-combustion engine came along." It was as if evil could not travel over water. Evil came on four wheels and couldn't be bothered with crossing that sweet and innocent little Cut bridge, but as soon as Route 128 and the A. Piatt An-

drew Bridge arrived, it roared over those spans in a tsunami of modernity
and changed this place forever. Then came its two-wheeled cousin the
motorcycle and its lesser relation the all-terrain vehicle. These mon-
strosities could have settled for Cape Ann's roads, but their owners
simply could not resist the appeal of Dogtown's great Eden of dirt roads
and open space. There frolicked deer, wild turkey, and every form of
New England wildlife possible, including, Joe Orange informed me,
moose. "Here in Gloucester, October 20 used to be a virtual local national holiday, when the gunnin' season opened up." (I was tempted to
tell Joe Orange he dropped a *g*, but I didn't think he would appreciate
my calling this to his attention.) "Gloucester was a great hunting community," he continued, "and Dogtown was a hunter's paradise. These
were good people, but I'm afraid that we just have too many people,
frankly. If I were Mother Nature I would probably want to diminish the
human population to what it was in about 1900 because we are a disaster when it comes to the environment. Humans multiply like maggots
in the sun. There are too many of us and we're too advanced. See, I have
a very hard-ass philosophy about mankind, don't I?"

Yes, I said, I agreed about the cars, and that line about the maggots
was a real zinger. But Joe Orange was not listening to me. He was charg-
ing forth with a head of steam and I couldn't get a word in edgewise.

"Everywhere you go nature is being assaulted and exploited, encroached upon. It's just a sad fact of life but right now we're quite
proud of what we've done with Dogtown because, barring the sun falling out of the sky, it's what you see is what you get and it's there forever. It's beautiful and it's a paradise. How long it will remain so depends
on how well we feel about it. It depends upon public opinion. It's sad
to say, but most people in Gloucester don't even know what Dogtown
represents, believe it or not. It's only the ardent minority that really
cares and the sportsmen. Other than that, I think you'd find perhaps
even indifference. In the main, people are somewhat indifferent about
it. But you find that no matter where you go, don't you think?"

Yes, I did think so, I said. I rarely, if ever, saw anyone else in Dogtown
and it certainly seemed that if more people actively cared about the
place it would be in much better shape.

With this, Joe Orange suddenly wanted to know more about me. I
had to exercise some self-control and not mention Marsden Hartley, his
paintings, or his great Dogtown epiphany because I was done with liv-

ing my life according to such illusory, romantic things. Instead, I told Joe Orange about having lived in Maine, growing up in Georgia by Kennesaw Mountain. Joe Orange then interjected that he went to paratrooper school at Georgia's Fort Benning and was soon saying that the woods in Georgia are far more extensive than on Cape Ann, as if I wouldn't know this already. I was about to shoot back that Georgia's woods have changed, but woods alone were not the point, in my opinion. Meanwhile, Joe Orange was busy yammering on, rattling off a list of America's great forests that I should go see instead of messing around in Gloucester. It seemed futile to state what seemed so glaringly obvious: Dogtown cannot be compared with the White Mountain National Forest or the John Muir Wilderness because it is wholly unlike those areas. I wanted to tell Joe Orange that when I first set foot in Dogtown, it made me feel part of some great continuum of human and geologic time and how much that inspired me, but this would have been pointless because Joe Orange sounded utterly consumed by his vision of the area as part of some great northern woods.

"If somebody jumped out of the grave from 1623, he'd feel very much at home there because it looks exactly the same," he boldly exclaimed. "But for a little bird problem you have," I thought. This was thanks to all the rules the Steering Committee had implemented and that he had officially started enforcing in the mid-1990s when he was appointed watershed constable. If I really wanted to know more about them, he advised, I could read all about it in back issues of the *Gloucester Daily Times*. Joe Orange did not say when or why this ordinance had been put into place, but I already knew what the catalyst was. Tragedy had inspired, of all things, an ordinance, which he recited koanlike: no camping, fires, motorized vehicles, poaching, dumping, swimming ("after all, that's our water supply"), or littering, and hunting allowed in-season only. These rules, he reminded me, are posted at the main entrance "in very simple declarative English language."

I had been to Dogtown many times by now but I had hardly even noticed these posted rules. Moreover, I had seen or heard many people violating nearly every one of them, or getting their dogs to do it for them, as with the time I saw a man tossing sticks into the Goose Cove Reservoir for his three dogs to fetch.

"I'm not going to suggest that it's Disneyland, because it isn't," Joe

Orange conceded. "Plenty of people are still going up there to get drunk. Or they shoot up and get to be a pain in the ass. You got to go up and root them out and some of them get lost, but those are isolated, unique incidents."

Joe Orange's delivery may have been hard-edged, his manner misanthropic, strict, and relentless, and his vision of Dogtown one-dimensional and unyielding, but he always came back around to how much he loved the place. "It is a very unique little time capsule here. I'm sure if you get off [the trail] in Appalachia, the backcountry of Georgia, you find similar places with people who are pretty much the same as here. You should feel at home here coming from Georgia and Maine. The trees march down to the shore"—there they were, those walking trees I had thought I was about to hallucinate earlier—"it's just a hunk of the Maine coast that just sort of slipped down and reattached itself to Massachusetts."

I had previously thought how easily one could compare Cape Ann to Appalachia. Like the mountains themselves, starting or ending with Kennesaw at their southern extreme, Appalachian culture took some sharp turns, twisted into impenetrable lairs, and fell into steep gullies as it extended all the way into Maine. Perhaps Appalachia's older, self-contained culture had taken a ride to Gloucester on those glacial errat-ics, some of which originated from the northern Appalachian town of Jackman, Maine. Moreover, Cape Ann's intense insularity and bewilder-ing interior made it seem closer to New England's Appalachia than other seafaring towns.

His sermon complete, Joe Orange suddenly, abruptly, said, "Let me wish you a long and happy life, dear," and hung up the phone.

For all his barking relentlessness, Joe Orange's sign-off was surpris-ingly tender. Coming from the tough-guy protector of the woods, I figured that this warmth was nothing to take lightly. But the brusque-ness with which he ended the call also led me to believe that Joe Or-ange had wanted to get me off the phone out of fear that anything I might publish would contribute to Dogtown's demise. Dogtown would no longer be lost unto itself; it would be on the map. And Joe Orange liked his landscapes as wild and woolly, unfettered, and as unpopulated as they could be. Though these qualities occasionally made Dogtown less hospitable to "city bred tenderfoots" who were full of romantic no-

tions and couldn't hack the mosquitoes or the place's disorienting peculiarities, such as me, to Joe Orange, they were what made it so
endearing and worth protecting.

A foghorn sounded, lowly, repeatedly. The day had cooled off con-
siderably. I turned and looked out the window. A clotting mist was
quickly moving in from the sea and thickening to a chowderlike fog.

I walked down to the little dock below Carolyn's house. Water
bathed the rocks audibly, but I could barely see across the cove. Even
the houses where Hartley had stayed, which were a mere thirty feet
away, had disappeared in the haze.

Chapter Twenty-seven

Confabulation

WITH PETER HODGKINS'S TRIAL set to turn over to the defense, Kalis prepared to call his sole witness, psychiatrist Dr. Stevan Gressitt, who had stated in his report that Hodgkins exhibited some of the characteristics of a false confessor. While prosecutors and law enforcement officials consider confessions to be solid statements of guilt, forensic psychiatrists such as Dr. Barbara R. Kirwin, author of *The Mad, the Bad, and the Innocent: The Criminal Mind on Trial*, consider them to be "the most suspect and unreliable forms of data." Kalis was hoping that Gressitt's testimony would reflect this theory. It was exactly what he needed to challenge Hodgkins's multiple confessions. It also happened to be precisely what Gribouski sought to avoid.

With the confessions, the prosecution had a nearly airtight case, but if Kalis were able to sow doubts about Hodgkins's statements within the minds of the jury, the prosecution's case would be significantly weakened. The diluted blood evidence was practically useless to Gribouski. Without the confessions, his case would rely solely on the hairs and fibers found on the bike. Moreover, Kalis was a formidable opponent who had more years of experience as a defense attorney—thirty-two—than the thirty-year-old Gribouski had in life. Twenty-four years later, James Gribouski would state that he would never see such a completely innocent victim as Anne Natti or such a brutal, senseless killing in his entire career. At the time of the trial, though, and with having lost the only two cases he had tried, Gribouski was nervous. But he set out to review every bit of case history on expert testimony, and picked up the telephone the night before Dr. Gressitt was scheduled to testify and made a few calls, most notably to a psychiatrist with whom he discussed each potential weakness in Dr. Gressitt's three-page report.

Back in court, just before the jury was summoned and the defense's presentation began, Gribouski filed a motion with Judge Rutledge against having Dr. Gressitt testify. The doctor's testimony would violate the jury's role as the sole determiners of Hodgkins's credibility, Gribouski argued. Kalis countered that Dr. Gressitt's testimony would help the jury understand Hodgkins's confessions in all of their complexity as forms of evidence, not as clear-cut admissions of guilt.

Judge Rutledge decided to hold a voir dire, a direct testimony and cross-examination without the jury present, to enable him to decide whether to allow Dr. Gressitt to testify.

AS KALIS CROSS-EXAMINED Dr. Gressitt, a bolder outline of Peter Hodgkins's life story began to take shape.

Peter was angry as a child. He had developmental difficulties. When he was six or seven years old, an eleven-year-old boy molested him. He repeated the first grade. For as long as anyone Dr. Gressitt had interviewed could remember, Peter C. Hodgkins Jr. had been a loner, and he often made up stories that did not "jibe with reality" in order to impress people.

By junior high school, Hodgkins had developed a "nasty disposition." Over the years, he became the subject of numerous allegations of sexual abuse and exposure. "He has exhibited himself, masturbated in front of people, [and] scared people for, truly, a long period of time," Dr. Gressitt stated. His arrest reports made it clear that Hodgkins simply behaved "in a truly bizarre manner."

Between 1978 and 1979 he had a series of temper tantrums and went around smashing windows and doors. He was also fired from a fish-processing job for attempting to put nuts and bolts into the fish. Family and friends said he believed the world was against him.

Hodgkins ran up bills and put down payments on expensive cars and never showed up to pay them off or to reclaim his deposits. He once told his father that he had a thousand dollars on him, but when he reached into his pocket, he found that the money was not there. He believed that the money had suddenly disappeared.

Though Hodgkins told people that he had served in the army for two years and often boasted that he flew helicopter missions in Vietnam, in reality he had served for less than a year, from August 1979 to June 1980, and went AWOL several times. His father had never seen his discharge papers.

Hodgkins had lied to the doctors at Bridgewater, too. What he told them about his life and upbringing in 1984 was inconsistent with things he had said when he was previously evaluated at the institution in 1980. And in 1984, he informed them that his girlfriend was pregnant—the same girlfriend that many people who knew Hodgkins had never seen and questioned if she ever existed. Kalis then asked Dr. Gressitt if he had come to an opinion on Peter Hodgkins. "I find a pattern of simply lying," Dr. Gressitt replied. "He is a disturbed man," the doctor concluded, "and has been for a long time." He then stated his belief that Hodgkins was a confabulator, someone who either invents a fiction because he does not remember the truth or simply lies to keep from getting into trouble, like a child who has stolen some candy. In the former instance, the made-up story is "a true defect, an inability in recalling and having any access to the memory and creating something spontaneously," whereas in the latter it is "volitional, deliberate."

"Would you consider Peter Hodgkins a chronic confessor?" Kalis asked.

"I don't have enough evidence to say that he's a chronic confessor," Dr. Gressitt replied. "A chronic liar, yes." But he could not venture much more. Dr. Gressitt admitted to having a poor relationship with Hodgkins because he believed that Hodgkins was afraid he would send him back to Bridgewater.

The testimony that Kalis had hoped for from Dr. Gressitt—that Hodgkins could have confessed to a crime he did not commit—suddenly collapsed. Kalis pressed Dr. Gressitt some more on whether Hodgkins could be a chronic or compulsive confessor, but it was clear that the doctor simply did not have enough information or a good enough relationship with Hodgkins to support any such theory with confidence. And as much as Dr. Gressitt believed that Hodgkins's motives for lying were not without psychological complexity, this did nothing to help the defense's case.

When it came Gribouski's turn to cross-examine Dr. Gressitt, Gribouski poked so many holes in the doctor's ideas about Hodgkins's confabulation and his knowledge of his client, there was nothing but the shell of an expert left on the stand. Dr. Gressitt admitted that confabulation was not a psychiatric disorder or one of the diagnostic categories in the then-current third volume of the American Psychiatric Association's *Diagnostic and Statistical Manual of Mental Disorders*. Gribouski then waived a copy of Hodgkins's criminal record and showed Dr. Gressitt that Hodgkins had in fact lied to *him* about the charges on his record. Gribouski also told the doctor that Hodgkins had avoided the courtroom at his arraignment and during his trial because news cameras were present. Why would someone so obviously publicity shy falsely confess as a way to gain personal notoriety, Gribouski asked. Given what Gribouski had laid out—including reminding the doctor that even he had admitted to having a lack of understanding of his client—Dr. Gressitt said that he could no longer support the theory that Hodgkins was someone who would confess to a crime for the sake of attention. When the doctor could not come up with any other motive for Hodgkins's potentially false statements, Gribouski had no further questions.

After hearing this lengthy voir dire, which took up the better part of the morning, Judge Rutledge ruled to allow Dr. Gressitt to testify.

KALIS CONFERRED BRIEFLY with Hodgkins, who had been sitting in the anteroom with two officers; their talk did not go well.

Once Hodgkins's trial returned to full session, Kalis approached the bench and informed Judge Rutledge and Gribouski that when he told Hodgkins that Dr. Gressitt was going to take the stand, Hodgkins was "almost violently against my using him." With no choice but to support his client's wish, Kalis turned to the courtroom and announced, "The defendant rests."

The jurors stared at Kalis in shock.

Testimony in Peter Hodgkins's trial was complete. Closing arguments would begin the following morning.

To the jury and members of the court who had sat through nearly two weeks of the prosecution's testimony, Peter Hodgkins would remain as enigmatic as Dogtown, the place he loved so dearly. Hodgkins seemed to want it that way.

LATE THAT NIGHT the herdsman Boötes led his hunting dogs Asterion and Chara across a field of stars as he has for millennia. Of the many legends that have been attributed to the Boötes constellation, the Homeric one states that Boötes drives an oxcart leading all the celestial creatures across the sky, just as dreams move ordinary men. What dreams drove Peter Hodgkins? What made him tick? Robert Kalis had wondered night after sleepless night. He never came up with a satisfactory answer.

Another legend concerning the Boötes constellation maintains that the stars represent an Athenian farmer named Icarius, whom Dionysius instructed in the art of winemaking. Icarius invited some shepherds who had never tried wine before to taste his new concoction. The men drank so much that they felt violently ill the next morning. Convinced that Icarius was trying to poison them, the shepherds murdered him as he slept under a tree. Icarius's dog Maera went running for help. In one of the oldest tales of cynomancy, the art of divination based on canine behavior, Maera led Erigone, Icarius's daughter, to her father's bludgeoned corpse. Grief-stricken, Erigone hanged herself from a tree. Maera wandered off and died of sorrow. People wondered what Woofer had seen that day. What did he do when Anne was attacked? The dog had to know the truth of the matter, they believed. He must have watched over Anne, tried to comfort her and keep her warm, people said. Long after the incident, Woofer continued to tuck his tail and cringe at the sound of motorbikes, as if he remained traumatized by the event.

The following morning, the Salem Jail guards searched Peter Hodgkins a final time and escorted him into the sheriff's cruiser for the ride to Newburyport. Outside the window, forests and fields flew by. So much land. Open and inviting. Full of birds taking wing and clouds streaming by, as if in flight. They reached downtown Newburyport, where the Merrimack River coursed on a path through town that paralleled High Street where the courthouse stood. The river's surface was smooth and placid, in spite of a growing swell underneath. The spring melt that often drives the Merrimack to crest its banks come April or May had only recently begun. For now, the river calmly flowed on, cool and pulsing, straight to the sea.

Hodgkins was handed off to the court guards. While he was being patted down a final time, Officer McCurdy had checked to make sure that sets of leg irons and belly chains were at the ready for when Hodgkins's verdict would be read. Increasingly concerned about Hodgkins's statement that he would not leave the courthouse alive if he were found guilty, McCurdy entered the courtroom to assess the scene for any potential hostages Hodgkins might try to take. There were Erik Natti and his children, sitting in a far corner as per usual, and three young, pregnant women sitting in the middle of the front row not far from where Hodgkins would be. Gribouski's wife, who was pregnant with their second child, had decided to come to hear her husband's closing statement and brought her sister-in-law and a friend along for company. Officer McCurdy did not want to give the women any reason for alarm, but asked them to move to the back of the courtroom. Much to McCurdy's relief, they obliged; being in the back meant being closer to the door and the ladies' room.

As soon as Hodgkins was escorted into the courtroom, the air felt tense. Judge Rutledge began delivering a lengthy set of instructions to the jury. Closing statements began with Kalis.

When he had received Hodgkins's signed and videotaped confessions Kalis had initially thought, "It's pretty cut and dried. What is there to try?" But examining the chain of events leading to the confessions made him think otherwise. Soon Kalis began to piece together the story of a deeply troubled man who he believed had played into the wishes of the Gloucester Police with no regard for his own life. He described Hodgkins's time in the woods with the helicopter bearing down on him, the barking dogs and men going by with guns. Hodgkins was so terrified of dying, so worn down by his nights without sleep or food, that he had let himself be interrogated for nine hours without a lawyer and signed every document put in front of him after turning himself in. In those nine hours the police had offered him food but no rest, though Hodgkins had essentially been on the run since Tuesday night, when he had asked Brian Langley to take him over the Route 128 bridge. Hodgkins was under such mental and emotional duress when he arrived back in the woods with the police that he turned to Detective Reardon and asked him, "What do you want me to do?" as if Hodgkins had not the foggiest idea why he was there. Moreover, Kalis argued that "an awful lot of blood had to be on the person who killed Anne Natti." Yet the FBI, "with the finest laboratory in the world, couldn't find a speck of blood" on the murder weapon. The blood that they did find could have been anyone's. "I haven't the intelligence to tell you why human beings agree to do these things," Kalis said. "I can't explain those mental processes on June 29 when he [Hodgkins] walked into the police station to commit suicide. Don't be part of it."

Where Kalis found a complicated case full of holes and psychological mystery, Gribouski saw a cut-and-dried collection of evidence that repeatedly illustrated Hodgkins's guilt. Blood was found in eleven locations on the bike, including places necessary to operate it. Whoever rode that motorbike had blood on his hands, Gribouski proclaimed. Additional tests proved that Hodgkins had blood on each and every one of his fingers, in the webbing between them, on his palm, and also on his jeans.

Most important, Gribouski argued, chemists matched microscopic characteristics from the damaged hair discovered on the motorbike to Anne Natti's. While Kalis had argued that the hair was that 1 out of 1,000 instance in which a faulty evidence match had been made, Gribouski stressed the inverse, that the odds were 999 out of 1,000 that the match was accurate.

Guilt drove Peter Hodgkins to confess, Gribouski proclaimed, not fear. He had walked into the police station and confessed immediately, not after nine hours of interrogation or being offered enticements of food or rest. The police noticed that he was hungry and therefore offered to feed him a generous three times. And Hodgkins not only told the police a story that matched the evidence, he also led them to the scene of the crime and showed them the murder weapon, a forty-pound rock, as big as a watermelon, which sat on a table in front of Gribouski.

Gribouski picked up the rock and paced back and forth. He noticed the sunlight tracking across the courtroom and thought about the legendary orator Daniel Webster, who had tried cases in the same room, a thought that filled him with a sense of auspice and might. But this was no "Devil and Daniel Webster," Stephen Vincent Benét's story in which Webster goes up against the devil in front of a jury that included the Indian chief Metacom, sachem of the Wampanoag from King Philip's

War, and the pirate Blackbeard in front of Judge John Hathorne, the Salem Witch Trial adjudicator (and Nathaniel Hawthorne's ancestor). This was the story of one man who had made his own deal with an internal demon in Gloucester's woods and was being tried in front of a jury of ordinary Newburyport folk. But that did not keep Gribouski from seizing upon all the drama in this tale as he wielded that most primitive murder weapon, the rock, and suddenly slammed it down on a table, jolting everyone in the courtroom to attention.

All eyes were fixed on Gribouski as he argued that Hodgkins freely confessed to all three criteria for first-degree murder in the state of Massachusetts. In thinking about attacking Anne Natti and deliberately picking up the rock and following her, Hodgkins had premeditated, Gribouski proclaimed. Hodgkins then freely, casually stated how he shoved Anne Natti, slammed the rock down on her skull, and hit her again, this time in the face. Gribouski pounded the table a second time, visibly upsetting the courthouse superintendent who was responsible for the care of the venerable old edifice. Hodgkins, seated, appeared as detached from the proceedings as before. Gribouski went on to explain that the defendant had also freely admitted to searching Anne Natti for money in an attempt to rob her, which meant that the murder was carried out while he was committing a felony. And Anne Natti was writhing in pain on this unseasonably cold, rainy June day, but Hodgkins removed all of her clothes and further brutalized this perfectly innocent woman by tying her rain gear around her neck and dragging her bludgeoned, naked body through the forest like some caveman while she was moaning in anguish. Then he left her for dead. It was unusually cruel, atrocious behavior, Gribouski declared.

Look at her here: Gribouski produced a photo of Anne Natti in the full bloom of health and happiness. Her chestnut hair flowing. Her eyes bright and full of life. Now look at what Peter Hodgkins did to her: Gribouski produced the most graphic crime scene photos for all to see. Face swollen beyond recognition, blood caked and bruised. "Look at your watches for thirty seconds," Gribouski said. Imagine that length of time multiplied to a full half hour. "Think of her pain so far off the path where nobody was going to find her when he pushed her face three inches into the ground and left her there to die." And with that, Gribouski closed his statement.

Yes, think of that story, if you will. Can one senseless death harness

four centuries of history and drive them forward? The outcast Hodgkins wanders among the rocks, cursing the place with his presence as
though he were the social descendant of those Dogtown witches. He
became a sound heard in the trees, a sight unseen then fully revealed.
Many people believed he lived in Dogtown because he seemed always
to be there, but he was sleeping wherever he could, even where his feet
poked through the wrought-iron bars of a bed frame under the watch-
ful eye of his teddy bear, as if he were prisoner to some childhood
trauma.

"I did not know what I was thinking," Hodgkins said in both of his
confessions, as if he had mentally fled the scene of his crime while he
was committing it. Then he claimed with enduring persistence that he
had watched someone else, a man in a yellow suit, kill Anne Natti. As
forensic psychiatrist Abby Stein explains in her book *Prologue to Violence*, the criminal's perspective shifts to this self-protecting mode because, no matter what kind of atrocity one has committed, it is hard for
the mind to see itself as evil.

Turn this story toward Anne Natti as she walked through Dogtown's
woods in search of a little peace and quiet and some precious time to
herself. But time stepped aside as death moved deliberately and suddenly. It had been there for centuries, haunting the abandoned village,
silently crossing those ancient paths, sleeping in the old cellar holes, and
overseeing the lichens as they slowly pulverized those imposing rocks
that reminded people to "Be On Time" and "Be True." Death did not
look Anne Natti in the eye. Its movement was shame-filled, coarse. Her
killing was senseless, just as its perpetrator seemed to be.

After Gribouski had finished his closing argument and Judge Rutledge instructed the jury and sent them to deliberations, Peter Hodgkins asked to go to the bathroom. An officer stood by the bathroom
door, which was kept slightly ajar while another officer sat nearby.

Slamming doors echoed up the stairs as the building emptied. The
guard took in the silence for a few moments. It was unusually quiet. He
knocked on the bathroom door. There was no response. "Peter?" he
called. The guard pushed the door, but it would not budge. The second
officer leaped up from his nearby seat. The two men called out. Kalis
had left the courtroom already. Gloucester detectives David Reardon
and Kenneth Ryan, who were sitting in the courtroom, immediately
jumped up and ran to the side room. The court officers pushed the

bathroom door open. Hodgkins lay prostrate and bleeding, but still conscious. In his right hand he clutched a small Gillette Trac II razor blade.

The guards reached for towels and applied pressure on the gushing wounds. Hodgkins had sliced from his jaw to his left ear and made an additional three-inch cut across the inside of his left forearm just below his elbow. This second incision was an inch deep.

Paramedics arrived. They wrapped swaths of bandages around his arm, made a mummylike casing for his neck and head, and attached a bag of intravenous solution. Hodgkins was manacled, placed in leg irons, and strapped onto a stretcher. Three men carried him down the steep courthouse stairs. Three walked alongside as guards. A seventh held the IV bag aloft. With lights orbiting, but no sirens blaring so as not to alarm the jurors, an ambulance silently carried Hodgkins away.

Gribouski's wife, sister, and friend, who had left the courthouse early to get some lunch, were on their way back to the building when they came upon the quiet scene of police lights flashing and the ambulance's trailing, spinning lights. The women panicked. Kalis, Gribouski, Judge Rutledge, and McCurdy had all believed that Hodgkins would attempt to take a hostage. In spite of Hodgkins's previous suicide attempts, though, Kalis and Gribouski later claimed that no one had anticipated that the life Peter Hodgkins would try to end that day would be his own.

PETER HODGKINS HAD now tried to kill himself three times since confessing to the murder of Anne Natti, and he failed in this attempt, too. By 3:00 P.M., officers escorted him back to the courthouse. The jury, who knew nothing about the suicide attempt, continued their deliberations. Though his face, neck, and arm were heavily bandaged, Hodgkins was fine. Wearing leg irons and handcuffs, he listened to the radio and tapped his toes and joked with the court officers as if nothing had happened.

Hodgkins told the officers that he sneaked the razor blade into the courthouse by placing it inside a matchbook he carried in his cigarette pack. But when he talked to Kalis, Hodgkins said that he had tucked the blade inside a slit he made in the seam of his prison dungarees. And Hodgkins changed his tune yet again when he talked to Detective Reardon and claimed to have carried the blade in his mouth between his gum and cheek. It seemed as if there was no story that Peter Hodgkins would ever tell straight.

Kalis, Gribouski, and Judge Rutledge agreed that for everyone's safety it would be best if Hodgkins were not brought into the courtroom for the verdict. Kalis worried that Hodgkins might appear to have been brutalized, but he was also concerned about what would happen next for his client. McCurdy told Kalis that the previous defendant who had attempted suicide in the courthouse ended up being committed to Bridgewater. Because of Hodgkins's strongly stated aversion to being sent there, Kalis made a special request to Judge Rutledge that, if the jury found Hodgkins guilty, he not sentence him to the facility. At this point it was all Kalis could do to help his client.

Before anyone could tell Peter Hodgkins that he would not be allowed in the courtroom, he requested to listen to his verdict from the side room.

Meanwhile, people milled about the courthouse awaiting the results of the jury's deliberation. With each passing hour, the courtroom atmosphere grew increasingly anxious. For what seemed to many to be an open-and-shut case, the jury was taking an inordinately long time. Erik Natti began to fear the worst.

Around 6:00 P.M., the foreman of the jury entered the courtroom and asked for clarification on the assault-with-intent-to-rob charge.

Approximately ten minutes later, just as the New England March twilight was beginning to fade to darkness, the jury filed back in.

Hodgkins sat next to an open door. The foreman stood. Peter C. Hodgkins Jr. was found guilty of first-degree murder and assault with intent to rob.

The Natti family rejoiced.

Officers escorted Hodgkins into the courtroom for his sentencing. He received the mandatory sentence of life without parole for the murder charge. Gribouski pushed for an additional eighteen-to-twenty-year sentence for the assault charge. After a review of Hodgkins's probation record, Judge Rutledge filed a complaint for the assault charge so it would remain on his record, but did not issue an additional sentence. Gribouski maintained his professional demeanor, but he was ecstatic. Not only had he won his first case, he had put Hodgkins away for good.

Hodgkins was whisked away to Cedar Junction, Massachusetts'

maximum-security prison, sixty-five miles to the south in the town of
Walpole, but five days later he was back in the Newburyport Superior
Courthouse with Kalis at his side, filing a motion for a retrial. The mo-
tion was promptly denied.

ON MARCH 29, two days after Hodgkins lost his appeal, boulders were
rolled across the entrances to Dogtown. The Steering Committee had
successfully passed a temporary ordinance to block off the woods from
motor vehicle traffic. Even though Peter Hodgkins was now gone, his
shadow continued to hang over this forsaken place. For some Cape Ann
residents he may as well have gathered every boulder, birch tree, white
pine, and blueberry bush and penned them in behind rebar and cinder
blocks with him, because they never wanted to set foot in Dogtown
again.

Chapter Twenty-eight

Mountains in Stone

AFTER PETER HODGKINS was sent away, the Dogtown Steering Committee made significant strides in its efforts to restore the area's reputation, if not the place itself. The private fund-raising campaign named Save Dogtown was closing in on its title-clearing efforts and its goal of raising $85,000 to purchase 150 Dogtown acres for conservation. Gates were installed across Dogtown's various entrances to keep out motorized vehicles, which were now banned from the area, with the exception of snowmobiles. The area's protective ordinance cleared the City Council and was put into immediate effect.

Steering Committee member Peter Anastas began publishing a new round of *Gloucester Daily Times* articles on the various facets of Dogtown's history. The Cape Ann Historical Association (now the Cape Ann Museum) put together an exhibit of Hartley's Dogtown paintings that was accompanied by lectures on Hartley and his and Charles Olson's Dogtown poetry. Nearly a year to the day after Anne Natti was killed, Ted Tarr led a crew of volunteers into the highland to clear and mark trails in preparation for an event called Dogtown Day. Bad weather dampened the day's proceedings, which included map-reading classes, guided walks, and a 5K fun run, but the event suggested that in the space of a year people had successfully begun to take back the woods.

This Dogtown renaissance did not end there. Gloucester choreographer Ina Hahn began creating a series of Dogtown-inspired modern dances, and composer Stephen Scotti wrote what Carolyn O'Connor called "the Dogtown musical," or *Dogtown in Song and Story*, as Scotti's song cycle was officially titled. Harry Chapin and Yoko Ono had previously released songs entitled "Dogtown," but Scotti's inspiration came from poems about the area by Hartley, various local poets, and Percy MacKaye, whose 1920 narrative poem "Dogtown Common" tells the story of a minister's son who falls in love with a Dogtown witch.

Before the premiere, Scotti took soprano Carla Bee up to Dogtown to rehearse by Babson's "Help Mother" rock to help her better connect to the source of his inspiration. They placed their hands on the boulder and sang as if they were channeling music straight from the rock.

The Annisquam Village Church performance of the Scotti work began with "Away on the Dogtown Road," a cheerful, melodic piece that could inspire even the crankiest old soul to skip straight up to the highland and start looking for four-leaf clovers. "The Wraith of Dogtown," the final song, which had been mistakenly printed in the program as "The Rape of Dogtown," took things to the opposite end of the spectrum. A singer walked up the church's darkened center aisle holding a candle under her chin, her face lit up like a phantom's. "Ooo, ooo, ooo," she wailed mournfully into the night. On this evening, Dogtown's two natures were fully expressed.

Members of the Dogtown Steering Committee continued inventorying and debating these two natures along with every living and nonliving thing in and related to Dogtown as they put the final touches on a thick report about the area to help guide the mayor, City Council members, and others in making decisions about how to manage the area. Representing the History Subcommittee, Peter Anastas and coauthor Martha Oakes attempted to set the record straight on the topic of Dogtown's mysticism: "Romantic fantasists who see in Dogtown's boulders a counterpart to Stonehenge and other Druidic ritual sites have wished also to locate primitive rites and practices here among the barren spaces between Dogtown's dolmen. Such practices exist, however, only in the imagination of those who are drawn to the peculiar quality of Dogtown's light, the underbrush that clings to its gravelly soil and to the seemingly ageless geologic formations of its rocks and hilly places." When I read this report nearly twenty years later, it seemed also to be describing Marsden Hartley, Thomas Wentworth Higginson, Charles Olson, and people like me. However, "legends and stories about magical practices on Dogtown," they continued, "may be somewhat closer to the facts." How the committee differentiated between "primitive rites" and "magical practices" was unclear. At the very least, from what I could gather after seeing the men in capes, witches had remained part of this place.

AFTER THAT WALK with Shep Abbott back in the autumn of 2001, I waited at a restaurant in downtown Gloucester to meet the "warlock" that Shep had recommended that I contact, Gerrit Lansing. Gerrit was a charming older gentleman in his midseventies with a head of neatly trimmed snowy white hair and crystalline blue eyes. Dressed in a button-down shirt, cardigan sweater, and khakis, he looked like your average upper-middle-class North Shore retiree, not what I had expected from a local expert on the occult. A poet and former Columbia University Press editor who first came to Gloucester by invitation from inventor John Hays Hammond Jr., Gerrit began studying the occult in the 1940s when he was an undergraduate at Harvard and started the university's first parapsychology club. The topic was also an interest he shared with Charles Olson, with whom he became friends.

"There is a geophysical electromagnetic anomaly under Dogtown, which makes it a very powerful place for meditation," Gerrit told me as he tore at a popover. When I asked if Gerrit could explain his take on this further, he replied, "I can't explain why there are certain power spots of breakthrough to another dimension up there [in Dogtown] or anywhere; scientific explanations are merely metaphors to my mind. One must allow for irrational explanations and magical explanations."

As for the two caped men, Gerrit did not know anything about them, but told me, "Some say that witches escaped the Salem trials and took shelter in Dogtown. Who knows if this is true, but Dogtown has been used and is used today by covens of witches for certain feasts, as it has for years. Most of these rituals are private, of course."

I never had much luck tracking down any of the kinds of rituals Gerrit referred to, but every so often I came across evidence of a different kind of woodland ritual: drinking around a campfire. Five years after Anne Natti was killed, one of these campfires burned so hot something previously unthinkable occurred.

THE WHALE'S JAW had endured hundreds of thousands of years of heat and ice and still managed to surge out of the earth as though it were defying gravity. That is, until one August 1989 night, when a fire, fed by a group of men drinking themselves into oblivion, raged under the rock's lower jaw. The flames feasted on branches, logs, and stumps, heating the overhanging monolith. The roaring conflagration made enough noise that the revelers could not have heard the telltale ethereal tinkling sound of molecules in the granite's crystalline structure breaking apart. The whale's lower jaw snapped in two and came crashing down, nearly crushing several drunken men.

"People were shocked. Perplexed. We didn't know what to make of it," Gloucester resident Cheryl Davis said. "Did it mean we should stay out of Dogtown? Was it dangerous? An omen? Foretelling what? Most suspected that over time we might figure out what it meant. But there was a huge sense of loss in the community." More than a massive hunk of granite broke that night. The Whale's Jaw had long been an icon of Cape Ann. It represented the various facets of Cape Ann's history from the Laurentide ice sheet to fishing and granite quarrying. It also conjured up notions of that mythic era described in the Book of Genesis when "there were giants in the earth." Many Cape Anners had an immediate, personal connection to the stone leviathan, too. Memories and photographs of parents and ancestors visiting the monolith, such as Charles Olson's picture of his father pushing the whale's jaws apart, had given them a palpable sense of belonging to this place and its continuum of history.

Residents discussed whether to mortar the rock back together, using the same technique that had been employed to reattach pieces that have fallen off Plymouth Rock over the years. John Tuck, who was Anne Natti's brother-in-law at the time of her murder, proposed making massive quantities of superglue and raising the whale's lower jaw with a pulley system modeled on one that archaeologists theorized the Easter Islanders had used when carving their monoliths. But the Whale's Jaw could not be repaired.

For many, the breaking of the Whale's Jaw signaled the end of an era, if not of Dogtown itself. "It was another trashing of this sacred space," Rockport resident Babette Brackett said, Anne Natti's death being the implied first event. "It was so powerful. Whenever I go by there now I always have this feeling of sadness and loss." One Gloucester resident who has never been back since the break claims, "I wouldn't be able to bear it."

ALTHOUGH MY ONLY experience of the intact Whale's Jaw came from photographs and Hartley's paintings, the story of its breaking further illustrated how much Dogtown had represented to people. And as much as I had strived to see the Dogtown beyond Hartley's frame, I realized that I had only wanted to love these fabled woods for what they represented to me: the possibility that they could somehow help recapture that hopeful sense of discovery and wonder that had been lost to me for so long. The more I had wanted Dogtown to provide this feeling, the less I was actually capable of appreciating its reality. Even the starlings, though ominous, were part of what made the place so deeply, weirdly fascinating.

A couple of months after that walk with Ted Tarr, I came across a note in my research about Hartley's working method. Hartley once stated that when he found a place that he wanted to paint, he "did as I always have to do about a place—look at it—see it—and think of nothing else." That was where I had failed in my Dogtown endeavors. As much as I had tried, I had never truly succeeded in emptying myself of expectations. I also revisited those three lines from T. S. Eliot's "Ash Wednesday" that Hartley had quoted in his letters and on the back of one of his 1931 Dogtown paintings: "Teach us to care and not to care / Teach us to sit still / Even among these rocks." Following Eliot's instructions, Hartley had studied this land, trying to absorb as much of it as he could. And on an unseasonably warm December day when I was back in Gloucester to attend a holiday party, I returned to Dogtown to also try to look at it, see it, and think of nothing else.

Tromping through the woods, I wandered off trail to explore parts of the area with which I was less familiar. Eventually I came to a boulder field where densely packed rocks spread across the highland like extensive earthworks sculptures. This was the terminal moraine of the Laurentide Ice Sheet, which Nathaniel Southgate Shaler had described in 1888 as "appearing in the landscape like the ruins of Cyclopean masonry." I continued walking into an adjacent little valley strewn with boulders, as if a giant had sown a handful of Brobdingnagian seeds across the land. Taking a seat atop a large rock, I realized I had never been in this place or seen the moraine from this perspective before. I sat for a while, attempting to look at the land in the same way as Hartley had, trying to sit still, to care and not to care.

The silence of this rock grove was so deep it seemed as though I could hear the sound of the trees drawing up water through their roots, the lichen and moss breaking rocks into dust, the soft burrowing of every animal. It was as though the Earth's hidden, most essential forms had risen up from deep inside its core and spilled over into this little valley. I took in this place and watched the pale winter sunlight move through the trees. The forest continued settling into itself. Only by sitting and looking and spending time in this way did I start to notice how the rising and falling contours of this land became increasingly visible. In some places it appeared as if the place were somehow buried underneath itself. And that was how I noticed that a nearby band of boulders, now half concealed under decades worth of underbrush and growth, would have once stood in tall relief, twisting and rising from the earth in nearly the same shape and thrust as those in *Mountains in Stone*.

"Oh, potent Art!" exclaimed Nathaniel Hawthorne's portrait artist in "The Prophetic Pictures" while admiring one of his creations. "As thou bringest the faintly revealed Past to stand in that narrow strip of sunlight, which we call Now, canst thou summon the shrouded Future to meet her there?" I imagined Hartley making quick sketches of this place back in 1931, when there would have been no trees, making for a more impressive scene worthy of "painted sculpture and no ordinary painting"—the landscape demanded this of him. That summer and autumn he painted late into the night at his Rocky Neck studio, quarrying the rocks from his memory, and shaping them into form as though working out the essence of his subject from surrounding matter like a sculptor. Something of the immensity of Hartley's solitude and suffering, its chill and its fire, flowed off his brush and into these paintings to summon me here years later.

I thought about the many people that *Mountains in Stone* and this zuihitsu had led me to, and how each of them had such a powerful relationship to this place. The living ones had repeatedly described Dogtown as the "soul" or the "shadow" of Cape Ann; it was not just one or the other, it was both light and dark, earth and eidolon, past and prophecy, a place they could not live without.

As for me, I was not so sure I would continue seeking inspiration from Dogtown, but knowing that this forgotten corner of America continued to exist and understanding some of its strange past filled me with a sense of auspice and wonder. Dogtown was now mine, just as it had belonged to Hartley and many others.

Epilogue

A YEAR AFTER Anne Natti died, Isabel Natti and John Tuck loaded a little red wagon with a metal plaque that they had made up, and wheeled it into Dogtown. It states:

ANNE'S PATH
HER LAST BREATH WAS LOVING
THE SMELL OF PINE

Arriving at the trail juncture where Peter Hodgkins first struck their sister-in-law, they set the plaque flush to the ground, where it still sits today.

Despite the sudden, devastating loss of his wife and his tragic memories of her murder, Erik Natti never abandoned the land his father had reforested. Years after the murder, he built a house not far from the trailer where he and Anne had been living that 1984 summer. Though Erik is an extremely shy and private man, he openly talks about his love for and connection to this land and his Finnish heritage. When I last saw him, in the summer of 2008, he had recently planted four hundred additional tree saplings and had nearly finished typing a transcript of his father's translation of the *Kalevala*. As for what happened in 1984, he would only say, "The murder has moved to the past, but it will never become history."

When Bob Kalis was leaving the courthouse the day that Peter Hodgkins's trial closed, Isabel Natti approached and gave him a brown paper bag. Inside the bag Kalis found a box of Tuck's Candy, the candy her in-laws made, and a thank-you note that she had designed. Kalis opened the card, which read, "Dear Mr. Kalis, I observed that you did your part to ensure that Hodgkins has received a fair and impartial trial. If I were ever charged with a crime, guilty or not, I would be fortunate to have you represent me. Thank you, John Tuck."

"It was the most extraordinary thing," Bob Kalis said as he handed this card to me when I interviewed him in his Marblehead home. Kalis, now in his eighties, appeared fit and as sharp as the pushpin that has fastened this note to a bulletin board next to his desk since the day he received it.

"Peter," Kalis said, slapping his knee, as if the frustrations he had experienced twenty-five years ago were right under his skin. "I never could figure him out." Hodgkins's was the last murder case Kalis tried. "It was so debilitating," he said.

The trial was an equally memorable experience for James Gribouski, who now practices law in Worcester. For twenty-two years, Gribouski kept a photograph on his office wall showing him, Kalis, and court of-ficials standing in the woods and staring at that unmistakable depres-sion in the ground on the trial's second day.

"They've got me made out to be psychotic, a maniac, unable to con-trol myself," Peter Hodgkins told *Boston* magazine reporter Wendy Qui-ñones a few months after his trial, as he sat inside a gymnasium-like space at Cedar Junction. "If I had that kind of problem, I would have to be real screwed up, big time, ending up in an institution or something.

"I know what people are telling you, and I'm telling you something different," he went on. "I love the woods. I always knew what I was doing. I would never say there was a point up in the woods when I was out of control, when I needed help. . . . I never have any incidents; I've been accused of going up there and doing stuff, but I never have. . . . I'm not the only person, but . . . the cops would think of me. . . . It happens every summer: somebody says I'm there, and I wasn't."

In 2006, I wrote Peter Hodgkins asking if he would be willing to share his perspective on Dogtown and this event. He responded im-mediately. "That area had a significant effect on my life," he wrote. "I often escape there in my dreams."

That May, I traveled to the medium-security Massachusetts Cor-rectional Institute at Norfolk, where Peter Hodgkins is now serving out his life sentence. After I had waited more than half an hour for Hodg-kins, Diane Wiffin, the Department of Corrections public relations of-ficial who was my escort, told me that inmates sometimes agree to an interview and change their minds at the last minute. It seemed that Peter Hodgkins was doing just that, but after nearly forty-five minutes of waiting, a guard let us pass through a prison gate.

Ms. Wiffin and I walked down a long corridor that passed through the facility's nineteen-foot-high outer walls and were granted passage through a sally port. Once inside the prison, we were met by Norfolk's community outreach coordinator, an affable young man who explained that most offenders at Norfolk live in a dormitory-like setting and are allowed to roam freely throughout much of the facility's confines. Thus, when I had arrived earlier that morning, Peter was not in his cell. It merely took a while to find him.

Never having been in a prison before, I had expected to enter a room with cubicles divided by Plexiglas windows and connected by telephones, but my two escorts led me into a typical office conference room, where I took a seat at a long table near a window. I had imagined that a guard would escort an orange jumper–clad, handcuffed Peter Hodgkins into the room and that he would look like an aged version of the wild-eyed young man that I had seen on his confession video and in 1984 editions of the *Gloucester Daily Times*. But after I waited another twenty minutes, a tall man dressed in jeans, a denim shirt, work boots, and a metal bracelet walked sheepishly into the room and took a seat across from me. This man with long, thinning gray hair was older and seemingly gentler than the Peter Hodgkins who had been fixed in my mind's eye.

Hodgkins stared at the middle distance between us as we talked. His unusually pale blue eyes, which had been described to me many times before, possessed a haunted, distant quality. Every so often he looked at me, but as soon as our eyes met he would quickly turn his head away, as if he were embarrassed or painfully shy. At times it seemed as if he were not fully, mentally present, but he came across as an extremely likable person full of a childlike love and tenderness for Dogtown. Talking about the area made him spring to life with stories that I have quoted elsewhere in the book. Dogtown was and continues to be the one place where he feels safe. When I asked what he needed to feel safe from, he said he did not know.

Though seemingly docile, Peter struck me as a person with the kind of vulnerability that could turn extremely dangerous. The thought that I was sitting across a table from a convicted first-degree murderer was never far from my mind.

As Wendy Quiñones pointed out at the time of the murder, all of the institutions that should have prevented Peter Hodgkins's decline—

the schools, the police, the military, the courts, mental health and probation agencies—essentially failed. Where the law and social services
could not help him, people attempted to do so, but in the end, it was
not enough. After Anne Natti was killed, there were some serious dis-
cussions about how the Cape Ann community could improve its social
service agencies, do more outreach with the mentally ill, and prevent
violence against women, but this talk did not command as much attention or newspaper ink as what to do about Dogtown. This emphasis on
Dogtown struck me as remarkable, but it most likely had to do with the
fact that it is far easier to fix a place than these societal ills.

As I was leaving the prison the day of my interview, Peter turned to
me and said, "Don't feel bad for me for being here, kid. I made this
choice." Though I got the impression that the structured life at Norfolk
was doing him some good—which is not at all to suggest that life im-
prisonment is easy—I was not convinced that Hodgkins's "choice" was
a fully conscious one.

A few days later, I received a letter from Peter in which he elabo-
rated on his feelings about the area. "Something calls to me," he wrote.
"The trees are calling me near, I have to find out why. The gentle Voices
I hear . . . Draw me to going to the woods . . . I would hear the Elders
of the trees speaking to me Strange but that is how I connect myself
with the woods. One has to beleave [*sic*] in the Forces." Perhaps the
region did in fact wield a peculiar psychic influence over him, as Peter
Anastas had suggested. In a subsequent letter, I asked Hodgkins what
exactly the elders in the trees had said to him, but he never responded
to this question.

Gloucester detective David Reardon later told me how masterful
Peter could be at telling people what he thought they wanted to hear. I
had wondered if Peter was just putting on a good show for me that day
at Norfolk, but my gut-level instinct told me Hodgkins was in fact sincere. As for his letter, I was not so confident. The various letters Peter
and I have exchanged over the years have confirmed Reardon's statement. They left me with an impression of a man who is extremely eager
to please. Hodgkins tells me what he thinks I want to hear, then immediately says or does nearly the opposite. Every so often he seems genuinely sincere and expresses a fervent desire to have a friend. Then I
won't hear from him again. He seems to be truly, deeply confused.

David Reardon eventually became a lawyer. One day, he received a phone call from a Peter Hodgkins. Reardon presumed that the man on the line was Peter's father, but in fact it was Pete Jr. asking if Reardon would represent him on an appeal. "I put you there, Pete," Reardon said. "I'm not going to be able to get you out."

Peter Hodgkins has tried to appeal on at least three occasions with the help of various lawyers, but his case has gotten tossed out each time. In one of these appeal attempts, his lawyer argued that Hodgkins was a Vietnam veteran prone to suffering post-traumatic stress disorder dissociative states. Three letters of support from psychiatrists, ministers, and prison officials who worked with incarcerated veterans were filed with Hodgkins's appeal papers. None of these individuals bothered to check his service record, where they would have learned that Peter Hodgkins never went to Vietnam. One of these letters cited the same molestation incident with a neighborhood boy that Dr. Gressitt mentioned in his voir dire. The letter also reported that Hodgkins claimed to have had an abusive relationship with his father. But given that the letter was also full of flagrant lies about Hodgkins's Vietnam service, it was hard to know what to believe. (Hodgkins's family declined interview requests for this book.) In spite of the ubiquity and accuracy of DNA testing, Hodgkins has never filed an appeal using this line of defense.

At some point after the murder, a couple who had recently moved to Hodgkins Street believed that a ghost occupied their home. They invited a local healer who knew something about the history of the area to come and investigate. The healer confirmed the presence of a male ghost and deduced that it was the Hodgkins forebear who had built the house and was buried in a cemetery just beyond the backyard. All wondered if Peter C. Hodgkins Jr.'s actions had roused the specter from his rightful resting place. This added to the spooky chill the couple felt moving through their home. While burning smudge sticks and incense to coax the spirit back to the cemetery, they heard a rattling sound, until suddenly the house quieted down. It has seemed normal ever since.

Dogtown's mysterious aura has not been chased away. The Dogtown Steering Committee did manage to acquire some more land, but not much. Today, roughly sixteen hundred Dogtown acres, a mixture of private and publicly owned land, have some form of conservation protection, leaving at least fourteen hundred acres vulnerable to development. Significant tracts of Dogtown land remain of unknown ownership, though one conservationist has been quietly researching these parcels over the years. These unprotected acres remain the last place where anyone can put up new construction on island Cape Ann. New houses continue to go up along the area's periphery, including a subdivision with the perfectly inhospitable name "Thorn Hill."

Recently, a Rockport selectman garnered support to pave Dogtown's old Rockport Road in order to open up greater emergency access and reduce traffic on Eastern Avenue, the primary artery in and out of Rockport. But the old Rockport Road runs through the heart of Gloucester's watershed and part of land that Roger W. Babson bequeathed to the city. Many Gloucester residents were outraged over the proposal. Ted Tarr thought the road was "not such a bad idea," which created another opportunity for him to butt heads with Joe Orange, who is now chairman of Gloucester's Watershed Committee. Though well into his eighties, Joe Orange is as hearty and robust as ever and, as Dogtown's ever-vigilant constable, continues to kick any and all ne'er-do-wells out of the area. When the road-building issue came to a head, Joe Orange continued his flair for hard-edged hyperbole by stating, "Nine months out of the year, there is more traffic going in and out of Mongolia than Rockport. Rockport doesn't have a problem; they have to live with it." The road-building project was abandoned, but local conservationists stress that it was abandoned merely for now.

While people continue to express concern for Dogtown, few actually actively tend to the place or work behind the scenes to halt its development. The area is in true need of more hands-on volunteers like Joe Orange and people like the individual who has quietly colored in the statue of St. Peter's beard over the years—effort and a little artifice are required to enable Dogtown to continue to provide a seemingly authentic, stumbled-upon, wild experience.

"What a distinguished spot my Dogtown is—I could work in it for a lifetime," Marsden Hartley wrote to Alfred Stieglitz on November 5, 1931. Hartley went back to Dogtown during the summer of 1934 and also returned to the subject from memory in 1936. Though he revisited Dogtown more than any other subject in his career, the place never had as powerful a hold on him as it did that 1931 summer. Hartley continued his peripatetic ways and eventually settled down in the small coastal town of Corea, Maine, until 1943, when he died at age sixty-six.

Cape Anners wanted to take back the woods from this 1984 tragedy, but until this horrific crime took place, few had been willing to
take the necessary action to halt the area's decline. Peter Hodgkins's
inexplicable actions changed Dogtown forever, or at least people's perceptions of it. But in actuality, are not the place itself and people's
perceptions one and the same?

Author's Note

THIS IS A WORK of narrative nonfiction in which I attempt to tell the story of a landscape—Gloucester, Massachusetts' Dogtown—and the relationships of people, including myself, to this unusual setting. Although I attempted to square the area's folklore with its sparse historical records, I eventually concluded that the history of Dogtown is inseparable from the emotional truth of this lore and people's perceptions of the place.

Throughout the ten years that I worked on this book, I interviewed close to a hundred people. To better allow the text to read as a narrative and to keep the story from getting overcrowded with sources, I decided to sometimes use constructions such as "people said." Sources for these statements are referenced in the endnotes.

Gloucester is an incredibly insular island community. Although it is technically a city, it has a small-town culture that is intensified by its island character. It is also the sort of place where family resentments can last for generations. And while many people were forthcoming with me with their feelings about Dogtown or Anne Natti's murder, some asked not to be named, or not to be named in particular contexts. I obliged these requests and changed names when asked.

Although this book focuses on its 1984 nadir, Dogtown is no longer the place it was back then. Cape Anners were successful in "taking back the woods" in spite of Dogtown's lingering bad reputation, but development pressure on Cape Ann has only increased over the years. Most of Dogtown is still in desperate need of conservation protection and better management, but I hope that it will never become a highly mediated tourist destination marked with signposts and paved trails. If you choose to go there, I hope you will discover something akin to what I did, "one of these strange wild places," as Marsden Hartley so evocatively described it, where "the chemistry of the universe is too busy realizing itself."

Appendix
Notes on the Term "Dogtown"

TO COME UP with my list of unincorporated communities known as "Dogtown" (see Chapter Sixteen) as well as my general definition of the term, I searched the *Getty Thesaurus of Geographic Names*, the U.S. Geological Survey and state historical place name indexes, W.P.A. guides, Civil War gazetteers, and additional lists such as the Commonwealth of Massachusetts' "Unincorporated and Unofficial Names of Communities." Additionally, I surveyed newspaper archives and caught stray bits from geographers' online message boards. I also came across volumes or resources on individual communities formerly or, in at least in one instance, currently known as Dogtown, such as the following:

Robert A. Birmingham, *Dogtown: A Historical and Archaeological Study of a Late Historic St. Croix Chippewa Community*. Burnett County, Wisconsin, Historical Society, May 1983.

Martha Callahan, *Excavations at Dogtown: A Pueblo III Pithouse Village in the Klethla Valley*. Unpublished M.A. thesis, North Arizona University, November 1985.

Bob Corbett, St. Louis Dogtown website: http://www.webster .edu/~corbetre/dogtown/dogtown.html.

Don Darnell, *Born, Raised, Lived, Learned, & Loved in Dogtown*. Lincoln, NE: self-published, 1993.

Wayne Pimentel, *Dogtown and Ditches, Life on the Westside*. Los Banos, CA: Loose Change Publications, 1987.

In my tabulation of American Dogtowns, I did not include such place names as Arizona's "Dogtown Tank" or Texas's two "Dogtown

Windmill"'s unless they appeared to relate to a neighboring community of some sort. Since 1999, when I began the research for this book, more historic newspapers have entered digital archives. As access to these resources increases, it seems likely that more than my conservative estimate of sixty communities once called Dogtown will come to light.

As for the term's meaning, open any contemporary American dictionary and you may find "dogtown" defined as a prairie dog community. Although my research located a few places named for prairie dogs, none of the places I included in my list of Dogtowns refers to this meaning.

The definition of "Dogtown" that seemed to best capture its menacing and pejorative overtones is in Mitford M. Mathews's *A Dictionary of Americanisms on Historical Principals* (Chicago: University of Chicago Press, 1951), which lists the 1841 "Spirit of the Times" article that I quote in Chapter Sixteen. As stated in the "Spirit of the Times," the term "Dogtown" once meant "a town literally overrun by dogs," but most nineteenth-century Americans had different ideas about dogs than we do today. Not only were minorities and women often equated with dogs, with the exception of the aristocracy's lapdogs, nineteenth-century dogs were kept primarily for protection, work, or sport. Companionship was something of a secondary benefit.

Sometimes a community's name was changed from "Dogtown" to something more respectable, as in Wellfleet, Massachusetts. More often, Dogtowns were places that fell into decline, like Gloucester's Commons Settlement. Most of these places were minority slums and wayside hamlets that never became much of anything and were populated by residents who likewise never amounted to much. "The next villages are Helltown and Dogtown, which well deserve their names," an undated article from a newspaper called *The Pacific* states in reference to two Butte County, California, villages. A theological student asked one area resident, "Have there been any religious meetings held lately at Dogtown?" "Done-no," the man replied. "There's a poker game going on now." The student then asked about the area's preacher. "Stranger," the man responded thoughtfully, "he's the best hand I ever seen.... The boys think a-heap o' Hoskins!"

Humorous accounts such as this made me think of Al Capp's comic strip about the Appalachian hillbilly Li'l Abner, who lives in a place called Dogpatch. I have since wondered if Dogpatch was a riff on a term that Capp's audience might have been well acquainted with when his comic was first published in 1934. Around that same time, the popular swing-era bandleader Bob Crosby (singer Bing Crosby's younger brother) also had a big hit with the tune "Dogtown Blues."

While Mitford Mathews dates the first published reference of the name to 1841, Sarah Dunlap of the Gloucester Archives Committee located the town's earliest official record of the term on a May 1, 1814, list of town valuations in Harbor Parish (i.e., First Parish).

As for the term's decline, according to Maria Leach in her book *God Had a Dog,* (Piscataway, N.J.: Rutgers University Press, 1961), throughout much of early and nineteenth-century America, cynomancy, or the folk art of divination based on canine behavior, was full of references foretelling of death. Thus, perhaps it's fitting that this term all but died until it was taken up in the mid-1970s by a small group of renegade skateboarders—another outsider group—in an abandoned area of Santa Monica, California, called Dogtown.

Notes

Various sources and authors are abbreviated as follows:

AAA   Archives of American Art, Smithsonian Institution

BG   *Boston Globe*

C&R   Melvin T. Copeland and Elliott C. Rogers, *The Saga of Cape Ann* (Freeport, ME: The Bond Wheelwright Co., 1960)

CLH   Christine Leigh Heyrman, *Commerce and Culture: The Maritime Communities of Colonial Massachusetts, 1690–1750* (New York: W. W. Norton & Co., 1984)

DHF   David Hackett Fischer, *Albion's Seed* (New York: Oxford University Press, 1989)

DR   David Reardon

EIHC   *Essex Institute Historical Collections* (The Essex Institute, Peabody Essex Museum, Salem, MA)

EN   Erik Natti

GDT   *Gloucester Daily Times*

GloArc   City of Gloucester Archives

JJB   John J. Babson, *History of the Town of Gloucester, Cape Ann* (1860; reprint, Gloucester, MA: Peter Smith, 1972)

MANN   Charles E. Mann, *In the Heart of Cape Ann or the Story of Dogtown* (Gloucester, MA: Procter Brothers, 1896)

MH   Marsden Hartley

PH   Peter Hodgkins

RWB   Roger W. Babson

SHAP   Marsden Hartley, *Somehow a Past*, ed. Susan Elizabeth Ryan (Cambridge, MA: The MIT Press, 1997)

SJC   Trial transcript SJC-04097, *Commonwealth of Massachusetts v. Hodgkins*, 7873–7874; transcription on file at Social Law Library, John Adams Court House, Boston

TEB   Thomas Edward Babson, "Evolution of Cape Ann Roads and Transportation," in *EIHC*, vol. 16

WQ   Wendy Quiñones, "Murder in a Small Town," *Boston* magazine, August 1985

YCAL   Yale Collection of American Literature, Beinecke Rare Book and Manuscript Library

Prologue

1   "the most gifted": *New York Times,* 2/2/03.
1   "Hartley's best art": *The New Yorker,* 2/3/03.
2   three-thousand-acre expanse: Shari Page Berg and Gretchen G. Schuler, Massachusetts Historical Commission (MHC), *Inventory Form: Dogtown,* March 2007, and Dogtown Steering Committee (DSC), *Developing a Management Program for Dogtown,* August 1, 1985. MHC and DSC consider Dogtown (alternately called Dogtown Common[s]) to measure 3,000 acres, roughly two-thirds of the island's unpopulated interior. Of these acres, 1,600 comprise the colonial ruins and their immediate surroundings. Yet many refer to Cape Ann's full, unpopulated interior, which measures roughly 5,000 acres, as Dogtown or Greater Dogtown.
2   population from 2000 U.S. Census figures: 7,767 in Rockport and 30,730 in Gloucester. Cape Ann's population has remained relatively stable for the past twenty years, if not longer.
2   nearly the same size as Manhattan: TEB, pp. 303–304. TEB claims that "island" Cape Ann is twice the size of Manhattan. According to my measurements, "island" Cape Ann covers 18.2 square miles. Manhattan Island covers 22.7 square miles.
2   fifty miles of shoreline: TEB, p. 304. This figure includes rivers and coves.
2   pre-Cambrian mountain: Nathaniel Southgate Shaler, *The Geology of Cape Ann, Massachusetts* (Washington, D.C.: U.S. Geological Survey, 1888), and Brian J. Skinner and Stephen C. Porter, *The Dynamic Earth,* 2nd ed. (New York: Wiley, 1992), pp. 307–316.
3   "most peculiar scenery": Henry David Thoreau, *The Writings of Henry David Thoreau Journal, vol. XI,* ed. Bradford Torrey (Boston: Houghton Mifflin, 1906), p. 179.
3   "borders of the known world": wikipedia.org, Thule entry.
3   "so original": *SHAP,* p. 144.
4   "Are you telling . . . living": Nathaniel Hawthorne, "The Prophetic Pictures," in *Twice Told Tales* (1837; reprint, New York: Modern Library, 2001), pp. 126–127.
6   place Hartley had compared to Easter Island and Stonehenge: *SHAP,* p. 145.
6   "blaze orange hat . . . return": Dogtown Advisory Committee, *Dogtown Common Trail Map* (Gloucester, MA: Dogtown Advisory Committee, 1987, 1996).

1: The Birth of Tragedy

11   Main Street fire: *GDT,* 6/25/84.
11   "would enjoy a good day": EN testimony, SJC vol. III, 3/18/85.
13   twenty-four large boulders: If one includes the rocks inscribed "To Rockport" and "DTSQ," there are twenty-six Babson boulders in all.
13   Daniel Bulba's tenth birthday: Susan Bulba interview.
13   "Everything I've been running": Anne Natti letter to Kenneth Riaf, 9/10, no year but likely 1982.
13   "I feel kin": Anne Natti to Kenneth Riaf, 10/26, no year but likely 1982.
14   wedding details: Jan Seppala, Peter Parsons, Jack Chase interviews.
14   "taking the heat": a frequently used Cape Ann expression for taking a sauna.
14   Natti family history: EN interview.
15   "forest people": Jan Seppala interview.
15   The Nattis had another claim: EN interview.
15   Main Street fire: Mark Adrian Farber interview, *GDT,* 6/25/84.

16 woodland calling card: Linda Ryan testimony, SJC vol. III, 3/13/85.
17 Dogtown's elevation: From John Henry Sears, *The Physical Geography, Geology, Mineralogy and Paleontology of Essex County* (Essex Institute, 1905), p. 399, and *Dogtown Common Trail Map.*
17 police had to borrow a map: *GDT,* 7/10/51.
17 "deep woods": Linda Ryan testimony.
17 Professor Norton's life, forest, and relationship to EN: Marcia Norton interview; *GDT,* 11/28/86.
18 crime details: DR testimony from PH signed statement, SJC pretrial motions, vol. III, 12/19/84; PH signed statement, SJC vol. VI, 3/18/85.
20 downtown scene details: Mark Adrian Farber interview, *GDT,* 6/25/84.

2: Follow the Brush

21 "In the early 1980s Dogtown Common": Dogtown Advisory Committee, *Dogtown Common Trail Map.*
23 MH general biographical details unless otherwise noted: Townsend Ludington, *Marsden Hartley: The Biography of an American Artist* (New York: Little, Brown, 1992).
25 "fine insanity": Philip Hale as quoted in Ludington, p. 54.
25 "at last, an original American": Gertrude Stein as quoted in Ludington, p. 81.
25 "In Berlin": *The New Yorker,* 2/3/03.
25 MH's peripatetic nature: Barbara Haskell, *Marsden Hartley* (New York: Whitney Museum of American Art, 1980), pp. 8–9.
26 "meant to go for a look . . . everywhere": MH letter to Alfred Stieglitz, 8/12/31, YCAL.
26 "record[ing] the genius . . . object": Paul Rosenfeld, *Port of New York,* pp. 91–92, quoted in Gail R. Scott, "In the Moraine: Marsden Hartley at Dogtown Common," *Arts Magazine* 54, Oct. 1979, p. 160.
26 "a sad recollection": MH to Alfred Stieglitz, 8/2/28, YCAL.
26 Henry McBride response: Haskell, *Marsden Hartley,* p. 79.
26 "[I] lost most . . . as long as I live": MH letter to Rebecca Strand, 10/11/30, AAA.
27 MH prognosis: Haskell, p. 82.
28 "new Druidism": Elizabeth Mankin Kornhauser, (Hartford, CT: Wadsworth Athenaeum Museum of Art, 2002), p. 245. Hartley painted *The Old Bars, Dogtown* in 1936.
31 Old Peg Wesson: JJB, p. 321.

3: Cynomancy

33 old Victorian house: Liz Bisch and Kenneth Ryan interviews.
33 "I thought . . . explanation": Linda Ryan testimony, SJC vol. III, 3/13/85.
34 search details: Linda Ryan, John Tuck, and EN testimonies, SJC vol. III, 3/13/85.
34 Erik had both a scientist's eye: EN demonstrated his knowledge of and sensitivity to his environs when we walked together in Dogtown during the summer of 2003.
36 additional crime scene details: DR testimony, SJC pretrial motions vol. III, 12/19/84; EN testimony; DR interview; Kenneth Ryan interview.
37 "pretty much the boonies": DR interview.
37 Mr. Pike: DR interview; Kenneth Ryan interview.

4: The Painter of Dogtown

39 "New York–itis": MH to Adelaide Kuntz, 7/6/31, AAA.
39 "I must see if I can work again": Ibid.
39 "Teach us to care": Ibid.
39 "alone and empty-handed": MH to Rebecca Strand, summer 1931/no date, AAA.
39 "did as I always have to do": *SHAP*, p. 144.
40 "to pull through": MH to Adelaide Kuntz, 8/2/31, AAA.
40 "general resurrection": MH to Alfred Stieglitz, 8/12/31, YCAL.
40 third most densely populated state: U.S. Census 2000.
41 "essentially druidic": *SHAP*, p. 145.
41 "casting off . . . chrysalis": MH to Rebecca Strand, 9/31/31, AAA.
41 "I think I have set": MH to Alfred Stieglitz, 8/12/31, YCAL.
41 "I think I am succeeding . . . more intense than ever before": MH to Adelaide Kuntz, 10/22/31, AAA.
42 "A sense of eeriness": *SHAP*, p. 144.
42 "a real connection": MH to Rebecca Strand, 11/27/31, AAA.
42 "Return of the Native," Gail R. Scott, ed., *The Collected Poems of Marsden Hartley, 1904–1943* (Santa Rosa, CA: Black Sparrow Press, 1987), p. 251.
42 "Dogtown is mine": MH to Rebecca Strand, 12/12/31, AAA.
43 "I want to paint the livingness": MH as quoted in Gail R. Scott, "Introduction," *On Art / by Marsden Hartley*, p. 41, from Bruce Weber, *The Heart of the Matter: The Still Lifes of Marsden Hartley* (New York: Berry Hill Gallery, 2003), p. 55.

5: Le Beauport

46 Fisherman's Memorial: www.nps.gov/nr/travel/maritime/glo.htm.
46 Gloucester history: JJB.
46 In 2005, Gloucester archivists Sarah Dunlap and Stephanie Buck discovered that the painter who has long been known as Fitz Hugh Lane was actually named Fitz Henry Lane: Sarah Dunlap and Stephanie Buck, *Fitz Henry Lane: Family and Friends* (Gloucester, MA: Church & Mason Publishing and Cape Ann Museum, 2007).
46 artists on Cape Ann: James F. O'Gorman, *This Other Gloucester: Occasional Papers on the Arts of Cape Ann, Massachusetts* (1976; reprint, Gloucester, MA: Ten Pound Island Book Co., 1990).
47 "suburb of the sea": TEB, p. 302.
47 "four hundred years . . . destructive": All Jack Chase quotes from interview.
47 Fiesta preparation: *GDT*, 6/84, various; and Sarah Day, *St. Peter's Fiesta Through the Years* (Cambridge, MA: SYP Design & Production/Young Men's Coalition, 2001).
48 "Slain Woman . . . head": *GDT*, 6/26/84.
49 "shattering experience": Josh and Babette Brackett interview.
49 "Of all the nice ladies": Sarah Dunlap interview.
49 "who had that rare gift": John Tuck interview.
49 stabbing victims: *GDT*, 6/26/84.
49 Donald Pinkham: *Boston Globe*, 6/16/05, erroneously reports Pinkham's date of death as 1983. Gloucester vital records state that Pinkham died "on or about October 1, 1982." GloArc.
49 "Lanesville royalty": Gregory Gibson interview.
49 Natti family history and reputation; Finnish culture: EN, Isabel Natti, Annie Melancon, Gregory Gibson, and anonymous interviews.

50 Virginia Lee Burton biographical information: Barbara Elleman, *Virginia Lee Burton: A Life in Art* (Boston: Houghton Mifflin, 2002).
50 "more Finnish . . . Finland": Annie Melancon interview.
51 artists living in Dogtown during the summer: Jan Seppala interview, Lee Steele and Annie Melancon interviews.
51 peering through her windows: Annie Melancon interview.
51 "stivering": C&R, p. 33.
52 "It was so open": Bill and Dot Noble interview.
53 "Sometimes it was spooky": Bob Quinn interview.
53 "the soul of Cape Ann": Phoebe Rowe, Peter Parsons, and various interviews.
53 "a paradise": Peter Anastas, *GDT*, 3/30/85.
53 more than one hundred fishermen's wives: Rosie Verga and members of the St. Peter's Fiesta Women's Committee.

6: The Baron in the Trees

55 "And the people went there": *The Confessions of St. Augustine*, as quoted in *Retrospective Exhibition of the Paintings and Drawings of Rockwell Kent* (New York: Wildenstein and Co., 1924).

7: Ghost Dog

64 police response: DR and Kenneth Ryan interviews.
64 police warnings: *GDT*, 6/26/84.
64 the professor refused to budge: Marcia Norton interview.
65 "older, weirder America": Greil Marcus, *The Old, Weird America: The World of Bob Dylan's Basement Tapes* (New York: Picador, 1997).
65 Bernard Taylor: Kenneth Riaf interview.
65 smuggled to get around: C&R, p. 14.
66 John McKean: JJB, p. 387.
66 Arthur Oker: *GDT*, 10/6/01.
66 "The leprechauns": Phoebe Rowe interview.
66 "I could tell . . . but I won't": *BG*, 10/30/05.
66 "one of Dogtown's tending spirits": Jack Chase interview.
67 details about Linda Crane's teachings and life: Cheryl Davis, Jill Wodehouse, Janet Finch, Phoebe Rowe, Thorpe Feidt, Gerrit Lansing, Jack Chase, Peter Anastas, Ellen Solomon, Michael O'Leary, and Josh and Babette Brackett interviews.
67 "doing some hand jive . . . booga": Jack Chase interview.
67 "Do you feel it?": Cheryl Davis interview.
68 "as though it were a weapon": Thorpe Feidt interview.
68 "If you scream": WQ.
68 "glowed yellow": Peter Anastas interview.
68 police details: DR and Kenneth Ryan interviews.

8: Rollicking Apparitions

69 Ebenezer Babson: According to JJB, p. 59, Ebenezer was born in 1668, but *Vital Records of Gloucester, Massachusetts, to the End of the Year 1849* (Gloucester, MA: Topsfield Historical Society, 1917), p. 75, states December 8, 1667.
69 "remote and lonely spot": JJB, p. 143. JJB uses this language to describe John Rowe's land at the Farms, where Ebenezer also lived on his father James Babson's land. RWB and others also consider James Babson to have been Dog-

town's first settler, though some limit their definition of Dogtown to the triangle formed by the Dogtown Road, the Commons Road, and the Back Road, which were officially laid out later. Charles E. Mann's definition of the area includes much of present-day Riverdale, an area that extends beyond these roads. In their definition of the area, C&R also include the common wood lots, which covered much of the northern stretches of Cape Ann's interior highland.

69 King William's War: CLH, p. 54.

69 Puritan worldview in Gloucester history: Ibid., pp. 102 and 106.

70 "The man of the house": Cotton Mather, *Magnalia Christi Americana or the Ecclesiastical History of New England* (1702; reprint, Whitefish, MT: Kessinger Publishing, 2006), p. 621.

70 Ingersoll family: JJB, p. 106.

70 "an house burnt . . . dashed in pieces": George Ingersoll to Leif Augur, Sept. 10, 1675, from Jill Lepore, *The Name of War: King Philip's War and the Origins of American Identity* (New York: Knopf, 1999), p. 239.

71 garrison house description: A Gloucester garrison is described in the GloArc as a well-built log cabin. Other area garrisons were fortified in the fashion described here: www.dover.lib.nh.us/DoverHistory/garrisonsarounddover.htm.

71 the Green: C&R, pp. 19–30.

71 James Babson: JJB, p. 59.

71 Puritans' attitudes toward wilderness: Keith Thomas, *Man and the Natural World* (New York: Oxford University Press, 1983), p. 194.

71 "Some affirm . . . devils or lions": Duane Hamilton Hurd, *History of Essex County, Massachusetts: With Biographical Sketches of Many of Its Pioneers and Prominent Men* (Philadelphia: J. W. Lewis & Co., 1888), vol. 2, p. 1483.

72 five hundred Wampanoag warriors: Samuel Gardner Drake, *The Old Indian Chronicle: Being a Collection of Exceeding Rare Tracts* (Boston: Antiquarian Institute, 1836), pp. 82–83. Ebenezer Babson's brother Thomas served in King William's War: JJB, p. 59.

72 "saw several men . . . commotion": Mather, *Magnalia Christi Americana,* p. 622.

73 "gray tradition . . . were once the resort . . . impious baptismal rite": Nathaniel Hawthorne, "The Hollow of Three Hills," in *Twice Told Tales* (New York: Modern Library, 2001), pp. 151–152.

73 large boulders and Noah's flood: Trustees of Reservations: www.thetrustees .org/pages/4_agassiz_rock.cfm.

73 boulders . . . what is now Jackman, Maine: John Henry Sears, *The Physical Geography, Geology, Mineralogy, and Paleontology of Essex County, Massachusetts* (Salem, MA: The Essex Institute, 1905), p. 336.

73 no French or Indian attackers: There was never a year-round Native American population on "island" Cape Ann or any reported violence between the European settlers and the Wabanaki, Penobscot, and other Maine and Massachusetts Algonquin groups that came to Annisquam, Bay View, and West Gloucester to fish and harvest shellfish during the summers. Dogtown Steering Committee, *Developing a Management Program for Dogtown,* August 1, 1985, p. 11.

74 "Village scolds, misfits, and poor widows": CLH, p. 105.

74 "rollicking apparitions . . . horrible molestations": Mather, *Magnalia Christi Americana,* p. 623.

9: Taking Care of Its Own

75 "there was a creep": Liz Bisch interview.
75 "Lots of times . . . exposed himself": WQ.
75 PH "haunted" Dogtown: WQ.
76 "completely Gloucester normal": Phoebe Rowe interview.
76 Horace Edward Hodgkins Jr. bio: *GDT,* 4/15/08.
76 Peter's mother: WQ; GloArc.
76 "You would look . . . different": WQ.
76 "He was strange . . . he was doing": Ibid.
76 "disappeared for the entire day . . . considered me part of the area": PH interview.
77 "Every year . . . forget them": Ibid.
77 "the kids . . . a lot [to avoid it]": WQ.
77 "the Boar. . . . Your heart just broke": Ibid.
77 "Who would . . . no clothes on?": Joe Walsh interview; also Kenneth Ryan interview.
77 "There are times . . . behind those eyes": WQ.
77 "He was one strange duck": Kenneth Ryan interview.
77 "He always gave me the creeps . . . a little odd": WQ.
78 boyishly aggressive antics: Ibid.
78 Barrel Ball: PH interview.
78 "kids would say . . . as hard as they could": WQ.
78 "always off to the side": Ibid.
78 "once in a great while": PH interview.
78 "make a bed . . . all it did was mess it [Dogtown] up": Ibid.
78 "a certain girl . . . and alone": Ibid.
79 "Peter was a pretty good worker . . . your friend": Jim O'Neill interview.
79 Hodgkins's adult character: Ibid.
80 attempted suicide: Stephen G. Moore, M.Ed., and Dr. William Brickhouse, behavioral report on PH, Old Colony Correctional Center, no date. Essex County Superior Court House, Salem, MA.
80 "I had *one* mother . . . replace her": PH interview.
80 "sunbathing": WQ and Wendy Quiñones interview.
80 Terry Rubin story: Annie Melancon interview.
80 arrest history: WQ.
81 "near-nude chase . . . please help me . . . tormented": Ibid.
81 "A community can absorb . . . should be": Ibid.
81 "comfort strange people": Jan Seppala interview.
81 Dan Ruberti: WQ, Sarah Dunlap interview.
81 Eino Leino: Sarah Dunlap, Mike Scagliotti, and Gregory Gibson interviews.
81 "Doctor Pet" . . . "Sweet Pea": Charlie Campbell and Bill and Dot Noble interviews.
81 John Hays Hammond Jr. and his ghost ship: www.hammondcastle.org; *GDT,* spring 1965 (no date specified), GloArc People file; John Hays Hammond, *Current Biography,* 1962 (no source specified), GloArc People file.
82 "Like any seaport . . . what to expect from them": Bill Noble interview.
82 "I knew the family . . . to live in that kind of place": WQ.
82 "Peter was strange . . . law enforcement perspective": DR in Ibid.
83 tensions with his stepmother: WQ, Joe Walsh and Jim O'Neill interviews.
83 additional boardinghouse details: Joe Walsh interview.
83 "say anything but good . . . Jolly Green Giant": WQ.
83 "Frank did a lot for him": Jim O'Neill interview.

83   change for the better: WQ.
83   tellers at the bank: Jim O'Neill interview.
84   "We were scared . . . neighborhood": WQ.
84   "Oh, he had been living here . . . looking out for him": Wilma Upham inter-
     view.
84   "Don't you know . . . feel safe!": Ibid.
85   Tuesday night details: Brian Langley testimony, SJC vol. V, 3/15/85.

10: In the Time of Pirates

86   April 14, 1724: George Francis Dow and John Henry Edmonds, *The Pirates of
     the New England Coast 1630–1730* (1923; reprint, Mineola, NY: Dover Publi-
     cations, 1996), p. 310.
86   "make fearful depredations": from a letter written by Gloucester's Reverend
     John White in 1711 describing French and Indian activities in the North At-
     lantic and their impact on Gloucester's fleet in JJB, p. 380.
86   Haraden's grandfather: JJB, p. 98.
86   five Gloucester vessels: JJB, pp. 272 and 380–381.
86   "prosecuting his intended Rogueries": Daniel Defoe, *A General History of the
     Pyrates* (1724; reprint, Mineola, NY: Dover Publications, 1999), p. 341.
87   Phillips's biography: Ibid., pp. 341–347.
87   "splitter": Ibid., p. 341.
87   "desolate and woody": Ibid., p. 347.
87   "the Hardness . . . very much": Ibid.
87   black strap and chowder beer: described in Benerson Little, *The Sea Rover's
     Practice: Pirate Tactics and Techniques, 1630–1730* (Washington, DC: Potomac
     Books, 2005), p. 248, and Ibid.
87   August 29, 1723: Dow and Edmonds, p. 315.
87   "If any Man . . . present Death": Defoe, p. 343.
88   Gloucester captains: Dow and Edmonds, p. 322; JJB, pp. 59, 84, 88–89.
88   "dance about the Deck": Defoe, p. 348.
88   "pestered": Bartholomew Gosnold as quoted in JJB, p. 16.
88   Gloucester trade: JJB, p. 384, and C&R, p. 15.
88   "That certainly . . . in a few Ages more": Reverend John Wise quoted in CLH,
     pp. 14–15.
88   *Sea Horse*: JJB, p. 289.
89   Isle of Shoals: Dow and Edmonds, p. 310.
89   "death's head": Little, p. 114.
89   the *Squirrel*'s capture: Dow and Edmonds, pp. 310–311.
89   "a modest sober young Man": Defoe, p. 346.
89   "broke his mind": Ibid., p. 349.
89   Philmore's relations: JJB, p. 288.
89   Cheeseman volunteered: Defoe, p. 349.
90   "to their next merry meeting": Dow and Edmonds, p. 312.
90   the mutiny: JJB, Defoe, and Dow and Edmonds.
90   heads hanging from the *Squirrel*'s mast: Dow and Edmonds, p. 313.
90   the trials: Ibid., pp. 322–327.
90   "a multitude of spectators": *Boston News-Letter*, May 28–June 4, 1724, as
     quoted in Ibid., p. 324.
91   Samuel Elwell and Joshua Elwell: Mann, *Beginnings of Dogtown* (Gloucester,
     MA: Proctor Bros, 1906) from Batchelder's Survey, pp. 10–11; JJB, pp. 84–88.
91   "the rocky surface . . . relieve the eye": JJB, p. 6.
91   1721: CLH, p. 58, remarks that town leaders agreed to divide the land in 1719

but that lots were not laid out until 1721. See also Mann, *Beginnings of Dog-town*, p. 19.

92   1729 dispute: Mann, pp. 1–17.

11: The Green Man

93   Stephen Amaral meets PH: DR testimony, SJC pretrial motions vol. III, 12/19/84, and SJC vol. VIII, 3/20/85.

93   Hodgkins's grandfather had died: Horace Edward Hodgkins Sr. died on April 18, 1984, see Gloucester Deaths, vol. 12, p. 34, GloArc.

93   "his castle": DR interview.

94   Details of Reardon's meeting with PH: DR testimony, SJC vol. VIII, 3/20/85; *Events Leading to Arrest*, Docket #7873-7874, Essex County Superior Court; DR interview.

95   "I think you know . . . telling me, Peter": DR testimony.

95   Brian Langley's: Brian Langley testimony, SJC vol. V, 3/15/85; Ronald Cunha testimony, SJC vol. V, 3/15/85; and trooper Mark Lynch testimony, SJC vol. V, 3/15/85.

96   Honda XL 250 trail bike: Jeff Clew, *Honda XL 250/350 Trail Bikes Owners Workshop Manual* (Haynes online, 1979).

97   Hodgkins's phone call: Brian Langley testimony.

98   "massive skull . . . substantial and severe force": *Cause of Death*, Docket #7873-7874, Essex County Superior Court, and John G. Guillemont testimony, SJC vol. VI, 3/18/85.

12: Dooming the Seats

99   Nathaniel Coit's age: JJB, p. 71.

99   "Ye are the light . . . be hid": Puritan leader John Winthrop, governor of the Massachusetts Bay Colony, invoked these lines from the Book of Matthew in his famous sermon to the *Arbella*'s passengers in 1630. The line was inter-preted as a Puritan mandate. DHF, pp. 18–20.

99   meetinghouse purposes: DHF, pp. 118–125.

99   announcements and wolf heads: DHF, p. 118.

99   meetinghouse as powder magazine/surprise attack: DHF, pp. 118–120.

100   "Perhaps no duty . . . meeting-house": Alice Morse Earle, *The Sabbath in Puri-tan New England*, 8th ed. (New York: Charles Scribner's Sons, 1898), p. 45.

100   "dignify": Earle, p. 49.

100   "doom": CLH, p. 148.

100   seating chart matrix and importance: CLH, pp. 148–149, 170.

100   "there be no Grumbling at them": Earle, p. 46.

100   Coit's opposition to relocating the First Parish meetinghouse: CLH, pp. 143–181. See also Mann, *Beginnings of Dogtown*, pp. 1–17.

100   1729: CLH, p. 145.

100   the town's population: JJB, p. 542.

100   harbor growth: CLH, p. 189; JJB, p. 453.

101   Four-vote margin: PR 7:11. Gloucester First Parish records compiled by Cape Ann Museum librarian Stephanie Buck in "First Parish Meeting House Time-line, 1729–1743."

101   meetinghouse construction and delayed use: CLH, p. 146.

101   one of the town's wealthier: CLH, pp. 143–181.

101   General Court suit against him: JJB, pp. 8–9; CLH pp. 154–155.

101   new seating committee: CLH, p. 171.

101 "Up in Town"/"Upper Town": used throughout CLH and Mann, *Beginnings of Dogtown* to refer to the villages at the Green and the Commons Settlement which were both uphill from Gloucester Harbor.

102 wood-framed houses: MANN. Only one area house had two stories. p. 36.

102 doors in line with the noonday sun: DHF, pp. 161–162.

102 plaster for walls: TEB, p. 319.

102 signs to keep away evil spirits: DHF, p. 129.

102 economic life: Irving Sucholeiki, *A Return to Dogtown: A Look at the Artifacts Left Behind by Some of Cape Ann's Early Settlers* (Gloucester, MA: Chisholm & Hunt Printers, Inc., 1992); C&R, pp. 19–30, 37, 162, and 172.

102 commons system: Herbert Baxter Adams, *Village Communities of Cape Ann and Salem: From the Historical Collection of the Essex Institute* (Baltimore, MD: Johns Hopkins University, 1883), p. 37; JJB, pp. 234–236; Richard W. Judd, *Common Lands, Common People: The Origins of Conservation in Northern New England* (Cambridge, MA: Harvard University Press, 1997), p. 42.

103 "fence-viewer": Gloucester Town Records, GloArc.

103 boiled dinners: DHF, p. 136.

103 Benjamin Allen's possessions: Sucholeiki, p. 46.

103 Descendants sold shares: Sarah Dunlap interview; GloArc.

103 "Ye major part . . . and children": Nathaniel Coit (11/12/1738), Massachusetts General Court Records III:127, quoted in Buck.

104 "fit for little else . . . all Art to Destroy the Whole": An Answer of the Town of Gloucester to Nathaniel Coit, Massachusetts General Court Records II:531 (12/23/1738), quoted in CLH, p. 179.

104 Upper Towners disruptive: Letter to the General Court by Epes Sargent and Daniel Witham from 1740, General Court Records 3:131, quoted in Buck.

104 "Sail with every Wind": Andrew Robinson et al. (12/1/1738), Massachusetts General Court Records II:510–512, quoted in CLH, p. 161.

104 "candle-lighting," "nightwalking": DHF, p. 162.

104 "not great . . . bread on shore": Letter to the General Court by Epes Sargent and Daniel Witham.

104 harbor economy and population: CLH, p. 198; JJB, p. 453.

105 Upper Town parishioners not under oath: Mann, *Beginnings of Dogtown*, p. 13.

105 taking children to the grave: DHF, p. 113.

105 reaction to new parish: CLH, p. 202; Mann, *Beginnings of Dogtown*. Mann's thesis is predicated on the reaction to this divide.

105 A new meetinghouse in 1752: JJB, p. 316.

13: Shadow Hunting

106 PH walk: PH signed statement, SJC vol. VI, 3/18/85.

106 PH clothing: Karl Sjoberg recorded what PH was wearing, SJC vol. VI, 3/18/85.

106 PH academic record: WQ.

106 Robert Pino's tests: state chemists' report, Robert E. Pino, Essex County Superior Courthouse, Salem.

107 vernal pools: Rick Roth of Cape Ann Vernal Pond Team interview.

107 blankets at gravel pit: PH signed statement, SJC vol. VI, 3/18/85.

107 officer reading a warrant: John J. O'Rourke testimony, SJC vol. V, 3/15/85.

107 Quincy Market Cold Storage: Kenneth Ryan testimony, SJC vol. VI, 3/18/85; Kenneth Ryan interview.

108 Six other officers searched: Mark Lynch testimony, SJC vol. V, 3/15/85.

108 manhunt details: *GDT* 6/28/84, Mark Lynch testimony, SJC vol. V, 3/15/85; Kenneth Ryan testimony, SJC vol. VI, 3/18/85.

108 helicopter unknowingly nearly touched down on PH: PH signed statement, SJC vol. VI, 3/18/85.

108 Vietnam flashback: PH filed a motion for a retrial based on a claim that he suffered combat-related post-traumatic stress disorder. Letters from La Salette Vietnam Veteran Ministry (4/15/91), Trauma and Stress Consultants, Inc. (1/9/91), the Boston VA Medical Center and Outpatient Clinic, and Old Colony Psychological Services, a division of the Commonwealth of Massachusetts' Department of Corrections (12/14/89), also supported this claim. Essex County Superior Courthouse, Salem.

108 "Let me come to you . . . did you do it?": Brian Langley testimony, SJC vol. V, 3/15/85.

108 details of Hodgkins's evening: PH signed statement, SJC vol. VI, 3/18/85.

109 "You got a cigarette?"/William Spinney scene: William H. Spinney testimony, SJC pretrial motions vol. II, 12/18/84, and SJC vol. VIII, 3/20/85.

110 "How are you, Pete?"/Lawrence Davis scene: Lawrence E. Davis testimony, SJC pretrial motions, vol. II, 12/18/84.

14: God's Burning Finger

112 "I feel a healing relationship with Dogtown": Jill Wodehouse interview.

112 "It has a tendency": Bill Noble interview.

112 "It's a beautiful . . . vortex": Janet Finch interview.

112 "time . . . when it was very dark": Jill Wodehouse interview.

113 David Pearce, Gloucester's wealthiest merchant: JJB, p. 267.

113 *Gloucester* details: JJB, p. 413.

113 "the most important enterprise": JJB, p. 412.

113 Commons Settlers as privateers: JJB, p. 313; James R. Pringle, *History of the Town and City of Gloucester, Cape Ann, Massachusetts* (1892; reprint, Gloucester, MA: Ten Pound Island Book Co., 1997), p. 83.

113 outfitting by donations: JJB, p. 416.

113 privateering and the U.S. Navy's beginnings: Gardner Allen Weld, *A Naval History of the Revolution* (Boston: Houghton Mifflin, 1913), vol. 1, pp. 43–49.

113 story of the *Falcon*: JJB, pp. 393–396. Peter Lurvey, a Commons Settlement resident, was one of two Gloucester fatalities from the *Falcon*'s attack. See also Joseph E. Garland, *The Fish and the Falcon: Gloucester's Resolute Role in America's Fight for Freedom* (Charleston, SC: History Press, 2006), p. 52.

113 legalized pirating: Weld, pp. 43–45.

114 Massachusetts privateers: Weld, *Massachusetts Privateers of the Revolution* (Boston: Massachusetts Historical Society, 1927).

114 Gloucester privateers' prizes: JJB, pp. 397, 410–411.

114 "could only prevent . . . wound": JJB, pp. 425–426.

114 "was driven . . . about 'burned down'": JJB, p. 89, states that this 1779 ship was commanded by Isaac Elwell, but does not mention in the telling of this story if it was or was not a privateer. Elsewhere (p. 424) he states that Elwell commanded a privateer.

114 watched their former shipmates: JJB, p. 391.

114 crawl into town: JJB, p. 423.

115 town suffered: JJB, p. 397; JJB, *Notes and Additions*, p. 151.

115 women's hardships: JJB, pp. 375, 409, 471; Carol Berkin, *Revolutionary Mothers* (New York: Vintage, 2005), pp. 43, 51.

115   women and children relocated to mainland West Gloucester and Ipswich: JJB, p. 375.
115   "on a sudden . . . invincible Armada": Letter from William Whipple to James Lovell, quoted in William James Morgan, ed., *Naval Documents of the American Revolution, vol. IX* (Washington, D.C.: Naval Historical Center Department of the Navy, 1986), p. 707.
115   William Whipple: Whipple also was a Continental congressman and a signer of the Declaration of Independence. http://bioguide.congress.gov/.
115   "balsam peru . . . capivi": *Rivington's New-York Loyal Gazette*, December 6, 1777, quoted in Michael J. Crawford, ed., *Naval Documents of the American Revolution, vol. X* (Washington, D.C.: Naval Historical Center Department of the Navy, 1996), p. 675 and p. 949.
115   much-needed salt: Gloucester had set up a saltworks in 1777 because the mineral was so scarce during the war. JJB, p. 415.
116   Captain Fisk: Weld, *Naval History of the Revolution*, pp. 237–238.
116   Isaac Day: Charles E. Mann, "More Historical Notes Concerning the Deserted Village of Dogtown," *GDT*, no date, but published sometime between November 10 and November 15, 1898.
116   *Spark* seized on Grand Banks: Crawford, p. 345; see also JJB, p. 413.
116   clethra: Ted Tarr interview.
116   unpaid salaries and donations: JJB, pp. 398, 412.
116   "One dark night . . . unfortunate crew": JJB, p. 413.
117   Scientific theory: *Scientific American*, 9/22/97.
117   corposants: George Ripley and Charles Anderson Dana, *The New American Cyclopaedia: A Popular Dictionary of General Knowledge, vol. V* (New York: D. Appleton, 1869), p. 730.
117   "death-fires . . . witch's oils": Samuel Taylor Coleridge, *The Rime of the Ancient Mariner* (New York: Newson, 1905), p. 10.
117   "God's burning finger": Herman Melville, *Moby-Dick* (New York: Harper & Brothers, 1851), p. 558.
117   "The number . . . gloom": JJB, p. 413.
117   "a large troop . . . destitution": JJB, p. 441.
118   one-sixth of its residents: JJB, p. 440.
118   pitch black: JJB, *Notes and Additions*, John J. Babson, *Notes and Additions to History of Gloucester* (Gloucester, MA: M.V.B. Perley, Telegraph Office, 1876), pp. 150–151.
118   extensive forest fires . . . "dark day": Erin R. McMurry et al., "Fire Scars Reveal Source of New England's 1780 Dark Day," *International Journal of Wildland Fire* (2007), 16 (3): 266–270.
118   335 were now widowed: Mary Ray and Sarah Dunlap, *Gloucester, Massachusetts, Historical Time-Line 1000–1999* (Gloucester, MA: Gloucester Archives Committee, 2002), p. 73.
118   widows by parish: Marshall W. S. Swan, "Cape Ann at the Nadir (1780)," *EIHC*, vol. 15, 1983, p. 255.
118   Commons Settlement's post-Revolutionary gloom: JJB, pp. 313, 450.

15: Confession

119   weather: *GDT*, 6/29/84.
119   since 6:30 A.M.: DR testimony, SJC pretrial motions vol. IV, 12/20/84.
119   "there is no . . . Cyclopean masonry": Nathaniel Southgate Shaler, *The Geology*

of Cape Ann, Massachusetts (Washington, D.C.: U.S. Geological Survey, 1888), p. 547.

120 No one said a word: Lawrence Davis testimony, SJC pretrial motions vol. II, 12/18/84.

120 "I think . . . coming now": DR testimony, SJC pretrial motions vol. IV, 12/20/84.

120 PH demeanor: DR and Carl Sjoberg testimony, SJC pretrial motions vol. IV, 12/20/84, SJC vol. VI, 3/18/85, and SJC vol. VIII, 3/20/85.

120 "You okay, Peter? . . . No, not now": DR testimony, SJC pretrial motions vol. IV, 12/20/84.

121 "Reardon's shock": DR interview.

121 "We have been . . . a story?": DR testimony, SJC pretrial motions vol. II, 12/18/84.

121 "I first saw her walking": All PH quotes and reported speech in this chapter from PH signed statement, SJC vol. VI, 3/18/85, unless otherwise noted. Additional details from DR testimony, SJC pretrial motions vol. III, 12/19/84, Carl Sjoberg, SJC pretrial motions vol. IV, 12/20/84, and DR interview.

124 Samuel Hodgkins: JJB, p. 104.

124 ferry details: TEB, p. 308.

124 another was a cabinetmaker: MANN, pp. 19–22.

125 hard to discipline: Dale Follansbee interview.

125 helped Peter: Jim Walsh interview.

125 "mentally challenged": Jim O'Neill interview.

125 shopping for PH: DR testimony, SJC vol. VIII, 3/20/85.

125 never saw his son again: Wendy Quiñones interview; PH interview.

126 Gribouski response and quotes: James Gribouski interview.

126 PH response to media presence: DR testimony, SJC vol. VIII, 3/20/85.

126 video cameras: DR testimony, SJC pretrial motions vol. VIII, 12/19/84; SJC vol. VIII, 3/20/85; DR interview and James Gribouski interview.

127 "Murder in the murderer": Ralph Waldo Emerson, *Essays* (Boston: Houghton Mifflin, 1883), p. 79.

127 "There's where I left . . . hit her with": PH quoted in DR testimony, SJC vol. VIII, 3/20/85.

127 "looked like . . . fieldstone wall:" DR testimony, SJC vol. VIII, 3/20/85. Reardon testified that the rock weighed sixty pounds. Elsewhere it is described as weighing forty pounds.

128 "utterly chilling": James Gribouski interview.

128 took some swabs: Kenneth Ryan testimony, SJC vol. VI, 3/18/85.

128 Erik Natti was still there: *GDT*, 6/30/84.

128 Judge Lawrence Jodrey ordered: *GDT*, 6/30/84.

16: In Gypsy Ways

129 "very choice vocabulary": MANN, p. 24.

129 "torrents of vocal pyrotechnics": Ibid., p. 23.

129 Luce George: Ibid., pp. 24–25.

130 "in a neglected State . . . only one": William Bentley, *The Diary of William Bentley, D.D.: Pastor of the East Church, Salem, Massachusetts* (1905; reprint, Gloucester, MA: Peter Smith, 1962), vol. 2, p. 307.

130 became known as Dogtown: Gloucester Archives volunteer Sarah Dunlap discovered the earliest mention of Dogtown that I know of in a May 1, 1814, list of property valuations: "12 acres Pasture—D. Town" in GloArc.

130 "sweet-faced": MANN, p. 4.

130 "The name 'Dogtown' . . . the ocean": Ibid., p. 10.

130 "gypsy ways": RWB, *Dogtown: Gloucester's Deserted Village* (address to the Gloucester Rotary Club, 1927), booklet, p. 13.

130 list of states with Dogtowns: See appendix.

131 "This is emphatically . . . squat": *Spirit of the Times*, August 21, 1841.

131 "good enough for dogs to live in": Erwin G. Gudde, *California Place Names*, 3rd ed. (Berkeley: University of California Press, 1969).

131 the Igarots: Bob Corbett, professor emeritus of philosophy at Webster University, has a website documenting St. Louis's Dogtown: www.webster.edu/~corbetre/dogtown/origins-2.html.

131 "Dogtowner" insult: RWB, *Dogtown: Gloucester's Deserted Village*, p. 4.

131 "warn out"/"put in their place": Ruth Wallis Herndon, *Unwelcome Americans* (Philadelphia: University of Pennsylvania Press, 2001), pp. 4–22.

132 indentured servants: Even children of economically stable families were sent away, not as servants, but to learn trades. Sarah Dunlap, GloArc.

132 Gloucester constructed a poorhouse: JJB, pp. 279–280.

132 Life in the poorhouse: Louise Chipley, " 'Enlightened Charity': William Bentley on Poor Relief in the Early Republic, 1783–1818," *EIHC*, vol. 128, 1992, pp. 162–179.

132 "dire drink": MANN, p. 31. All accounts of these Dogtowners are from this Mann source, unless otherwise noted. Only direct quotes will be cited.

132 "became convinced that his legs": Ibid., pp. 25–26.

133 "buccaneers and lawless men": Ibid., p. 17.

133 "If a person sawed a barrel": Mann, "More Historical Notes Concerning the Deserted Village of Dogtown," *GDT*, no date, but between November 10 and November 15, 1898.

133 American witches: Barbara Ehrenreich and Deirdre English, *Witches, Midwives, and Nurses* (New York: Feminist Press, 1973).

133 "shrewish . . . against their neighbors": CLH, p. 112.

133 "bodily diseases": JJB, p. 275.

133 women healers in Gloucester: JJB, p. 275.

133 "Now, ducky": MANN, p. 31.

133 Dogtown plants: Elliott Rogers, *GDT*, 8/13/54, and *Cape Ann Summer Sun*, 8/27/54; Richard W. Judd, *Common Lands, Common People* (Cambridge, MA: Harvard University Press, 1997), p. 30.

134 "seem to have done": MANN, p. 45.

134 "Now, ye hell birds": Ibid., pp. 61–62.

134 Dorcas Foster: Foster's was the only family known to relocate to the Commons Settlement during the Revolution. Ibid., p. 45.

134 Isaac Dade: Ibid., pp. 47–48.

134 "entertained": Ibid., p. 41.

134 "a parcel of girls": Ibid., p. 39.

135 "coverlet white with snow": Ibid., p. 55.

135 slaves in 1740s Gloucester: CLH, pp. 187–188; Gloucester historian Joe Garland in *GDT*, 2/17/89.

135 At least three hundred slaves: James R. Pringle, *History of the Town and City of Gloucester, Cape Ann, Massachusetts* (1892; reprint, Gloucester, MA: Ten Pound Island Book Co., 1997), pp. 86–87.

135 granted their freedom: JJB, p. 456; see also *Gloucester Vital Records*.

135 Robert Freeman: Valuations 1801, West Ward/Harbor Parish, Box 62, GloArc.

136 "tumble down old house": Charles L. Hill, "Slavery and Its Aftermath in Bev-

erly, Massachusetts: Juno Larcom and Her Family," *EIHC*, vol. 116, 1980, p. 127.

136 In 1790, Gloucester's census: GloArc. Larcom's home had no known connection with the Underground Railroad.

136 1801 federal census: Phillips Library, Peabody Essex Museum.

136 Cornelius Finson's death: Gloucester Vital Records, vol. III, p. 132. Though there is a separate section for "Negroes," Finson is listed in the white section of this volume. His race is not specified.

136 slave owner named John Woodman: *Vital Records of Newbury, Massachusetts to the End of the Year 1849*, vol. I (Newbury, MA: Essex Institute, 1911), p. 564.

136 "heavy toil": MANN, p. 43.

136 "never had white flour . . . physical condition": Susan Babson, *Along the Roads of Cape Ann* (Gloucester, MA: F. S. and A. H. McKenzie, 1923), p. 39.

137 "to whimper": MANN, p. 21.

137 "panicky": Ibid., p. 22.

137 1839: Ibid., p. 51, states that Finson died in 1830, but Gloucester Vital Records record his death as occurring on February 7, 1839.

137 "was full of ice . . . old age and fright": Ibid., p. 51.

137 "They say . . . deserted village": *Boston Sunday Herald*, 9/15/1897.

17: "Viva San Petro!"

139 St. Peter's Club: Shep Abbott's Fiesta film and Sarah Day, *St. Peter's Fiesta Through the Years* (SYP Design and Production/Young Men's Coalition, 2001).

139 "crazy lumper": Giancarlo Salucci interview.

139 no one remembers exactly: Fiesta's start date differs in accounts from Day, *St. Peter's Fiesta* (p. 6) and those published in *GDT*.

140 Addison Gilbert Hospital: DR testimony, SJC pretrial motions vol. III, 12/19/83, and SJC vol. IX, 3/21/85; Kenneth Ryan testimony, SJC vol. VI, 12/19/84.

141 Fiesta details: from interviews with Joe Palmisano, who also watched Fiesta with me in 2008 and pointed out which traditions were the same as they had been in the early 1980s; and *GDT* articles from June 1984.

141 "If I wash thee not . . . clean, but not all": John 13:1–10.

142 Simone Sanfillipo: This event, which I witnessed, took place in 2008. I have included it here because it captures how Fiesta is as much about grieving and loss as it is a celebration, an idea that was as strong in 1984 as it is today.

143 elders calling up spirits: EN interview.

143 memorial service: Scott Campbell and Phyllis R. Silverman, *Widower: When Men Are Left Alone* (Amityville, NY: Baywood, 1996), p. 50.

143 "Don't anyone go in the woods": Isabel Natti quoted by Ellen Solomon in an interview.

143 "[S]end away evil . . . redound upon himself": Elias Lönnrot, *The Kalevala*, trans. Francis Peabody Magoun (1849; reprint, Cambridge, MA: Harvard University Press, 1963), book 45: 218–220, 233–236; p. 303.

144 St. Peter biographical details: Michael Grant, *Saint Peter: A Biography* (New York: Scribner, 1995).

144 "A year ago I hovered . . . celebration today": *GDT*, 7/2/84.

144 suicide attempt: Robert Kalis to the court, SJC vol. VIII, 3/20/85.

145 procession: *GDT*, 7/2/84, and interview with the St. Peter's Fiesta women's committee.

145 "What can Hawthorne mean . . . interior of Cape Ann": Thomas Wentworth Higginson, *Oldport Days* (Boston: Lee & Shepard, 1882), p. 251.
146 "couchant monsters . . . summer after summer": Ibid., pp. 253–254.
147 "You win the greasy pole": Spoken to me by a very "happy" greasy pole participant in 2008.
147 "happy people": *GDT*, 7/2/84.
147 "put him to bed": Joe Palmisano interview.

18: Life's Book

148 "I'm beginning to feel things!": Sarah Comstock, "The Broomstick Trail," *Harper's Monthly* magazine, December 1919, p. 12.
148 "New World Salisbury Plain": Ibid., p. 11.
148 "spellbound victims": Ibid.
148 "the monstrous shapes of prehistoric beasts and birds and reptiles": Ibid.
148 "true home of the witches": Ibid.
148 "a few of whom so blackened . . . its records": Ibid., p. 12.
149 "the very dwelling . . . darkness": Ibid.
149 "wonder-world": Ibid., p. 11.
149 "real history . . . fine people": RWB, *Dogtown: Gloucester's Deserted Village*, address to the Gloucester Rotary Club, 1927, booklet, p. 2.
149 Roger W. Babson biography: RWB, *Actions and Reactions: An Autobiography of Roger W. Babson* (New York: Harper & Brothers, 1935).
149 "Babson Break": Though RWB regularly forecasted crashes, his September 5, 1929, prediction, known to economists as the "Babson Break," is considered by some to be especially prescient. Some maintain that Babson was merely repeating what others had been saying for a while, only he happened to say it at the right time and place. John Kenneth Galbraith, *The Great Crash, 1929* (Boston: Houghton Mifflin, 1997), pp. 84–86, 95.
149 "Boston Millionaire Deserts": *Boston Sunday Post*, 7/28/29.
150 "more tragic than the history of almost any other American community": RWB, *Dogtown: Gloucester's Deserted Village*, p. 13.
150 "many great lessons . . . catch its spirit": Ibid.
150 "by the light of a kerosene lamp": RWB, *Actions and Reactions*, p. 8.
150 "twisting up pins for the teacher to sit on": Ibid., p. 32.
150 "liquor actually flowed in the streets": Ibid., p. 29.
150 Hannah Jumper: John Hardy Wright, *Gloucester and Rockport* (Charleston, S.C.: Arcadia Publishing, 2000), p. 86.
150 "the greatest event of my life": RWB, *Actions and Reactions*, p. 31.
150 "old-fashioned": Ibid., p. 32.
150 "Some phase of every industry . . . a story of romance": RWB, *Dogtown: Gloucester's Deserted Village*, p. 13.
151 Grazing cattle had knocked down: *Boston Sunday Post*, 7/28/29.
151 "Good Cheer Library": RWB, *Actions and Reactions*, p. 254.
151 Gutzon Borglum: Simon Schama, *Landscape and Memory* (New York: Vintage Books, 1995), pp. 386–387.
151 Stone Mountain and Walker Hancock: http://stonemountain.com/history.
151 "debauching outdoor poster talk": Roger W. Babson quoted in *Springfield Union & Rep.*, 8/14/32.
151 "many other cities": RWB in *Springfield Union & Rep.*, 8/14/32.
151 "picturesque geyser": *GDT*, 6/5/30.
152 "There is a scarcity": Thoreau, *Journal*, September 23, 1858, p. 180.

152 "Our main fire protection": RWB, *Actions and Reactions*, p. 125.
152 emergency meeting: *GDT*, 6/7/30.
153 "several other things . . . that diseased place": *GDT*, 6/26/30.
153 Alewife Brook protest: *GDT*, 7/20/30.
153 engineers and state health officials' response: *GDT*, 7/23/30.
153 "unusual purity": *Cape Ann Summer Shore*, 7/11/30.
153 Tammy Younger was still at work: *Cape Ann Summer Shore*, 7/11/30.
153 the deal's costs: August 1930 article, source uncited, in Cape Ann Museum scrapbook #28, p. 56, GloArc.
153 "a natural park and bird sanctuary" to be accessed "on foot only": Memorandum of Agreement Between the City of Gloucester and Roger W. Babson and Gustavus Babson, 1/31, GloArc.
153 Charles Olson: Charles Olson, *The Maximus Poems*, ed. George F. Butterick (Berkeley: University of California Press, 1983), I: 21, p. 25; Tom Clark, *The Allegory of a Poet's Life* (Berkeley: North Atlantic Books, 2000), p. 19.
153 reservoir construction was complete: *GDT*, 12/8/30.
153 "an intervention of the worst sort": *SHAP*, p. 145.
154 "defacing of the landscape"; "Just look . . . foolish notions?"; "propaganda": *Springfield Union & Rep.*, 8/14/32.
154 "As a warning . . . two hundred years ago": *GDT*, 7/30/32.
154 1940 presidential election results: *Dave Leip's Atlas of U.S. Presidential Elections*, www.uselectionatlas.org.
154 "Dogtown teaches me": RWB, *Actions and Reactions*, p. 248.

19: Island Heart of Darkness

155 "I lost my woods": Annie Melancon interview.
155 "a very large, scary dog": Annie Melancon interview.
155 "a wonderful spirit": Liz Bisch interview.
156 "numerous 'close calls' . . . guns, and knives": Joe Orange, *GDT*, 7/12/84.
156 "In essence, a 2,300-acre area": *GDT*, 7/24/84.
156 "TAKE BACK THE WOODS": *GDT*, 7/26/84.
156 "The gate to Cape Ann's 'heart of darkness'": Ibid.
156 "In order for there to be wilderness . . . spirit into a place": Jack Chase interview.
156 "that multitude of couchant monsters . . . as the years go by": Higginson, *Oldport Days*, p. 253.
157 "quiet, gentle, and compassionate": *GDT*, 7/26/84.
157 "You will not find violence . . . problems in the woods": Ibid.
157 "There had always . . . strange people": Campbell and Silverman, *Widower*, p. 51.
158 developers: a U.S. Army defense site: *GDT*, 10/1/41; a small-craft municipal airfield: *GDT*, 2/11/50; an antiballistic missile site: *GDT*, 11/28/67; a wind farm: *GDT*, 9/23/80; a drive-in movie theater: *Cape Ann Summer Sun*, 7/15/55; and a colonial theme park: *GDT*, 11/4/74.
158 "the blossoming apple trees": Charles Olson, *The Maximus Poems*, ed. George F. Butterick (Berkeley: University of California Press, 1983), III: 22, p. 391.

20: Maximus, to Dogtown

161 Charles Olson general biographical details: Unless otherwise noted, from Tom Clark, *The Allegory of a Poet's Life* (Berkeley: North Atlantic Books, 2000).

161 "A Maximus Written to Throw Back a Hex": Clark, *The Allegory,* p. 276.

161 "Don't mind anything": Charles Olson to Elizabeth Olson, n.d., cir. 1959. Ibid., p. 275.

161 "all really essentially Dogtown": Olson quoted in George F. Butterick, ed. *Muthologos: The Collected Lectures and Interviews of Charles Olson,* vol. 1 (Bolinas, CA: Four Seasons Foundation, 1978), p. 188.

161 "It is impossible to describe . . . generation of writers": Steven Ratiner, *Christian Science Monitor,* 10/07/83.

162 "probably the most ambitious poems": *Los Angeles Times,* n.d.

162 "Sit on it and feel the energy . . . in the ass": Charles Boer, *Charles Olson in Connecticut* (Chicago: Swallow Press, 1975), p. 99.

163 "ushered in postmodernism": Paul Christensen, "Charles Olson," *American National Biography* (Oxford University Press), http://www.anb.org/articles/16/16-02171.html.

163 "A Foot Is to Kick With": Charles Olson, *Human Universe and Other Essays* (San Francisco: Auerhahn Society, 1965), p. 79.

164 "let them not make . . . as the nation is": Olson, *Maximus Poems,* I:9, p. 13.

164 Olson met Hartley: Olson described this event in a letter to Robert Creeley quoted in *Charles Olson & Robert Creeley: The Complete Correspondence,* vol. I, ed. George Butterick (Santa Barbara, CA: Black Sparrow Press, 1980), p. 145.

165 "But what he did . . . to such humanness": Olson, *Maximus Poems,* I:33, p. 37.

166 "Soft soft rock . . . this/park of eternal/events": Ibid., II:2, pp. 172–176.

166 "actual earth of value": Olson quoted in Butterick, *Muthologos,* vol. 2, p. 9.

167 "Anybody that's ever . . . our being.": Butterick, *Muthologos,* vol. 2, p. 196.

167 tree-stump-cum-writing-stand: Olson, *Maximus Poems,* II:37, p. 207, and III:22, p. 391; George Butterick, *A Guide to the Maximus Poems of Charles Olson* (Berkeley: University of California Press, 1980), p. 297.

167 dancing with Ferrini: Stephen Scotti interview.

167 "renewal by destruction": Olson quoted in Peter Anastas, ed., *Maximus to Gloucester: The Letters and Poems of Charles Olson to the Editor of the Gloucester Daily Times 1962–1969* (Gloucester, MA: Ten Pound Island Book Co., 1992), p. 49.

168 "A Scream to the Editor": Olson from *GDT,* 12/3/65, in Ibid., pp. 87–90.

168 restore its original selectmen: Olson from *GDT,* 12/28/65, in Ibid., pp. 93–96.

168 "I met Death . . . Not it being He": Olson, *Maximus Poems,* III:69, p. 436.

168 "forever . . . me": Olson, *Maximus Poems,* II:14, p. 185.

168 "a sense of auspice of life and being": Olson from *GDT,* 2/12/68, in Anastas, *Maximus to Gloucester,* p. 124.

169 Olson's additional efforts with the house: Anastas, *Maximus to Gloucester,* pp. 106–107.

169 literary cult figure: *New York Times,* 11/23/75.

169 "Big Fire Source": Robert Duncan quoted in Butterick, *Muthologos,* vol. 1, p. 63.

169 "The soul of man is worth more": Olson from *GDT,* 5/30/69 in Anastas, *Maximus to Gloucester,* p. 157.

169 Center for Personality Research: Clark, *The Allegory,* pp. 292–294.

169 "all the drinking and the pills": Ed Dorn quoted in Ibid., p. 333.

169 "working his way . . . two weeks": Robert Creeley quoted in Ibid., p. 323.

169 friends worried about Olson's health: Ibid., p. 342.

169 engineer from Apple Records: Ibid., p. 343. These recordings are available on the Smithsonian's Folkways label.

170 "I drink to live to go further": Ibid., p. 345.

170 "the fake/which covers . . . indistinguishable from/the USA": Olson, *Maximus Poems*, III:204, p. 599.

170 "I despise Gloucester": Olson in Anastas, *Maximus to Gloucester*, p. 59.

21: The Masked Man in Yellow

171 Dr. David Swenson's examination: John Brosnan testimony, SJC pretrial motions vol. II, 12/18/84, and *GDT*, 7/5/84.

171 exchange between PH and Brosnan: Ibid., also in Essex County Superior Courthouse, Salem, MA.

172 PH Vietnam service: Stephen G. Moore, M.Ed., and Dr. William Brickhouse, behavioral report on PH, Old Colony Correctional Center, no date. Essex County Superior Courthouse, Salem, MA. Filed with a motion for a retrial, submitted 10/1/93 by L. Stephani.

173 criminally insane or mentally competent: Ronald Roesch et al., "Defining and Assessing Competency to Stand Trial," American Psychology Law Society, University of Nebraska at Lincoln: www.unl.edu/ap-Is/student/CST%20assess.pdf.

173 *The Titticut Follies: Washington Post*, 8/2/91.

173 *BG*, 5/27/85 and 8/19/87. Bridgewater conditions: *BG*, 8/28/84.

174 Dr. Robert A. Fein competency finding: Report to Robert Kalis from Stevan E. Gressitt, 3/12/85, Essex County Superior Courthouse, Salem, MA. Dr. Fein's assessment is also quoted in SJC vol. V, 3/18/85.

174 "Joe, I fucked up": Joseph Aiello testimony, SJC pretrial motions vol. IV, 12/20/84.

174 PH to Hardy: Edward Hardy testimony, SJC pretrial motions vol. IV, 12/20/84.

174 Edward O'Reilly: *GDT*, 6/30/84.

174 Lawrence Maguire, PH's counsel: *GDT*, 7/5/84.

175 "I pulled off . . . to deny": WQ.

176 Dogtown cleanup: *GDT*, 9/8/84.

177 hire a private investigator: Robert Kalis interview; Essex County Superior Courthouse, Salem, MA; WQ.

177 Old Salem Jail history: *Salem Gazette*, 7/13/07.

177 "Stone Gaol": Barbara Howell Erkkila, *Hammers on Stone: A History of Cape Ann Granite* (Gloucester, MA: Peter Smith, 1987), pp. 6–7.

177 Kalis's feelings about PH: Robert Kalis interview.

178 "pretty docile," "a strange man": Robert Kalis interview.

178 "was what I thought they": PH to Robert Kalis, Robert Kalis interview.

178 DNA testing: Michelle Hibbert, "DNA Databanks: Law Enforcement's Greatest Surveillance Tool?" *Wake Forest Law Review* 34, Fall 1999.

178 "Can you give me three bucks for candy?": Robert Kalis interview.

178 Kalis and PH's commissary account: Wendy Quiñones interview.

179 suicide attempt: Robert Kalis testimony, SJC vol. VIII, 3/20/85.

179 Dr. Stevan Gressitt evaluates PH: Dr. Stevan Gressitt testimony, SJC vol. IX, 3/21/85.

179 PH military records: Dr. Stevan Gressitt testimony, SJC vol. IX, 3/21/85, and National Archives and Records Administration.

22: The Geography of Being

180 "Nothing gives . . . befalls us": Nathaniel Hawthorne, *The House of the Seven Gables* (1851; reprint, New York: Bantam Books, 1981), p. 122.

181 *gah-nee-saw*: http://www.nps.gov/kemo/.

183   "It's beautiful out. Let me show you around": All Carolyn O'Connor quotes from various interviews with her unless otherwise noted.
184   Joe Orange quotes: Everyone I interviewed had an opinion on Joe Orange and asked not to be identified regarding the topic.
185   "As for the Steering Committee, . . . 'God, go'": Joe Orange, *GDT*, 12/31/84.
188   Peter Anastas biography and quotes from various interviews with him unless otherwise noted.
189   oral history of Gloucester: Peter Anastas and Peter Parsons, *When Gloucester Was Gloucester: Toward an Oral History of the City* (Gloucester, MA: Gloucester 350th Anniversary Celebration, Inc., 1973). In addition, Anastas published a Penobscot Indian ethnography titled *Glooskap's Children* (Boston: Beacon Press, 1973), as well as various Gloucester-based works of fiction and literary nonfiction.
189   epic novel about Dogtown: The three published volumes of Jonathan Bayliss's epic quartet yielded 2,300 pages: *Gloucesterbook* (Rockport, MA: Protean Press, 1992), *Gloucestertide* (Rockport, MA: Protean Press, 1996), and *Prologos* (Ashburnham, MA: Basilicum Press, 1999).
190   1950s murder in Dogtown: Also referenced in Larry Ingersoll and Mark Foote, *Behind the Badge: The History of the Gloucester Police Department* (Gloucester, MA: Dogtown Books, 2004), vol. 2, p. 84.
192   trial photograph: *GDT*, 3/15/85.

23: Into the Deep Woods

193   Newburyport's Essex County Superior Courthouse history: www.mass.gov/courts/press/newburyport_cjmarshall.pdf.
193   Bartlet Mall: http://bartletmall.org.
193   Fred Hampton Unit of the People's Forces: *Newburyport Daily News*, 8/27/04.
194   Where PH sat: Robert Kalis to the court, SJC vol. III, 3/13/85.
194   "Now . . . tragedy": James Gribouski opening statement, SJC vol. III, 3/13/85.
195   Erik's children: Robert Kalis interview; Wendy Quiñones interview.
195   EN's feelings about the trial: Campbell and Silverman, *Widower*, p. 55.
195   "I touched her back" and all additional EN quotes unless otherwise noted: EN testimony, SJC vol. III, 3/13/85.
195   jury cries: *GDT*, 3/14/85.
196   green chamois shirt: Wendy Quiñones interview.
196   Dr. Gressitt's report: Essex County Superior Courthouse, Salem, MA.
197   PH response to Dr. Gressitt's report: Robert Kalis to the court in a lobby conference, SJC vol. VIII, 3/20/85.
197   Earl McCurdy's character: James Gribouski interview.
198   National Guard transport: *GDT*, 3/15/85, SJC vol. III, 3/13/85.
198   "stop, look, and listen": James Gribouski instructions to the jury, SJC vol. III, 3/13/85.
198   "Pay attention . . . here": James Gribouski, SJC vol. IV, 3/14/85.
199   "bear[ed] ackhorns": TEB, p. 313.
199   Professor Norton's forest: *GDT*, 8/26/80.
199   Natti family reforestation: EN interview.
199   "these woods . . . job on him": Marcia Norton interview.
199   "like a cast of the face": Robert Kalis interview.

24: City Bred Tenderfoots

200   City Hall referendum: *GDT*, 12/31/84.
200   New houses: *GDT*, 9/16/77.

200 "to develop . . . Acropolis": *GDT,* 12/21/84.
200 "clouded titles": The various struggles over ownership of this land play out across four decades of *GDT* articles. Of the acres mentioned here, 20 acres were purchased in 1973 (*GDT,* 9/7/73) and 36 in 1975 (*GDT,* 5/1/75).
201 "I Benjamin Ellery . . . more or less": Ellery deed quoted in George Butterick, *Muthologos: The Collected Lectures and Interviews of Charles Olson* (Bolinas, CA: Four Seasons Foundation, 1978), p. 454.
201 Granny Day and Abraham Wharf: *GDT,* 9/16/78.
202 grant: *GDT,* 1/18/85.
202 hunters' involvement in Dogtown: Peter Anastas interview; Joe Orange interview.
202 "All I want . . . fun for them": *GDT,* 12/13/68.
202 the Sportsmen's Club had long stocked: *GDT,* 1/18/69; *GDT,* 10/11/69; and others.
203 "trees . . . automobiles do": *The Guardian,* 5/13/04.
204 "savagery" and party details: *GDT,* 3/30/85.
204 Olmsted Historic Landscape Preservation Program: *GDT,* 12/24/84.
204 Dogtown Foundation's 1959 plan: Dated August 1958 but cited in *GDT,* 6/27/59.
204 "a group of city bred tenderfoots": *GDT,* 12/31/84.
204 "lock the place up": *GDT,* 12/29/84.

25: "No Intention of Leaving This Courtroom Alive"

206 "Okay . . . your own": Officer Earl McCurdy in lobby conference, SJC vol. VIII, 3/20/85.
206 mentally competent: Dr. David Swenson testimony, SJC vol. V, 3/15/85. All general reporting on the trial from SJC unless otherwise noted.
207 "consistent with having originated": Warren Oakes testimony, SJC vol. VII, 3/19/85.
207 EN's reaction: Campbell and Silverman, *Widower,* p. 56.
208 Kalis's reaction to meeting with Tierney and Salem jail guard: Robert Kalis interview.
208 "no intention": PH as reported by Robert Kalis in a lobby conference, SJC vol. VIII, 3/20/85.
208 Additional quotes from Robert Kalis, Judge Paul Rutledge, and Officer Earl McCurdy from same lobby conference, SJC vol. VIII, 3/20/85.
209 "I could finish . . . cameras are here": PH to the court, SJC vol. VIII, 3/20/85.
210 Natti family moved: *GDT,* 3/21/85.
210 "Well I . . . from behind": PH videotaped confession, SJC vol. VIII, 3/20/85 and video belonging to James Gribouski.
211 "I didn't know what I was thinking": PH videotaped confession, quoted in *GDT,* 3/21/85.
211 For Kalis, the video: Robert Kalis interview.
212 it was already too late: Robert Kalis in a lobby conference, SJC vol. IX, 3/21/85.

26: Nature Working Her Magic Unmolested

214 "church . . . a place for spiritual renewal": *GDT,* 7/26/84. All additional Ted Tarr quotes from various interviews.
218 "[T]his is another instance": *GDT,* 8/14/29.

219 "the fog . . . on earth": Dina Enos interview.
219 "I could write an . . . forests": David Rains Wallace, excerpt from *The Klamath Knot*, in *The Norton Book of Nature Writing*, eds. Robert Finch and John Elder (New York: W. W. Norton and Company, 1990), p. 858.
222 "This is Joe Orange": All Joe Orange quotes from Joe Orange interview.

27: Confabulation

227 "the most suspect": Dr. Barbara Kirwin, www.courttv.com/archive/movie/crowe/psychological.html.
228 Gribouski's preparation: James Gribouski interview.
228 "jibe with reality": Dr. Stevan Gressitt, voir dire, SJC vol. IX, 3/21/85, unless otherwise noted. All additional Dr. Stevan Gressitt, Robert Kalis, and James Gribouski quotes from the same unless otherwise noted.
230 "almost violently . . . him": Robert Kalis to Judge Rutledge, SJC vol. IX, 3/21/85.
230 "The defendant rests": Robert Kalis, SJC vol. IX, 3/21/85.
230 The jurors stared at Kalis: James Gribouski and Wendy Quiñones interviews.
231 Boötes's history: www.ianridpath.com/startales/bootes.htm. Boötes is visible in the sky starting in the spring.
231 Kalis's sleepless night: Robert Kalis interview.
231 Woofer's reactions: EN interview; Annie Melancon interview.
232 Gribouski's wife: James Gribouski interview.
232 "It's pretty cut and dried . . . try?": Robert Kalis closing statement, SJC vol. X, 3/22/85. All remaining quotes from Robert Kalis and James Gribouski from SJC vol. X, 3/22/85. Additional details from James Gribouski interview.
235 self-protecting mode: Abby Stein, *Prologue to Violence: Child Abuse, Dissociation, and Crime* (Mahwah, NJ: The Analytic Press, 2007).
235 details from PH's suicide attempt: SJC vol. X, 3/22/85; *GDT*, 3/22/85 and 3/23/85.
236 razor blade location: Robert Kalis interview; David Reardon interview; *GDT* 3/22/85 and 3/23/85.
237 The Natti family rejoiced: Wendy Quiñones interview.
238 Dogtown roads closed: *GDT*, 3/30/85.

28: Mountains in Stone

239 motor vehicle ban: *GDT*, 7/12/85, 7/24/85.
239 Peter Anastas began publishing: *GDT*, 6/4/85, 6/11/85, 6/18/85, 6/25/85.
239 CAHA exhibit: *Cape Ann Historical Association Newsletter*, vol. 5, no. 3, July–September 1985.
239 Dogtown Day: *GDT*, 6/24/85.
240 Scotti took soprano Carla Bee: *GDT*, 8/1/85.
240 performance at Annisquam Village Church: Stephen Scotti interview.
240 "Romantic fantasists . . . facts": Dogtown Steering Committee, *Developing a Management Program for Dogtown*, August 1, 1985, p. 11.
241 "There is a geophysical electromagnetic anomaly . . . rituals are private": Gerrit Lansing interview.
242 how granite breaks: Scotty Stuart showed me how granite breaks at his quarry on EN's land.
242 broke the Whale's Jaw: *GDT*, 8/11/89.
242 "People were shocked . . . community": Cheryl Davis interview.
242 "there were giants in the earth": Genesis 6:4.

242 plans to reattach the Whale's Jaw: *GDT,* 9/21/89, and John Tuck interview.
242 "It was another trashing": Babette Brackett interview.
242 "I wouldn't be able to bear it": Jan Seppala interview.
243 "did as I always have to do": *SHAP,* p. 144.
243 "Teach us . . . these rocks": T. S. Eliot, "Ash Wednesday," *Collected Poems 1909–1962 by T. S. Eliot* (New York: Harcourt, 1991), pp. 83–96.
243 "appearing in the landscape": Nathaniel Southgate Shaler, *The Geology of Cape Ann, Massachusetts* (Washington, D.C.: U.S. Geological Survey, 1888), p. 547.
244 "Oh, potent . . . there?": Nathaniel Hawthorne, "The Prophetic Pictures," in *Twice Told Tales* (1837; reprint, New York: Modern Library, 2001), p. 136.
244 "painted sculpture . . . painting": MH to Rebecca Strand, 9/31/31, AAA.

Epilogue

246 Erik Natti: EN interview.
246 "Dear Mr. Kalis . . . Tuck": John Tuck letter to Robert Kalis, no date.
247 "It was the most extraordinary thing": Robert Kalis interview.
247 photograph from the trial: James Gribouski interview.
247 "They've got me . . . I wasn't": WQ.
247 "That area . . . dreams": PH letter to Elyssa East, 4/12/06.
249 "Don't feel bad . . . choice": PH interview.
249 "Something calls to me": PH letter to Elyssa East, 5/09/06.
250 "I put you . . . out": DR interview.
250 Hodgkins's appeal attempts: Essex County Superior Courthouse, Salem, MA.
250 Hodgkins forebear's ghost: Phoebe Rowe interview.
251 "not such a bad idea": Ted Tarr interview.
251 "Nine months out of the year": Joe Orange in *GDT,* 1/21/08.
251 "What a distinguished spot": MH to Alfred Stieglitz, 11/5/31, YCAL.

Acknowledgments

THIS BOOK COULD not have been written without the support and generosity of many Gloucester, Massachusetts, residents. Most of all I would like to thank Sarah Dunlap of the Gloucester City Archives Committee, a great friend, researcher, and guiding force, who was always an incredibly generous host along with her late husband Steve Warshall, and a tremendous help with practically everything. The endnotes in this book are lovingly dedicated to Sarah.

Erik Natti never ceased to impress me with his wit, wisdom, courage, and trust. I am eternally grateful for his permission to quote from a previously published anonymous interview with him about this tragedy.

Other individuals stand out for their exceptional assistance, hospitality, and friendship: Shep Abbott, Carolyn O'Connor, Peter Anastas, Ted Tarr, Grace Schrafft, Noel Mann and Daan Sandee, Cindy Mom, Joe Palmisano, Vivien Low, and Mike Scagliatti.

Liz Bisch, Toppy Bott, Josh and Babette Brackett, Barbara Braver, Fred Buck, Susan Bulba, Charlie Campbell, Jack Chase, Cheryl Davis, Sheree DeLorenzo, Dina Enos, Mark Adrian Farber and Amy Farber, Thorpe Feidt, Henry Ferrini, Vincent Ferrini, Janet Finch, Dale Follansbee, Bob French, Joe Garland, Gregory and Ann Marie Gibson, Charlotte Gordon, James Gribouski, JoeAnn Hart, Vilma Hunt, Judge Lawrence Jodrey, Robert Kalis, Gap LaFata, Gerrit Lansing, Chris Leahy, Annie Melancon, Anne Millitello, Corey Moody, Ernest Morin, Isabel Natti, Bill and Dot Noble, Kate Noonan, Marcia Norton, Michael O'Leary, Jim O'Neill, Joe Orange, Peter Parsons, Judy Peterson, Louisa Poole, Bob Quinn, John Quinn, Judy Ray, David Reardon, Kenneth Riaf, Rick Roth, Phoebe Rowe, Kenneth Ryan, Giancarlo Salucci, Stephen Scotti, Dave Seiter, Jan Seppala, David Shaw, Ellen Solomon, St. Peter's Fiesta Women's Committee, Scotty Stuart, Julie Thibodeau-Bidart, Pat Towler, John Tuck, Wilma Upham, Rosie Verga, Jane and

Joe Walsh, Mary Weissblum, Marianne Wenniger, and Jill Wodehouse were all willing interview subjects or provided me with valuable information and perspectives at various points along the way. The contributions of each of these individuals make this book as much a community project as it is my own work. Additionally, I'd like to acknowledge the many people who worked with the Dogtown Steering Committee, the Dogtown Foundation, or in other capacities to ensure Dogtown's future, without whose efforts there would be no Dogtown as it exists today.

I would like to extend a special thank-you to Wendy Quiñones for her excellent *Boston* magazine story and assistance. Thanks also to Ray Lamont and the various staff members of the *Gloucester Daily Times* whose articles I have quoted here.

I would also like to acknowledge Peter Hodgkins for his trust and willingness to speak with me despite his initial reluctance.

Staff members at the following research institutions and organizations were particularly helpful: Melissa Watterworth and Kristin Eshelman at the University of Connecticut's Thomas J. Dodd Research Center, Kathy Flynn at the Phillips Library of the Peabody Essex Museum, Stephanie Buck of the Cape Ann Museum, members of the Gloucester Archives Committee, staff of the Sawyer Free Library and Gloucester Lyceum, George Hodgdon and Darlene McGrane of the Office of the Clerk at the Essex County Superior Court in Salem, Amanda Patterson at the John Adams Courthouse's Social Law Library, Diane Wiffin of the Massachusetts Department of Corrections, and Charlie Manuel at the Newburyport Superior Courthouse.

Grants and fellowships from the Ludwig Vogelstein Foundation, the Ragdale Foundation, and the Phillips Library; as well as the Rose and Sigmund Strochlitz Travel Grant at the University of Connecticut; and the Jerome Foundation's New York Mills Regional Cultural Center Arts Retreat all supported the research and writing of this book.

Alan Ziegler, Patty O'Toole, Richard Locke, Mike Janeway, Leslie Sharpe, Lis Harris, Nicholas Christopher, Maureen Howard, William Leach, and Honor Moore each had a hand in guiding this material or influencing my thinking about it. Karen Braziller offered some of the greatest support imaginable. Binnie Kirschenbaum was also of great help.

I am ever grateful to my agent, Brettne Bloom, and editor, Wylie

O'Sullivan, as well as Dominick Anfuso at Free Press, for their willingness to take on this project and to help bring it to life. Elisa Rivlin and William Drennan each gave the manuscript expert, careful review. Edith Lewis was extraordinarily patient and exacting, while Sydney Tanigawa consistently, gently nudged me to keep things moving along. Andy Dodds, Laura Davis, and Carisa Brunetto Hays are a fabulous publicity team.

At last, my friends: the staff and members of Paragraph Workspace for Writers; members of the Red House workshop; my classmates and fellow staff members at Columbia, especially Margot Kahn Case, Leslie Zubaty Anderson, Dave Beeman, and Anna Peterson. And those dear individuals who helped keep my head above water throughout the long course of writing this book: Melissa Heltzel, Nancy Rawlinson, Lynda Curnyn, S. Kirk Walsh, Anna Solomon, Susan Stellin, Maya Allison, Eve Bowen, Lauren Weber, and my family. And saving the best for last, Yulun Wang, my closest and most devoted reader and my true love.

Index

About the Author

Elyssa East grew up in Georgia and spent nearly ten years getting lost and finding herself again in Gloucester's Dogtown all because of an unusual painting she fell in love with as an undergraduate at Reed College. She has an M.F.A. in creative writing from Columbia University and lives in New York City.